Since 1986, Greig Pickhaver has appeared as H.G. Nelson in various radio and television programmes, usually with John Doyle appearing alongside him behind the card table as Rampaging Roy Slaven.

*This Sporting Life* was a regular weekend fixture on Triple J for 22 years, followed by five years on Triple M with *The Life* and *The Sporting Probe*.

John and Greig have presented a number of television shows including *This Sporting Life* (the TV show), *Club Buggery*, *The Channel Nine Show*, *Win Roy & H.G.'s Money*, *The Dream*, *The Monday Dump*, *The Cream* and *The Memphis Trousers Half Hour*.

In 2020, he started co-hosting *Bludging on the Blindside* on ABC Radio.

ALSO BY H.G. NELSON

*Petrol, Bait, Ammo & Ice*
*The Really Stuffed Guide to Good Food 2006 (ed.)*
*Sprays*
*My Life in Shorts*

H.G. NELSON

# The FAIRYTALE

## A REAL AND IMAGINED HISTORY OF AUSTRALIAN SPORT

MACMILLAN
Pan Macmillan Australia

Pan Macmillan acknowledges the Traditional Custodians of country throughout Australia and their connections to lands, waters and communities. We pay our respect to Elders past and present and extend that respect to all Aboriginal and Torres Strait Islander peoples today. We honour more than sixty thousand years of storytelling, art and culture.

First published 2021 in Macmillan by Pan Macmillan Australia Pty Ltd
1 Market Street, Sydney, New South Wales, Australia, 2000



NATIONAL LIBRARY OF AUSTRALIA

A catalogue record for this book is available from the National Library of Australia

Typeset in 12.5/16 pt Bembo by Midland Typesetters, Australia
Printed by IVE



Aboriginal and Torres Strait Islander people should be aware that this book may contain images or names of people now deceased.

FSC www.fsc.org MIX Paper from responsible sources FSC® C018183

The paper in this book is FSC® certified. FSC® promotes environmentally responsible, socially beneficial and economically viable management of the world's forests.

*To the here, there and everywhere duo of Lucille Gosford and Kate Gosford, with thanks for the wonderful Wagstaffe years.*

# Contents

# The FAIRYTALE

## *Introduction*

# THE FAIRYTALE

*A real and imagined history of Australian sport.*

SPORT HAS BEEN PART of Australian society for centuries. Everything was humming along nicely for tens of thousands of years, but in 1788 the whole shebang took a weird right-hand turn when the First Fleet burst in through the Heads under full sail with senior referee Arthur Phillip at the helm. He blew the siren on the old sporting codes and overnight different, new-fangled sports with crazy rules were on top of the weekend agenda.

Instead of nationwide participation by the whole community, the citizens of the new colony were suddenly only interested in the big game and the big game players. They liked the ones who could go hard early and kick clear as the field turned for home and headed up to salute the judge. The new settlers loved the excitement of seeing a conveyance come from behind and nab a convincing win in the shadows of the post. Suddenly the rules were there to be bent and exploited and it did not take long for the lurkers to unleash their cheating ways.

*The Fairytale* ambles along the winding track of time from Phillip's first colonial tweet on the Thunderer right up to and beyond the arrival of the Olympics to south-east Queensland in 2032.

A sporting nation is only limited by its imagination. Every time this story is told it changes; something is always added, embellished or dropped from the run-on side.

This is not a tale of who won and where. How it was won and why. Or why it went down to the wire before hitting the S-bend of disappointment and was flushed away. The real, full-time scores can look after themselves on other platforms in other books. The record-keeping industry provides valuable employment opportunities for those who stand back with the pencil poised over the blank sheet of paper.

From high in the grandstand, *The Fairytale* uses the eight-by-ten binoculars to cast a gaze across this wide sunburnt land of drought and flooding rains. From this magpie-eye vantage point it is easy to see that sport is now central to the very idea of Australian society. That is the 12.78 millionth time that fact has appeared in print in Australian media since 1788.

*It is a dip of the toe into the vat of victory featuring remarkable results and an improbable cast of characters, some of whom actually lived.*

Stating the bleeding obvious, these chapters are plucked from the nation's real and imagined sporting jamboree. It is not the whole story. It is a dip of the toe into the vat of victory featuring remarkable results and an improbable cast of characters, some of whom actually lived.

Horse racing was the first of the European introductions, with races run around Sydney's Hyde Park not long after the anchors dropped at Farm Cove. Punting was central to the race day experience. Sports betting kicked off as soon as the first convicts and crew staggered off the forgotten ships of the First Fleet, the *Lady Penrhyn* and the *Prince of Wales*.

Sporting types freed from the shackles of conservative England were prepared to bet on anything. This was soon demonstrated by the big turn-outs for fly races up the walls of the first pubs in The Rocks around Circular Quay in Sydney.

The whole 'long may we play' caper really took off in the early 1800s. The first Sydney Cup was run in The Fortune of War pub on 12 June 1811. The five-pound purse and a bottle of Arthur Phillip claret (1792) were won by The Pride of Potato Point, a big blowie from the Narellan area, who nailed Cracklin' Dopsie, a biting march fly from the Upper Hunter. The big buzzing noise from Scone was nabbed in the final bound in a desperate finish that went down to the pencil line on the cornice behind the swinging doors in the front bar.

Soon local megastars emerged from the pack. One of Australia's early greats, maybe our original GOAT (as in 'the greatest of all time') was William Francis King. Billy was known to anyone who put a bet on him as 'The Flying Pieman'. His record speaks for itself. Bill's sport was pedestrianism. This lark, now lost, was a big noise at the time when Billy went sauntering. No one could touch him on the stroll. He dominated over all distances, in all events and in all conditions. He was the Ian Thorpe, the Dustin Martin, the Bart Cummings, the Winx of his era, with a dollop of cream to go with the strawberry on top of the Royal Show blue ribbon–winning cake. He was that good.

Bill blew into town in 1829. He was a schoolteacher by trade, but gave the chalk away to slip behind the slab and pull beers at The Hope and Anchor. The demanding hours in hospitality meant he had no time to train. Bill dropped the bar work and turned his hand to making pies. He sold 'the four and twenties' waddling around Hyde Park in downtown Sydney. The park was developed as a central sporting venue in the early days of the NSW colony.

The waddling baker excelled at walking enormous distances in a very short time. He inherited the 'Pieman' mantle from Nathaniel McCulloch. Nat was an A-grade pie-making rambler but a bit silly with it. McCullouch was often up before the beaks of Olde Sydney Towne for running amok and disturbing the peace with his bad behaviour. On one occasion he was fined five pounds for attempting to cut his own throat.

The Flying Pieman, Billy King, made his mark early. On one occasion he sold pies to passengers boarding the ferry in Sydney, then ran the eighteen miles to Parramatta to off-load the remaining unsold tartlets, cinnamon scrolls, finger buns and savoury quiches to the same passengers as they got off the ferry. That is some effort. All that way on foot, keeping the pies hot and the flies off was an astonishing effort. With this fantastic display the mantel of top dog was passed from McCulloch to the King.

Bill saddled up Shanks's pony and walked because there were not many ways of getting around the NSW in the early days. Boat, horse and carriage were about it, apart from self-propulsion with the pedal extremities.

One of Billy's very big walks was a 192-mile canter in forty-six hours. The venue was the Maitland racecourse. He completed 206 laps, attracting big crowds as the nights turned into days. Remember these were simpler times. There were fewer must-see night-time attractions. Watching a fit pieman stagger about the local racecourse fuelled conversation for weeks.

The Prince of Pastries loved lugging weights, big weights. He was a whizz with weight. They say trackside weight is a great leveller; not for the Pieman.

As Bill outlined in a profile for 'The Walking Week', a column written by Devon Sprode and published in *The Argus*:

> Devi, weight is no heavy burden. It's all in the mind. Honestly when I pick a hundred-pound lump of Sydney sandstone that I have to deliver to a building site in Warwick Farm, of course I feel insane. Who wouldn't? But honestly, Dev, the first ten steps are the hardest; after that it becomes a blur. And remember I am carrying eight dozen hot pies to drop off at Casula along the way. So, I never go hungry.

The King of Flans loved company on the road. When he took on the great Campbelltown to Sydney Challenge in January 1830, he carried a thirty-two-kilo dog as a companion. He backed up and did the Sydney to Parramatta Christmas Eve Mini Sprint and was handicapped by the stewards with an adult goat. It was described by Sprode in that week's column 'as a double goat act'.

The Footloose Flyer had a crack at a range of novelty events. He once beat the mail coach from Sydney to Windsor using a single breath.

He loved making it fun. His run a mile, walk a mile, push a brick-laden wheelbarrow for a mile, drag a cow in a carriage for a mile, walk backwards for a mile and walk for a mile over stones placed five yards apart was a Easter happening that drew very big crowds. His best time for this early multi-discipline 'triathlon' style event was a swift twenty-three minutes. A record that still stands.

He created some of these idiotic challenges with the help of letter writers to 'The Walking Week' column who responded when he threw down the gauntlet and asked, 'Well punters, what do you want me to do next?'

Often as an extra wriggle tacked on to his promenading there was an eye-watering food challenge for the crowd who gathered at the finish line. He once polished off nine family-sized pies and a dozen beers after finishing first in The Gong and Back Charity Fun Run. This stomach-extending pie-a-thon completed a memorable day out for families, who got the crumbs. And it gave kids memories for a lifetime.

Billy King did much to establish the new agenda of sporting and culinary traditions in the colony.

He loved a flutter and took on all comers. Most of the bets were set against him achieving his impossible goals. Sadly for slow-learning punters, there were tears before bedtime as they usually lost.

By the way, is it time to begin a national conversation about celebrating the deeds and contribution to Australian culture of The Pieman, with a Day of Walking Wonder featuring all-age events over serious distances? What a great contribution this day would make to the build-up to the torch relay blast-off for the 2032 Brisbane Games.

The highest levels of state and federal government need to set up an all-party committee to probe the possibility of a waddle from Dubbo to Darwin via Uluru and The Alice. This ramble would bring the nation together as Australians would be glued to social media platforms for live updates as they followed the progress of a hot international field. The world would be watching.

Old-fashioned pedestrianism had echoes in the Melbourne to Sydney Run first staged in 1983, with the last international line-up flagged away in 1991. This one stopped the nation for days. It was a very popular saunter up the Hume sponsored by the Westfield shopping mall people. The idea was that Australians thinking about the Melbourne to Sydney amble would waddle off to the nearest Westfield in their area and buy up big. It was a 960-kilometre race and Cliff Young, the gum-booted Colac dairy farmer, set the pace from day one in 1983. Most of the subsequent runs were dominated by Yiannis Kouros, whose best time was five days, two hours and twenty-seven minutes. Yiannis was born in Tripoli in Greece, the home of the original marathon. He had a head start in the caper as he just loved putting one foot in front of the other.

Walking is a sport that has always observed the strict COVID-19 protocols, which may still be part of our daily life even in 2032. Walking is something everyone can do even in times blighted by a pandemic. We know how hard it is to walk to school, work or to the beach. The nation can appreciate the effort put in by the long-distance stars.

In the twenty-first century, it is hard to imagine any part of Australia being liveable without a raft of sporting options. At the height of the COVID pandemic, when all sport had been suspended, the leader of the National Party in NSW and deputy premier, John 'Bara' Barilaro, stumbled out of the ashes of the summer of the 2019/20 fires and the swamps of the recent east coast floods and admitted that 'NSW isn't NSW unless it is playing rugby league'.

That is how important a senior, well-respected politician with a great spread in the Southern Highlands believed sport was to the nation's most populous state.

Rugby league was a pioneer in the early days of the dreaded lurgy, continuing to play the game. Like horse racing, the league swerved around experts who thought they were mad proceeding with the season and found better experts, more in tune with the thinking of the code's head office, who thought that the blue paper on Project Apollo (the rugby league season 2020) should be torched for take-off without delay.

One senior member of the Legislative Council, the NSW Upper House, was right up behind the 2020 Footy Frenzy. He was an outspoken advocate of the 'Bugger COVID!' press-ahead pressure group. He spoke at length to ABC's *Insiders* host David Speers, setting out his case for the Project Apollo blast-off.

> Speersie, if we can keep the COVID deaths to around 2,150 per week we should be able to run the whole of the NRL season and stage the Big Dance at Homebush with a crowd of 85,000.
>
> Dave, COVID protocols are not rocket science. The social distancing, the hand washing, the use of the sanitiser bath, we know how to do it. We can all get our heads around it. Plus it won't be long before we are making a nice dollar from it and exporting our skills to the world.

> As to public discomfort, Speersie, the fully ticketed team of specialist Project Apollo staff on the gates at all rugby league grounds can have the public out of their clothes, immersed in a bath of the bug-killing sanitiser gear, hosed off, back in their clothes and seated with a full-strength beer in hand within seven minutes. Most Australians will be prepared to tolerate that degree of state-approved health controls to see a game of rugby league. You wouldn't object to any of that for you and the kids?

Rugby league players in 2020 responded and generally respected hub life. But as with any ambitious moon shot there are always a few glitches and malfunctions. After all, the players and coaches central to Project Apollo's success are only human. They have needs. They got hungry. They wandered away from the league-approved chuck wagon to get their snout into a trough at a local Bar Italia that did the carbonara the way they liked it, as in not too creamy, just the right combo of egg-and-bacon sauce and penne.

But rugby league's actions give pause for thought at a crucial moment in Australia's recent history in 2020. After the collapse of fire-ravaged ecosystems, before the east coast was battered by a once-in-a-thousand-years deluge and ahead of the 'unprecedented' worldwide pandemic that gripped the nation by the throat, the big topic in NSW politics was the central place of sport in the state's affairs and the future of rugby league.

COVID revealed how busted-arse most sporting organisations actually were. They had put nothing aside for a rainy day. Head offices across the nation had to slash staff and cut costs. The codes dumped millions from the budgets but asked the nation if they could imagine a modern multicultural, inclusive and diverse society without AFL, rugby league and horse racing in all states. Australia was saved from that catastrophe by very valuable work by club committees at the coalface of the boot. Many right-thinking Australians found themselves asking: If all those great sports stopped, where would the punting dollar go? How would Australia pay for schools, health and cybersecurity?

Politicians and sports administrators argued that all sports were providing a public service to the community. They were solving the mental health issues of the nation. They gave the nation something to think about apart from the annoying germ. Sport gave the nation moving images of humans in action trying their best. These often-spectacular pictures took the mind off the devastation of the recent fires, unprecedented floods and the collapse of the koala population.

*Sport gave the nation moving images of humans in action trying their best. These often-spectacular pictures took the mind off the devastation of the recent fires, unprecedented floods and the collapse of the koala population.*

The ruling elites know that sport is central to national political life because as well as filling hours of each day with mindless stupidity and offering an opportunity to win big, it offers opportunities for personal redemption. Nothing apart from religion can compete with sport in the redemptive space.

The need for redemption is always changing. The demand is never satisfied. Hub life confines in 2020 produced a whole new series of unforgettable images that required the gentle touch of the redemption persuader. With teammates crammed into five-star resorts like Pringles in a tube, sharp-eyed viewers on the couch at home were presented with an array of once-seen never-forgotten modified dick pics and date-hunting images, especially during the energetic renditions of post-hooter club sing-a-longs.

These old-style football high jinks were stamped on pretty quickly by club media managers well aware of the damage uncensored live television images can do. Occasionally they were too late to bring down the forehead curtain on the club chorus line doing the modified elephant walk. In a crisis, media managers swung into action to smooth over the damage done to the club's 'brand'.

Pundits and fans outside the hub-life experience began asking what the club brand stood for and wanted explanations from the new bad boys of footy. These delinquent players who had no idea of how close they came to shutting the whole shebang down appeared shame-faced at a packed press conference on Monday morning. There were apologies all round, using well-crafted lines embracing time-honoured themes and a plea for forgiveness, as a prelude to a redemption that only sport can provide:

> Everyone here? Everyone ready? OK . . . Hi, my name is Trevor 'Frosty' Pew. I am sorry about the todger tugging with Poxie and Crumpy. I was excited about the win against the premiers, but I went too far. I have let the jumper down. I have let the club down. I let the fans down. I let 'Big Flutey' our coach down. I let my family down. I have let my mates back home down. I let my suburb down. Most importantly, I let myself down. It just wasn't me out there!

> I've now got seven days to think about it. I want to put this episode behind me. Hopefully I can get a couple of goals next week and move on. After this experience, I am certainly going into the room of mirrors as soon as this is over to have a good hard look at myself.

By this stage, the press did not know where to look. 'Frosty', a likeable bloke but a known goose, had said more than enough. The football media could see it was just one of those things that had gotten out of hand after an unexpected victory.

Trevor had said almost too much. The wheels of redemption were now in motion. Any more than those carefully chosen words and the apology would suddenly sound insincere. It's a script that every club media manager has wedged in their hip pocket or handbag, ready to be pulled out and passed to the offending player on these embarrassing occasions.

Trevor was a role model before these hub incidents. He did a lot of work in schools helping younger kids to read and with sick kids in hospital. He did not have to do it. The top club role model is a tricky burden to carry. They have a place, but not all Australians can be stars. There have to be one or two passengers, even in a premiership team.

It is a national stupidity to imagine that every youngster who pulls on a pad in the school yard can play for Australia, or every teenager who pulls on a boot can win the Brownlow, or everyone who has sandshoes can win the 100 metres at the Olympics. These results are extremely unlikely. In fact, each year only twenty-two players can win the AFL Grand Final, only one horse can win the Melbourne Cup out of the twenty-four starters, unless there's a well-organised and well-managed dead heat, and only seventeen Australians can win the NRL flag. It is just not possible for everyone to be a winner. But the speculation gives hacks something useful for that hard-to-fill weekend think piece.

At troubled times like these, when things go wobbly, sporting clubs always talk about cultural change. It is code for 'we are having a run of outs, and Trevor's changeroom antics did not help. But we need to move and dump someone into the ash can and start winning. That is what the fans want!'

Cultural change has everyone ducking for cover as someone is bound to cop it in the neck. Usually, it is the coach who gets the flick and wanders off for a think about spending more time with their family. The new appointee talks at length at another hastily arranged press conference in front of the sponsor's logo about a new culture that they will be bringing to the club. A culture of winning is all that is required to turn the joint around.

No one will ever remember a team because it didn't break protocols and curfews. A side will not be remembered if none of the players skipped out of the hub, a five-star luxury resort on the Sunshine Coast, around the witching hour to take in the late show at Hollywood Showgirls on the strip in Mooloolaba. If, when the on-stage underpants stopped hitting the floor around 3.30 am, the boys, still on the loose and feeling peckish, didn't decide to nip across the road for a late-night kebab takeaway. Who doesn't feel like a kebab at 3 am? Have you tried one at that hour? That is the sweetest time in kebab land. At that time Aussie lamb is awesome.

*No one will remember any of this because the only thing that really matters is winning. That is a given.*

No one will remember any of this because the only thing that really matters is winning. That is a given. Even though this book is written in an era of alternative facts, there is no alternative to challenge that simple idea.

Sport forces supporters to live in the present. That list of jobs on the fridge – washing the car, clearing the gutters, doing the groceries – all of that can wait until the match is over. The list can even be forgotten completely after an impressive victory over the premiers; life can be put on hold until then. Live television coverage of sport is the only must-see TV, apart from a royal wedding. No one gives up hope until the final siren. And then there is always next week, and if the worst happens, as it usually does, there is always next year.

If your team is lucky enough to make the Grand Final – and there is a lot of luck involved – there is nothing more important to you, there never will be. Time stops.

If you win: jubilation. It was never in doubt. If you lose: there are months of pondering where it all went wrong, who was to blame. Winning doesn't illuminate much; after all, that is what every team is meant to do. Losing on the other hand, well, there is so much to contemplate. So many questions, so many angles, so many talking points, so few answers.

Sport is a great leveller. Walk onto a racetrack anywhere, and off goes your head, on goes a pumpkin. Stabbing a winner in the first and scoring a big collect makes everyone a deadset genius. Then by the end of the afternoon, after a run of outs across the rest of the eight-race card that hands back to the TAB what was won in the first and a lot more besides, suddenly solitude is sweet. The sorry punter staggers home shirtless wondering how it all went wrong, once again.

# THE FAIRYTALE

As English football great and Liverpool legend Bill Shankly blurted out when bailed up by a fan who asked how important sport is: 'Some people believe football is a matter of life and death. I am very disappointed with that attitude. I can assure you it is much more important than that!' The COVID pandemic proved the wisdom of that simple truth.

This is not a book about the stuff known by all genuine sporting Australians. There are no pages of football Grand Final scores, or descriptions of every ball and stroke from a memorable big innings from Australian tours of the subcontinent, or calculations of how much you would have won if you had invested a dollar on Winx at her first run and let it roll all the way to the end of her career. There is none of that because that is all available to everybody everywhere on Google.

*The Fairytale* is an historical record of great sporting moments and events that may or may not have happened. Sport buffs have to make up their own mind about whether these events, these stories and these personalities were real and whether they were significant.

The era of certainty in sport is well and truly over. This book is just a version of the truth. But it's a version of the truth that is definitely worth telling. It's a version of the truth that should be told somewhere. Even if it all seems unlikely, who is to say some of these facts did not happen?

Sport was once described as the most important thing of the least important things in our life. Hopefully this book proves it.

# *Part 1*

# HISTORY

# GRAND FINALS AND PRE-MATCH ENTERTAINMENT

*What a concept! An endless cavalcade of great musical ideas, few having anything to do with football.*

THE YEAR WHEN THE electrodes were applied to this lifeless lump and the creation rumbled from the slab and started wriggling about lewdly was 1977. This was a big year for Australian Rules football.

Back in the day, before 1977 – and let's face it, that's last century – the Australian game, Australian Rules football, was played in South Australia, Tasmania and Western Australia, but its heart and soul, according to the pundits who lived there, was nailed to the floorboards in suburban Melbourne.

It was a mystical landscape. The game's spiritual home was the MCG. The Australian game was always bigger, better and more meaningful when the august Victorian Football League controlled the players, the money and the rules.

The teams from the football suburbs of Melbourne did their thing during the home-and-away season and once the first weeks of the finals were cracked, boxed and buried, the twelve teams that started the annual journey towards that one day in September were whittled down to two.

The two finalists shared a dream. It was a dream shared by the whole competition when the field lined up for the starter back in late March. It was a dream of taking the Premiership Cup back to their club house for a wild summer-long shindig.

The VFL Grand Final (the Grannie) decided the champion team, and featured at the 'G' on that 1977 spring afternoon were the North Melbourne Kangaroos, dolled up in blue and white, and the Collingwood Magpies, who turned up in their traditional strip, featuring the prison bars of black and white.

On that September day, with another difficult, bleak city winter back in its box for six months, these two great Melbourne sides battled for the biggest prize in football anywhere in the known world. On that one day of the year the centre of the Universe was Melbourne.

But 1977 was about change. It was the first year the Grand Final was televised live in Victoria. The live, free-to-air coverage was predicated on the idea that if the Grand Final sold out, then the Channel Seven football tap would be turned on and everyone could see the game and listen to Peter Landy and Lou Richards call the action in the most liveable city on the planet. Everyone across the nation would be united around the television in a festival of the boot.

As the final Saturday in September approached there was great nervousness among Melbourne footy heads who did not have Grand Final tickets. They prayed that the magic groundfull number would be reached, lifting the TV curtain, allowing the modern world of sports broadcasting to catch up with VFL football.

The days rolled by. Suddenly, the MCG was stacked to the rafters. The game was a sell-out. Footy-mad Victorians would have the big show blasted into their lounge rooms from the sticks on Mount Dandenong. The Grannie would finally appear across Melbourne on Astor twelve inches and AWA Radiola deep image screens in vibrant living football colour.

As is often the case, the back story of these end-of-season events is often more exciting and dramatic than the actual game. So many VFL/AFL Grand Finals are lopsided affairs. The match is often done and dusted in the first quarter. By half-time, disappointed footy heads and serious punters are headed for the exits looking forward to the Boxing Day Test. But the big one in 1977 lived up to its top-of-the-table billing.

Before we come to the main course, let's nip backstage and see what the chefs and the fickle football gods had steaming on the stove by way of entrée …

IN 1976, COLLINGWOOD WERE simply a joke. They were the wooden spooners. The 'Side by Side' team propped up the whole competition. In the off-season the hard-working, desperate-for-success Victoria Park committee realised they were waist deep in football excrement.

The Pies did not see the funny side of being the joke of football and Melbourne. They wanted and expected respect. President Ern Clarke fell on his bayonet after the club hit rock bottom for the first time in their history. The Captain of the Skies, John Hickey, was cleared for take-off as president. Remember, this was decades before Eddie 'Everywhere' McGuire came lurching down the premiership cakewalk.

First item on the agenda for Wing Commander Hickey and the committee was to find a new coach. They moved on 1976 coach, Murray 'The Weed' Weideman, from his position as custodian of the club's clipboard. The Weed's numbers were not great. He had his hand on the levers for forty-five matches but only managed to get the chocolates in nineteen. This was unacceptable!

In an extremely controversial move, Richmond Tiger great, 'T-shirt' Tommy Haffey, was tapped and tipped into the black-and-white coach's box. He was the first outsider to take on the team, but he came with big raps, having coached Richmond during a golden age, bagging the big one for the yellow and black in 1967, 1969, 1973 and 1974.

Collingwood and Richmond were great rivals. In fact, they hated each other. With T-shirt in charge of the witches' hats at Victoria Park, the long-suffering membership believed the premiership window was thrown wide open.

All through the final series that September, there was talk in the Melbourne media of a fairytale finish to the season. The media, then as now, was always sniffing for an angle and latched on to the 'last in 1976 to first in 1977' rave. This was a modern football story told as a happy-ever-after saga. It was a powerful but slightly silly space-filling idea. Though then, as now, there was plenty of media space to fill.

Is there an actual fairytale that echoes the last-to-first football narrative? Does it matter that there are no near equivalents in the Brothers Grimm handiwork, the ancient Norse myths or in the popular versions of Rumpelstiltskin and Little Red

Riding Hood? It did not matter to the bright sparks with fingers poised over the keyboard starring at a blank sheet of paper in 1977.

Remember everything in football has been said 5274 times already. Newspaper editors in 1977 suggested to writers, never be afraid to reheat a golden oldie. But no one knew that the fairy-tale theme as developed by the media in 1977 football would go way beyond the ordinary. This Grannie was looming as the most important event in the history of the city.

*Is there an actual fairytale that echoes the last-to-first football narrative? Does it matter that there are no near equivalents in the Brothers Grimm handiwork, the ancient Norse myths or in the popular versions of Rumpelstiltskin and Little Red Riding Hood?*

The Pies had not won a VFL flag since 1958.

Their subsequent appearances on the big day were disastrous. They always turned up with hope. Every year was their year. But after the final hooter the team got on the bus and drove away for the long lie down, disappointed and dispirited. Outraged fans were, well, outraged. Commentators had a term that described their losing run of outs. The malaise was referred to as 'Colli-wobbles'. A disease so virulent it put diehard supporters into intensive care.

Coach Tom Haffey left nothing to chance in his quest for success in his first year at Victoria Park. Echoing the media approach to the looming fairytale finals he began reading Cinderella in chapters, by torchlight, to the players at the conclusion of training every night throughout that magnificent September.

Training, in the seventies, was not the scientifically based, medically supervised, diet-driven, sophisticated operation it is today. The teams would run laps of the oval, do a bit of circle work (that is, kicking the ball to each other as they ran around in a big circle), then come in close for a chat from the coach about the meaning of life, football, the opposition and why 'we have to win', before breaking into groups to do handball work and tackle practice. Forwards then practised marking and goal-kicking. Defenders practised spoiling and thumping each other. To finish up, it was forwards v backs or a game of skins and shirts. Football is a simple game.

That September the Pies won their final matches and the Collingwood players bought into the Cinderella concept. They were enchanted by the tale of the search for a foot that fitted the special glass shoe left on the stairs at midnight. The players saw this as a football analogy. The search for the perfect boot and a magical finish to the story was surely a metaphor for a flag-winning end to the 1977 season. No one at training was quite sure what the pumpkin coach represented. That and many other details were stumpers for specialist football writers to unravel in the seasons to come.

For decades, the Grand Final game day at the G was a football-focused three-pronged carnival of kicking. An early bounce got hostilities underway, not long after tip-out time at the North Melbourne Breakfast. The Breakfast was the must-attend event for everyone who moved or shook in Australia and Victoria since the mid-sixties.

In 1977, the early risers had packed into the Southern Cross Hotel for a bowl of Weet-Bix, an average fried egg, a sodden baked tomato, a rasher of over-crispy bacon and a slice of slightly burnt toast, washed down with tea or coffee, plus a few beers for the early starters who enjoyed a Fosters at 8.30 am. The festive room was always chock-a-block with media types, footy heads, soap stars, celebrities, politicians, comedians, tipsters and sporting tragics.

Over the years, the business end of the breakfast had featured a cavalcade of stars, but the guest speaker in 1977 was, surprisingly, ad man, filmmaker and notorious anti-sport identity, Phillip Adams.

Big Phil 'hated' football. Unsurprisingly, his running mate on this occasion was Football Personality of the Year, Hawthorn stalwart John Kennedy, the 'Don't think, just do!' man. John had coached the wee and the poo to flag wins in 1961, 1971 and 1976.

It was a genuine meeting of minds down the deep end of the Hotel's ballroom – something that only Melbourne can turn on. Phillip spoke for thirty electrifying minutes on the topic 'Why the Pies will win!' before controversially asking the room to stand and sing the Pies' club song, 'Good Old Collingwood Forever'.

Incidentally, Phillip cashed the cheque he wrote at the 1977 Grand Final Breakfast when he became the host of ABC Radio National's late-night chat show, *Late Night Live*.

Historically, as the last coffee was put away, the action was firing up at the MCG. First out kicking the dew off the grass were the Under 19s, then the Seconds and finally at 2.30 pm it was the big show, the VFL Grannie. Keen

*Phillip cashed the cheque he wrote at the 1977 Grand Final Breakfast when he became the host of ABC Radio National's late-night chat show, Late Night Live.*

supporters got there early and made a day of it. They saw the stars of tomorrow run around before the bounce in the big stink, which featured the stars of today.

But in 1977, out of the blue, the VFL, using all its footballing wisdom and marketing know-how, decided to expand its Grannie footprint worldwide. In a rush towards the bright lights of the modern world it tapped the show business arts to carry the game to a whole new audience. The Grand Final brains trust decided to unleash pre-match entertainment for the very first time.

In marketing terms, the committee could not change the game, so they decided to value-add by getting artists, who in the main had nothing to do with football, to come along and have a warble, a cough and a spit before the bounce. The strategy was, if the VFL cannot get eyeballs with the game, then maybe we can get them with the packaging. It was a very modern concept.

The wheeze evolved so that chart-topping artists could sing their hits and maybe do the honours with a couple of moving Australian classics before the teams ran on. If international viewers in Vladivostok or Salt Lake City were intrigued by the pre-match entertainment, they might stay for the football.

Our great stars and, in time, international stars were to build a bridge between the MCG and the wider sporting community in non-VFL states in Australia, and then onto the world.

The man driving this change was the new VFL President, Dr Allen Aylett. Allen was a dentist by trade and a shinboner by choice. The Doc turned out for the North Melbourne Kangaroos 220 times and slotted 311 majors. He saluted in the best and fairest in 1958, 1959 and 1961. These are very impressive career statistics.

Allen played in an era when players worked at real jobs instead of earning all their income by pulling on the shorts and kicking a Sherrin. He even worked with teeth on the boundary line as a service to footballers who got whacked in the mouth during the game. After an unintentional accidental-on-purpose thump to the jaw, players could often lose a couple of molars. Allen was a great believer in numbering teeth with Texta colour, so that, if the worst should happen, the medical staff would know the right order in which to reinsert the teeth in the jaw line.

If the Kangaroos were winning, Allen often did a filling or two at quarter time for battling members of the cheer squad. His secretary, Valmai, would make appointments for extractions at half-time. During the long break he would set up the chair in the rooms, reach for the pliers and have a yank while the rest of the team had an orange. One of the larger players was tasked to hold the patient still.

It was a different time. People from the Arden Street area of North Melbourne did not have the loot to see a dentist during the week. If they got work done out the back at the footy on a Saturday afternoon for free, it was a win-win, especially when the Roos got up. Doctor Allen loved drilling teeth, he loved fixing smiles and he loved footy.

Once his slippers were under the VFL's presidential table, Allen pushed through many changes. The Doc got night football up and running, moved the city of Sydney onto the VFL radar and made Sunday fixtures a regular part of the season. The 1977 Grannie had his dabs all over proceedings.

Doctor Allen established a Grand Final pre-match entertainment committee. He dubbed the operation Blueprint Blight after one of the Kangaroos' greatest players. Maz, Stumbles,

Choko, Scone and Fluff, all great football people, were chosen to sort out the Grand Final pre-match show and select the first line-up of talent. They met at football HQ in Jolimont House, Tuesdays at 6.30 pm. The Blueprint selection panel gathered for the first time in July 1977. They were given a spray by the boss, who highlighted the need for something special on the big day and told the panel to get cracking.

Fluff and Scone were early arrivals at footy HQ on the night. With nothing to do they wandered around poking into cupboards, and quite by chance discovered a couple of cylinders of nitrous oxide. This gas, used by dentists around the world, takes the edge off and the agony out of dental procedures. They found the gas stored in the cleaning closet behind a four-gallon drum of Exit Mould. President Aylett had parked the cylinders there for safe keeping and forgotten all about them.

The committee had dreams. Dreams that informed the whole development of Blueprint Blight. They promised the Doc they would support local Victorian and Australian talent. But they could see a day when the game was so big it could easily support international artists. Finally, their dream was that playing talent could be part of both the show business and footballing prongs on the day and maybe even sing the national anthem. That was the ultimate goal of the Blueprint Blight. Their nirvana merged show business and football.

*They promised the Doc they would support local Victorian and Australian talent. But they could see a day when the game was so big it could easily support international artists.*

This was all great in theory. Luckily, several hours later, with the meeting bogged down in the weeds of detail and getting nowhere, Fluff remembered the cylinders of gas.

Fluff, a former Coleman medallist with a great leap, cracked a cylinder with Stumbles's help. They turned on the gas and stared, passing the mask around the table. Giggles, laughs and ideas all round lifted the mood!

Nitrous oxide slows down the brain and the body's responses, inducing a feeling of euphoria, relaxation. When those two impulses weave their magic, fits of giggles often reduce imbibers to incoherent rabble. These were days when drugs played a different role in the community, especially in the alternative culture arts space.

The committee dubbed itself the Nitrous Oxide Five (NOF). The meetings were the stuff of legend. The National Film and Sound Archive recently unearthed a box of TDK cassettes that record the first two years of Oxide Five meetings. Sure, there is a lot of incoherent laughter, but the dreams, goals and principles of pre-match entertainment developed by the NOF come through loud and clear between the guffaws of stupidity.

On the chill-out gas, the whiteboard markers were busy and the sheets of butcher's paper were inundated with entertainment ideas and show-business names. Early names of interest were the punk rockers The Clash, who released their first record in March that year. They were slightly ahead of the Sex Pistols in the committee's must-have pecking order. The Pistols had dropped their smash 'God Save the Queen' to wild, spit-drenching acclaim in May. Fleetwood Mac had *Rumours* riding high in the charts but were considered unlikely to do the gig for free. There was a lot of interest in Elvis Presley. Everyone agreed the King would be a great get, and give the event a must-see international flavour. Overtures were made to Colonel Tom through back channels to sound out the King about an appearance. Sadly, the King dropped off the twig six weeks before the Grannie. Imagine the King at the G on the big day.

The superstars of the era flitted in and out of focus as the gas wove its magic. Suddenly, with the Clash, the Pistols, Mac and the King doubtful starters, Barry Crocker's name was on the radar. Then, as these things happen, because of time limits and sheer exhaustion, Barry was in the frame for a warble before the bounce!

From today's perspective Barry Crocker and the VFL Grannie do not seem a tight fit. But as they passed the gas around Barry made more and more sense to the NOF. His was the name they were looking for, in their gassed opinion. His was the name that all Melbourne wanted.

Fluff knew Barry was born in Geelong within walking distance of the Cattery. The singer was a Cats man, through and through. Fluff was convinced Barry would not let the VFL down. Crocker was even fiddling on a song called 'Come on the Cats', which would be released the following year.

This Crocker-penned Kardinia Park chart-topping cracker rehearsed the essentials of any great club song. Words like 'Geelong' and 'belong' are front and centre in the first verse. Then follows a list of the champs from the great Geelong sides.

The chorus – well no surprises – heavily features the central theme of 'Come on the Cats!' This tune slots in at number two in the charts of all-time great Geelong tunes. It makes you want to pick up the phone, ring the club and become a

Cats member. This simple musical chestnut was old school and very G-town.

Barry Crocker, the song-and-dance trouper, had been performing in musicals and television for over a decade. He won the 1970 Gold Logie for his lively work on Channel Nine's *A Sound of Music.* At that same night of nights, Johnny Farnham was tapped as best teenage personality again. Johnny suddenly became John and made this award his own for many years. Soon Farnsie would be tasked to play a part on football's biggest day. He strolled out for Grannie action for the first time in 1979.

Barry Crocker had struck pay dirt on the big screen with the dinky-di, true-blue character Barry McKenzie created by comic Barry Humphries. There were two 'Bazza' films: *The Adventures of Barry McKenzie* came out in 1972, and in 1974 Barry returned in *Barry McKenzie Holds His Own.* These were simple tales of a young Australian trying to make good in a wicked world in which everyone else was a no-good foreigner and completely clueless about beer.

Barry Humphries added to the language a number of urinal bon mots delivered by Barry McKenzie in these cinema classics, including 'Drain the dragon', 'Siphon the python', 'Unbutton the mutton' and 'Point Percy at the porcelain'. All those cans of Fosters had to go somewhere. They all ended up in the sewage system via a nearby urinal.

*The Logie and the King of Moomba hats were two pillars any great artist could hang a career on.*

Barry Crocker was crowned the King of Moomba in 1976. There was no bigger accolade in Australia during the seventies than being crowned with that impressive, jewel-encrusted bauble. The Logie and the King of Moomba hats were two pillars any great artist could hang a career on. The Oxide Five at the helm of Blueprint Blight knew if anyone could hold a crowd of 100,000 at the G, Barry could.

As the big day loomed ever closer, Barry was in England appearing on the West End in the musical *Man of La Mancha.* He brought the show together, knocking out the ten o'clock number 'The Impossible Dream'. That fact alone solved the committee's tricky song selection dilemma.

The VFL flew Barry from London to the G and let him loose before the bounce. Footy people thought, 'Well this is great! At last, the VFL is doing something right! How good is that Dr Allen Aylett? He is fantastic!'

Predictably enough, footy tragics saw 'The Impossible Dream' in footy terms. It was all about winning the flag against impossible odds. It spoke to the Collingwood faithful with the line about fighting an unbeatable foe – that is what they had done all season. They had done it all their life. From last to first 'no matter how hopeless' said it all. 1977 was going to be their year!

It's hard to find reviews of Barry's tonsil action on the day. But the fall-out from his 1977 Grand Final performance included a contribution to the nation's lexicon of rhyming slang. The name Crocker was tipped into the concept of 'a shocker', as in truly dud.

The Crocker appearance in 1977 let the pre-match entertainment cat out of the bag and there was no chance of stuffing the tabby back into the hessian sack. Barry's appearance changed Grand Final day forever.

## The 1977 Grand Final experience before the bounce was out of this world!

*What happened when the big men flew?*

Once the Crocker, B. 'Impossible Dream' fluff had been cleared away, the umpire bounced the ball and the Grannie was finally underway.

The Magpies were minor premiers, with eighteen wins from twenty-two matches, but North were a big noise in the seventies. The Kangaroos had turned out for the last three Grand Finals. When they fronted in 1976, they fell at the final hurdle, beaten by Hawthorn by 30 points. The old footy adage maintains a team will lose a Grand Final before they win one. If that was the case, then North Melbourne were overdue. They were Shinboner hungry.

It was a one-sided first quarter. North were up by 18 points at quarter time. There were 2 points in it at half-time. North, after a bright start, were having a miserable time in front of the goal. The usually reliable Shinboner boot radar in front of the big sticks had gone on the blink.

The third quarter was all Collingwood, and at three-quarter time the Pies led by 27 points. The Kangaroos did not boot a major in the second and third quarters. They had plenty of chances but kicked 13 points in a row. That is a lot of missed opportunities. A very nervous Arnold Briedis was the main culprit, ending up with 7 minors for the match. Once a star misses a couple of sitters in a big stink, the confidence goes and then the brain-to-boot axis fades to rubble. When technique is shot, it is all downhill ending in a shallow puddle of nerves. Sooner or later, North had to slot the Sherrin between the big sticks. But the yips were getting bigger.

Pies people went into the last quarter confident that the long twenty-year drought was almost over. Ah but the faithful, the army, had overlooked the dreaded Colliwobbles. Could the curse ring true once again?

In the last quarter the tide came in. The Kangaroos kicked five unanswered majors while the Pies stumbled forward, snaring just one. When the final hooter blew the scores were level, not a struck match between them.

Total devastation and deflation all round. Scores: North 9.22 (76), Collingwood 10.16 (76). This points-heavy scoreline anticipated the modern era in which accurate kicking is no longer a feature of the game.

As the final hooter honked, 108,224 spectators did not know where to look, what to do, whether to laugh or cry. Hardly anyone could remember the last drawn VFL Grannie. The first draw was thirty years before in 1948 when the Demons and the Bombers could not be separated at the death.

Post hooter, supercoach Ron said the Kangaroos should have won the Grannie, as his side had five more scoring shots than the Pies. Sadly, in those unenlightened times, the bookies did not pay on the number of scoring shots; they only paid out on the final score.

The VFL match committee replayed the draw the following week, which meant rustling up some acts to charm the fans before the bounce on that first day in October.

And the replay? Well, it was anti-climactic. North led from bounce to final hooter.

The Kangaroos took a firm grip on the match in the third quarter. Collingwood needed something.

They got it when Phil Manassa picked up the footy on the half-back line, swerved round Roo super boot Malcolm Blight, sprinted to the far end and booted truly. It was a stunning run, described by Channel Seven's Peter Ewin as the 'goal of the century'. And *The Age* newspaper rated Phil's swerve, run and goal as 'the fifth greatest Grannie moment of all time'. There is no pleasing some commentators.

Final scores in the replay: North 21.25 (151), Collingwood 19.10 (124). Pies lost by 27 points. This was Collingwood's fifth Grand Final loss since their 1958 win. There were more desperate days at the G to come before they finally won their next flag. The Pies kept wobbling until 1990.

Sadly, the 'goal of the century' did not help the Pies, but in honour of the effort the Phil Manassa Medal is dished for AFL Goal of the Year.

Grand Finals are often forgettable affairs unless the beanie on your bonce is in the club colours of a winning side. Losers can suit themselves.

But for the dedicated footy head, Grand Finals mark the great moments of life. Time passes with the turn of the season. Winning supporters know exactly where they were, who they were with and what they were holding when the final siren sounded and *Footy Records*, beanies and half-drunk glasses of beer are tossed into the MCG twilight sky.

And the thing that mattered most, the TV ratings, were incredible. The 1977 Grannie was a smash hit. Channel Seven paid the AFL $500,000 to televise the game and the same dollop again for the repeat the following week. One and a half million footy freaks tuned in, the greatest daytime TV audience at that time. One game, and suddenly the Melbourne television future was live-to-air footy.

In the early years, the Oxide Five were keen on cabaret stars, tapping Adelaide-born art teacher and musical theatre star Keith Michell in 1978 to follow Barry's sod-turning blast. Keith worked his magic. The cabaret vibe persisted when the Oxide team asked Peter 'I Go to Rio' Allen to do the honours in 1980. Diana Trask, Olivia Newton-John and the *Hey! Hey! It's Saturday!* man Daryl Somers all had a go in the first decade of Blueprint Blight pre-match action.

The Oxide Five's approach in a nutshell: familiar acts with familiar tunes talking to the people of Melbourne. If stuck, the cabaret collective could always unite the nation with a football-tinged rendition of 'Waltzing Matilda'.

Many performers, though keen to get involved, found the circumstances of the gig challenging.

The vast scale of the MCG, the distance between star and audience, the excitement of the football to come – all pulls the focus from the musical contributions. Unless the artist packs the bristle and brawn of AC/DC live no one hears a word. All the supporters see is an ant-sized artist stumbling about in the distance.

Everyone wants the singer to shut up and get off so the football can start. For the singer, it can be a thankless task, a cruel gig! Focus is hard to maintain as footy people drift off to have a jimmy in the nearby bushes or get a pie or a couple of beers that will see them through the first quarter before another mad dash to complete the toilet, food and beverage trifecta in time for the bounce for the second quarter.

The humble Crocker-inspired beginnings soon expanded into a day that combined old-fashioned show business with

Grand Final football. It evolved into a showcase for artists from around the world. The big names selected by the NOF committee soon graduated from a throwaway afterthought, forgotten as soon as the teams ran onto the G through the club run-through, becoming a sizeable strawberry on top of a three-layer sponge cake that was football's one day of the year. They became a crucial ingredient, almost as important as the game-day Sherrin.

*The humble Crocker-inspired beginnings soon expanded into a day that combined old-fashioned show business with Grand Final football.*

The annual build-up to the Oxide committee's announcement about which local or overseas artists would grace the Grannie card occupied media speculation for weeks leading up to the reveal on Channel Seven's six o'clock news. The announcement was usually made by the VFL/AFL CEO at a large press conference with music industry heavies like Mushroom chief Michael Gudinski in attendance.

In the aftermath of every Grand Final, especially if the act had put in a 'Barry Crocker', there was forensic analysis of what went wrong and how the NOF committee could get it right next year. This kicked off the 'Who's Next?' debate. Media speculation could run for months!

The VFL/AFL Grand Final entertainment journey has been a long, strange trip. One melody has anchored the ride from day one. That tune is Mike Brady's 'Up There Cazaly'. This footy-focused chart topper quickly became a Grand Final day staple. It is a genuine footy anthem, penned in 1979 to promote the Channel Seven season-long football coverage.

The title refers to the high-leaping South Melbourne ruckman, Roy Cazaly, who pulled on the boots for the blood-stained angels in the early years of the twentieth century. Roy was a great mark, with a spectacular vertical leap, often grabbing the footy with one hand at ruck contests.

The song topped the music charts in 1979. Given the Channel Seven free-to-air exposure, 'Up There' stayed on top for months. Musically, it's a tricky song to get your head around, with a couple of startling key changes. But no one doubts its long life or its pride of place as Australia's number one footy anthem.

*It harkens back to a time when football was not a vast international business but the suburban pastime that explained why Melbourne existed.*

It harkens back to a time when football was not a vast international business but the suburban pastime that explained why Melbourne existed. Once this humble harmony is heard and the great game glimpsed, who would be mad enough to live anywhere else? Honestly? Melbourne is a city full of attractions, but when you line everything up the footy wins hands down.

The follow-up, 'There's a Little Bit of Cazaly in Us All', spoke to every footy follower who needed convincing they were doing the right thing and not wasting their life by going to the game every weekend no matter what the weather.

On the one hand, the Oxide Five realised that Mike Brady and 'Cazaly' was a Grannie given, and on the other, it did not take long for international music managements to see the promotional potential of touring the big stars through Australia in late September on the off-chance they could snap up an afternoon gig at the G.

There were lean years when no one was around, the big stars were elsewhere, so on the day NOF had to rely on the Friends of the Grannie like John Farnham, Normie Rowe, Glenn Shorrock, Daryl Somers and Paul Kelly. Some years the crowd was serenaded by a choir in charge of the sing-a-long. There were almost as many on stage singing as playing the game.

In other years the pre-match entertainment was weird. In 1991, the MCG was closed for renovations and the Grand Final was relocated to Waverley Oval, nicknamed Arctic Park for the obvious reasons. This was a challenge for all concerned. The Oxide Five's handiwork on the big day at Waverley had a curious flavour.

It was the last go-round of the final five concept. The VFL, in an effort to squeeze another drop from the September action lemon, added another team and the final five became the final six.

On that history-making day, in a triumph of cross-promotion, hard-rocking Rose Tattoo's front man Angry Anderson was tapped to farewell the Australian team headed to the Olympic Games in Barcelona the following year. Angry, with help from Mikes de Luca and Slamer, had cooked a confection full of gold medal encouragement called 'Bound for Glory'. It climbed to number eleven on the charts. The sentiment, style and sound were unremarkable, but it was heartfelt and loud.

What was remarkable on the day was that the bad boy for love, bald-headed Angry, waddled out at half-time into a rain sodden venue accompanied by the Batmobile. The what? Well, it was a canny piece of cross-promotion, letting footy heads know that *Batman Returns* was going to be in town at a cinema near you. The cinema in 1991 still pulled big crowds, especially to superhero blockbusters. The suggestion was that this film was almost as good as football – just look at the car. The car still talks to Batman fans. It still goes and was sold in late 2020 on eBay where it attracted a lot of interest from speed freaks who had space in their double garage.

*Once the Oxide Five had a taste of the cross promotion-caper it was all systems go.*

Once the Oxide Five had a taste of the cross promotion-caper it was all systems go. The concept struck gold in 2010 when the AFL unveiled the Dreamliner. It's a huge plane and the future of flying. It swooped in from the Punt Road end at the MCG. The Big Bird looked as though it was about to touch down in the centre circle of the G before suddenly gaining altitude and swinging over the city and out of sight. The daredevil pilot had 100,000 supporters staining their underwear – the future of aviation was that close.

In 1995, Scott Morrison's favourite, Tina Arena, stepped out to her biggest audience when she wandered on and blasted an acapella version of 'Waltzing Matilda' with the help of many friends. This brave presentation was followed in 1996 by the big ensemble doing the Grannie standards. The hundredth year of the VFL/AFL Grannies was celebrated with a star-studded line-up of stars who had been having a sing on the day since 1977. This was the big one and it needed a big crew. Barry Crocker was back, John Farnham was in the house, along with Normie Rowe, Venetta Fields, Slim Dusty, Daryl Somers,

Glenn Shorrock, Lindsay Fields, Diana Trask, Norm Watson and Maroochy Barambah.

The joint effort on 'Matilda' had everybody chipping in a line or two before the massed voices of the Nitrous Oxide Grand Final All Stars chimed in for the chorus and brought it all home. Critics raved, 'Not a dry eye in the House!' The game, however, was another lopsided affair. The North Melbourne Kangaroos touched up the Sydney Swans by forty-plus points.

And as the years and seasons rolled by, more footy songs were added to the AFL canon. Hunters and Collectors contributed 'The Holy Grail' (this song is actually about Napoleon's retreat from Moscow, but it was clear to anyone who kicked a Sherrin that the Holy Grail was the AFL premiership). 'One Day in September', 'Rock 'N Footy (Rock the G)' and Paul Kelly's 'Leaps and Bounds' were all great additions to the songs that could be rolled out as part of football's biggest day.

Blueprint Blight's great Grannie successes are tempered by numerous totally forgettable moments and many completely forgettable games. But pre-match immortality was achieved in 2011 when the Oxide Five tapped Meat Loaf to appear on the Grannie boundary line. Hard to know if the Loaf knew anything about Australian Rules football or footy fans. For starters, Loaf freaks had to be middle-aged, as in about forty-seven, to have a clue who he was. It had been decades since Captain Meat had a hit on the charts. In his prime this great act had sold forty-three million records and was a Grammy award-winner.

The committee's nitrous oxide–fuelled concept reached a historic low (or high) with Meat Man's startlingly cod ordinary performance. It was a complete Barry Crocker.

Introduced in magnificent fashion on the big day by 'the Voice of the AFL':

> Ladies and gentlemen, Carlton Draught and the VFL are pleased to present a man who burst onto the world music stage in 1977 . . . [A list of achievements and hits followed.]
>
> Please welcome to the stage Grammy award-winner Meat Loaf!

One hundred thousand footy fans were scratching their heads as the Loaf roared into the G, leg over a Harley. He was a noisy speck in a sea of supporters' scarves. Suddenly, he was there with a twelve-and-half-minute medley of the best of Meat. It was *Bat Out of Hell* (1977) hits rammed together, including 'Two Out of Three Ain't Bad', 'Bat Out of Hell' and 'You Took the Words Right Out of My Mouth'.

It was all there: that voice surging like a runaway cement mixer, the leather threads, the Bat Out of Hell ensemble blasting away and letting the chips fall where they may, and those songs. It was a performance that baffled the knowledgeable MCG crowd, who would have needed an international musicologist to unravel the Loaf's sonic mess. As far as anyone at the G knew, the Mince in Motion Man was singing the team list from the Grand Final *Footy Record*.

On the upside, Australia has not stopped talking about the Loaf's unique Grand Final performance. His contribution to football gossip and folklore in those magical few minutes was outstanding. In a Best on Ground performance, he was the benchmark of both success and failure. Everyone in Australia claims they were at the G on that day when the train with

Meat Loaf up front, with his hands on the levers, crashed, leaving millions asking: Why?

The horrendous nature of Meat's performance did not give the Blueprint Blight committee pause to reconsider their strategy. They kept throwing acts at the wall and were delighted when one stuck. The pre-match entertainment had come a long way from the humble 'The Impossible Dream' days and the simpler times of Barry Crocker.

*The horrendous nature of Meat's performance did not give the Blueprint Blight committee pause to reconsider their strategy.*

Back in Jolimont House, after another pull on the nitrous oxide, the NOF suggested expanding the musical and artistic content of the day by shrinking the role of football. The committee always had that as a dream. It made so much sense: if you were paying a star for a warble before the bounce, why not roll the ensemble out at half-time for another blast of big hits? Or even better, get another act to do the half-time and then get the pre-match artists back for a big set after the game. Suddenly, it was Glastonbury, Sunbury and footy at the MCG.

Once the Norm Smith and the premiership medals had been dished out, the speeches boxed and buried, and the winning team had made a stumble around the boundary line greeting delirious fans, there was a football audience gagging for more. The Blueprint Blight committee tipped the footy crowd out, reopened the gates and let 100,000 music buffs back in.

The Blueprint's ultimate dream was to cement the link between entertainment and football. If only a player from the winning team, still wearing the jumper, could get up on stage and sing a big hit with the band during the post-game show.

Hopefully, the international act and footy star could find a chart-topper that the crowd knew and could join in the sing-a-long. What a 'sensational' finish to the day! This would climax the journey begun all those years ago when the Famous Five first assembled around the gas tank, breathed deeply and dreamed.

This marriage of footy and art climaxed when Tigers forward, Jack Riewoldt, still sporting his sweat-stained premiership winning jumper and shorts, sat in on vocals with Las Vegas chart toppers The Killers. The band and Jack swung through 'Mister Brightside' after the Tigers' flag success in 2017. This selection, The Killers' first song, has an autobiographical flavour, but what a choice it was! The opening line about coming out of a cage talks directly to the Tigers faithful. The rest of the song is pure yellow and black.

It was an absolute triumph, for the G, the Grannie, a Tigers' win, Jack and The Killers – and the soundman out front on the mixing board who had the sense to turn Jack's mike down.

## Live Performances at Rugby League Grand Finals

*On that one day in October, was the league just as insanely creative as the AFL?*

Rugby league, the AFL's great football rival, was keen to get involved with the pre-match entertainment romp. Over the years the Greatest Game of All (G.G.A.) had baked a wide variety of music into the promotion of game. There were plenty of acts to choose from for the big occasions.

The history of the G.G.A. Grand Final entertainment is littered with the great and, not surprisingly, on-the-blink moments. Mixed into the fiasco of feeble are some A-grade stinkers.

There are more big nights on the rugby league calendar than on the AFL schedule. There is a finals series, including the big tombola, three State of Origin matches and an assortment of Test Matches and All-Star games. All these fixtures require musical support. Game theory suggests a crowd will never be pulled simply by the drama of the game.

No one remembers the good nights when the show went to plan. Nights when the Provan–Summons trophy arrived without a hitch, when the game started on time after the musical act had quietly packed up and moved on. When the choking smoke of the fireworks was blown away on the spring breeze and when the parade of old players in ill-fitting suits passed without comment. There is no reason to remember those nights. It's the dud that lingers.

As in the AFL, pre-match entertainment in rugby league is a heady cocktail of moving parts. Performers, staging, PAs, lights, fireworks, dancers, road crew, musical equipment and power all have to be rushed on and then rushed off after a blast. The moving parts cannot collide with the players from both teams running on for their date with destiny.

The league got lucky early. The entertainment committee set the bar very high on the dud gauge when they booked the cast of *Neighbours* to sing the national anthem before the 1986 Grand Final. This memorable big rhumba was a try-less fling, Parramatta Eels 4, Canterbury-Bankstown Bulldogs 2. It was a defence masterclass, entertainment as only the league can turn on.

The afternoon kicked off with a choir that included Kylie Minogue, Jason Donovan and Guy Pearce. They lurched right out of their comfort zone when they lined up to unite the nation in song. When the booking was made, no one was asked whether the Ramsay Street song-and-dance troupe could actually sing. Rugby league people assume all actors can hold a tune and bring their A-game to the big watusi. Maybe the choir over-rehearsed or suffered from big-game pre-match nerves, but they contributed a unique rendition of the nation's big tune with a lot of guesses about notes and lyrics. Once heard never forgotten. Even the players who are most reluctant to comment on art and culture were gobsmacked by the originality of the read. This rendition featured some genuinely weird pitch selections which would have stretched the great jazz saxophonist John Coltrane's understanding of how music worked.

From 1988 until 1998 the league Grand Final was played at the Sydney Football Stadium and witnessed several distinguished displays of dud. The Navy apprentices' shed-erection competition in 1987 was a curious pre-match entertainment. Tradie teams from our senior service went at it hammer and tongs, showing what young Australians can do if given a chance. Sadly, the apprentices did the bolts up too tight during the erection phase. It took most of the first half plus a lengthy spray of WD-40 to loosen the bolts. Professionals rushed in to dismantle the structures before kick off could get underway.

At next year's final, the dome of doom featured a promotion of the cable channel Optus. It was a tight fit, as the cable channel was the new home of rugby league. It was decided that the best way to link the two was to suspend a giant television from wires running across from one side of the SFS to the other. It was all going swimmingly until the giant prop TV got caught up in the wires that held it in place.

Clearing the collapsed promotional prop required time-consuming work by skilled riggers. It was not easy. The league was so used to disasters by this stage that the teams ran on and began the game with the technicians and stage crew still trying to clean up the chaos. In a weird way, the whole shemozzle foretold the future of the Optus channel, which collapsed in debt and disappointment several years after its wobbly Grand Final launch.

In 1989 the big show in town was the musical *42nd Street*. The tap-dancing cast were tasked to get the big dance underway. The Street's big number was 'We're in the Money'. In the theatre the whole cast tap-danced their way in unison around the set. It was not the easiest routine to adapt to a football stadium, but Australian musical theatre thrives on challenges.

The cast, wearing their show clothes with taps on their shoes, assumed the start positions at all points of the Stadium. It was a 'ready, set, go' situation. Then nothing happened. No sound, just a pin drop and embarrassed looks. With no beat, the dancers could not move their feet. The crowd turned restless. Word filtered through with stage whispers that someone had left the all-important backing tape cassette in the glove box of the car. The cast finally got the message and, feeling stupid, sloped off, lugging their props with them to ironic cheers. They gave it their best shot on the day and came up short.

It was an early curtain for the tap troupe. Mercifully, the Canberra Raiders had their footy boots and heads on and cleaned up the Balmain Tigers. It was the Green Machine's first flag.

By 2002, the Grand Final had been relocated to Stadium Australia, at Homebush. It was not Billy Idol's fault that he laid a dump centre stage that had to be flushed before the match could get under way. There he was, looking stupid in his threatening, old-school punk garb. That look of menace, the bleached thatch, the song 'Rebel Yell'. An aging punk and rugby league – what a tight fit, it was going to be great!

Billy Idol zoomed on in a hovercraft. Fireworks bursting from the back of the lawn mower that floats. He jumped off the airborne Victa punching the air. His sneer was dialled up to nine. Fists pumping the air, he was ready to rock. But the only thing that worked was his mike! He blurted out a few lines of punk cabaret.

Awright! Sydney, are you ready to rock!

Are there any Warrior fans here?
[Very modest applause, given that the team come from New Zealand.]

Can't hear you!
[Pause, hoping something might happen.]

Are there any Roosters fans here?
[Louder applause.]

I love my footy.
Just waiting for the power!

A few drum fills but no rocking, no punking, no gobbing because there was no power. With Billy out in the middle dying, it dawned on the Stadium Australia stage management that someone had forgotten to run a power lead out to the stage.

Cut to the commentators who contributed to proceedings with the immortal observation: 'Billy Idol not having the best of nights on Grand Final night'.

By now, the crew upstairs were used to coping with disaster. After all, they had seen a fiasco or two. They once battled on bravely when the video-taping skydiver collided with the roof of the grandstand in an epic jump miscalculation.

But remember stadium management on Grand Final day has so many things to think about. Something is bound to go wrong. The rugby league public are very forgiving. They have come to see the big dance and could not give a stuff about an unpowered entertainer prancing about almost three kilometres away. Billy's cough and spit on the day was far more memorable because it contributed nothing except embarrassment.

The most recent calamity was in 2014 when the entertainment committee let Slash from the Guns N' Roses commune loose for a mid-pitch noodle on the Gibson Les Paul Standard. It was 2014, the year of the Rabbit. It was Slash in his hat with the Les, two Marshall stacks and a lot of other musical equipment that no one was playing. The crowd assumed the band was still loading up on the bus. But suddenly Slash was out there and hard at it.

How could Slash make such a racket by himself? The instruments were being played by unseen hands.

Everyone, including Slash, was relieved when the backing tape agony ground to a halt. The stadium applause for the television coverage was curiously produced by no one in the seats clapping. For those watching at home it was another league pre-match miracle.

The best, included for balance: well, there's Cold Chisel's sixteen excellent minutes of high-revving art delivered in 2015. They could handle the venue and had the technology to fill it. They knew how big it had to be to reach the far corners of the room. It was one of those nights when it all worked, because Johnathon Thurston led the big hats of the North Queensland Cowboys to the NRL title for the first time. It was a great climax to the season that Robbie Williams had promoted with his hit 'Let Me Entertain You'.

In rugby league, as in the AFL, plenty of artists came and went, barely leaving a mark in the guest book. Hopefully the entertainment committee do not lose their magic touch. On the big nights, there will be easily forgotten gems, but also if the past is a guide there will be magnificent duds. The latter providing footy heads with talking points and sonic flops, often far more memorable than the game.

# THE NATIONAL AGENDA

*The names Hawke, Howard, Menzies, Holt and Snedden set the bar at a gold medal height.*

SPORT IS ALWAYS NEAR the top of the national agenda. These great role models all had competition in their genes. Many are called to the highest office, but not every Australian can snare a run-on spot with the A-Team. This line up gives all potential starters an idea of what is required to snare a green and gold guernsey.

They came hoping to make a difference to their nation, their suburb or their street, and maybe to get a nice car park near the local railway station. On the way out they had a tearful goodbye promising to spend more time with their family (but only if other activities permit).

## The great all-rounder: Bob Hawke, PM 1983–91

Our twenty-third Prime Minister, Bob Hawke, was our great all-rounder. He could do the lot. Whether it was cricket,

*As Prime Minister he loved being part of any team, as long as it was a winning team, and he was part of any team, as long as it was a green and gold team.*

drinking, boats or bathers, he was up for it, on it and into it. As Prime Minister he loved being part of any team, as long as it was a winning team, and he was part of any team, as long as it was a green and gold team.

Early notoriety came at university, where many of Australia's greatest political stars got a start climbing the greasy pole to the top. Bob always had luck on his side. Like hard-living Australians of a certain age, he was an ice-cold lager guzzler. He got lucky when he established a spectacular world beer-drinking record at Oxford University. In 1953, Bob won a Rhodes Scholarship to the British Home of Brewing, University College, Oxford, to write a thesis on wage fixing in Australia. This was the sort of topic that needed serious alcoholic support and sustenance.

There were a number of students on campus who knew how to really put it away, but Bob demonstrated an exceptional talent in postgraduate grog tutorial. Sinking a long length of local brew was not a regular subject on the university curriculum, but students and staff felt the need to give the squirt a nudge during the difficult days of serious study and to ease the tension, especially when the final exams approached. Our future PM established a wonderful record. As a part of a 'sconce' penalty Bob put away 1.4 litres of beer in eleven seconds. The 'sconce' was an ancient form of punishment for college alcoholic infringements.

Not sure if his record still stands. Not sure if the attractive gauntlet that Bob threw down in the Uni refectory on that day in May has been picked up by other champions of the big gargle during the intervening years. That's a PhD thesis waiting to be written.

All real Australians know that sport and drinking have gone hand in hand since Arthur Phillip blew through the Heads at Sydney Harbour with the First Fleet on Invasion Day, 26 January 1788. They are the twin pillars of the European-controlled Australia and were unpacked with the first convicts.

Sport was in Bob's blood. He loved Test cricket. In his mind, the great game, especially the Ashes competition against the Old Foe, was best consumed with a beer in hand. Later, in his go-slow years, he would often waddle out to the SCG on a warm day three of the New Year's Test and entertain the crowd during a dull session between lunch and tea by sinking a pint of beer in one gulp.

He dropped a jar to prove he still had it, all that time after his original gullet-challenging records were set in those exciting Oxford years. The thirst-quenching feat was always relayed to the SCG faithful via the big television screens inside the venue. As the beer went down, cheers erupted from a crowd that was always keen to be involved.

Let's be honest: it was not a great act – a glass of cold beer on a hot day in your own time. It would be un-Australian to fail that Test match challenge. No records were broken at the SCG, but cricket fans, by that time of the afternoon, loved seeing a fit ex-Prime Minister do what they had been doing since 11 am. Sure, the packed Test crowd egged him on, but he never needed much encouragement. Simpler times, simpler pleasures.

Bob Hawke played cricket in his pre-Oxford, pre-wage-fixing student days for the University of Western Australia. He kept wicket. One afternoon, crouching behind the furniture, Bob pulled off that rarest of cricket tricks, dismissing a batsman twice with the same ball. It was a wicket the Uni side had to get against the local power side, Subiaco.

In a mid-pitch, mid-over confab with the bowler, who was doing a bit off the pitch from the Swan River end, Bob observed the clown with the willow in hand was getting a long way out of his crease. He tasked his wily medium pacer to put one down the leg side. Bob resumed the crouch, standing up to the wicket, hoping to remove the bails and effect a stumping. He went one better: he caught the ball the batsman snicked and took the bails off in the same motion. The umpire saw it Bob's way and put the finger in the air not once, but twice. The stumping was a brave decision from the non-striker's end, but the confirmation of the stumping came from the official standing at square leg.

*The umpire saw it Bob's way and put the finger in the air not once, but twice.*

The future PM would have given the twice-dismissed batter a solid send off to accompany 'this hopeless loser' on his long and lonely stroll all the way back to the pavilion.

Bob pulled on the pads and big gloves and crouched behind the furniture whenever time allowed during his political career. He turned out in the clash of a PM's Eleven against the Press Gallery in 1984. These Press v Pollie brouhahas were hotly contested fixtures, with prestige and bragging rights on the line. There were serious players turning out on both sides.

At the crease with the willow in hand, Bob was known for keeping his eye on the ball. On this particular occasion Bob was set and was looking to push deep past 50 for the politicians. Suddenly he misjudged the line and length of a ball from *Herald Sun* journalist Gary O'Neill. The delivery reared up off a length and caught Bob flush in the face, breaking his glasses.

It did not look good for the PM's good eye. Everyone went very quiet. Bob was rushed to hospital as the crowd held its breath. Given the all-clear by the cricket-literate, white-coated hospital eye staff, the PM was able to return later in the day as a spectator. There are dramatic photos of the moment the six-stitcher ball smashes Bob's OPSM gear.

In 1983 he had not been long in the job when an Australian yacht, imaginatively named *Australia II*, skippered by John Bertrand with navigator Iain 'Lard' Murray at the wheel, snared the America's Cup from the New York Yacht Club. This was a big thing! The arrogant NYYC had bolted the trophy in place, so confident were they of never being beaten. It was a best of seven series.

Our opponent in the twelve-metre war on water was *Liberty*, skippered by San Diego interior design expert (special subject, soft furnishings) Dennis Conner.

In the 1983 tilt, *Australia II* was in trouble early. Everything went wrong. Poor tactics, flukey winds, home track advantage, and suddenly after four races the gutsy Australian outfit were 3–1 down and Australian yachting types were looking down the barrel of another in a long line of America's Cup defeats.

But our tub packed a powerful secret where only the snook could see it. Boat designer Ben Lexcen had tacked on a magical winged keel below the water line. This 'hush hush' technology gave the Australian twelve-metre genuine grunt.

As it turned out, it gave our barge a winning chance. The winged keel took a while to master, but *Australia II* romped home in the next three races in a row to bag that bolted-down old mug 4–3.

Business tycoon and media mogul Alan Bond, who bankrolled the brouhaha, had to go to the local Bunnings in New York and borrow a set of Stillsons to loosen the nuts on the pewter carafe for the first time in 132 years.

No one in Australia took much notice of this 'unwinnable' watusi of wetness until we won. It was seen as a private stink for people with far more money than sense.

This was true until the last day of competition. The final race ran through the night, Australian time, keeping many Australians, including Bob, glued to the dramatic television coverage. Next morning Bob Hawke appeared on breakfast television. He was over the moon. It was a dream come true for the recently installed PM. What a win!

He appeared wearing a very attractive *Australia II* supporter's jacket. Bob could not contain his excitement. He declared to a deliriously, bleary-eyed and worse-for-wear nation that they could have a public holiday. He concluded this historic press conference with the immortal line, 'Any boss who sacks anyone for not turning up today is a bum!' One of the great quotes from any politician after an unlikely win in a sporting contest.

## The winning edge was a winged keel!

*The mystery from Down Under tacked to the bottom of the boat.*

Ben Lexcen's winged keel was a great bit of lateral thinking. The idea originally came from a Dutch floatation tank. Ben adapted the concept to twelve-metre racing yachts.

Great ideas are often very simple. Ben's winged keel lifted the boat up when travelling at speed giving it superior glide. It was a big help for heavy yachts with sail up tacking into headwinds. The advantage to *Australia II* in that magical America's Cup final series was measured at one minute every upwind leg.

The skipper of *Liberty*, *Australia II*'s America's Cup opponent, the San Diego draper, Dennis Conner, sent down cloak-and-dagger spies with the scuba gear to have a peek at what the boat was packing downstairs. Mercifully these cloak-and-dagger merchants could not penetrate the shroud of secrecy that surrounded the pen in which the Aussie challenger was docked between races.

There were suggestions in the American press with a fake news agenda that the keel was fitted with micro-motors powered by miniature lithium batteries to basically cheat. As if Australian yachting types would be caught at it red-handed like a bunch of boof-headed cricketers or international cycling showboats!

Not sure the winged keel had many applications. It seemed to be limited to racing yachts and power boats cruising in shallow waters.

Sadly, the innovation was not adapted to the popular Toyota Lexcen, which was Ben's next cab off the innovation rank. The car disappointed Australian car buyers who thought they were getting something very special in the speed department. They weren't.

Once the Down-Under glide genie was out of the bottle it did not take long for a new breed of twelve-metre designers to tumble to the idea that it was the actual water that created the drag that slowed the boats to a crawl. Racing yacht designs evolved, eventually removing any contact between the yacht's hull and the liquid source of the slows. Suddenly, the friction drag was reduced to nothing.

The next stage in design evolution got the hull up out of the water and the yacht flying, kite-surfing style. Twelve metres now go like the clappers, literally flying around the course. Twelve-metre buffs claim officials are planning to run the next series between two coastal airports.

Australia has always been a nation of great innovation. The Hills Hoist rotary clothesline, the Victa lawnmower, the Pope sprinkler, the wine cask, Interscan, over-the-horizon radar, the black box flight recorder, solar panels are just a few. The list of great ideas is endless.

They were not all hits. One great mystery was the Ralph Sarich orbital engine. Ralph's two-stroke orbital combustion engine was going to revolutionise the motor industry. Not sure what happened to the concept. Maybe it was a dud in a car.

All revheaded Australians wanted to see the Sarich orbital slaved up to the fantastic Peter Brock Energy Polarizer to see how fast these technologies could make the FJ Holden or the Ford Falcon XY GT-HO phase III go.

That is just one of many great ideas lying dormant, waiting for a new generation of bright sparks to come along and kick start Australian speed innovation all over again.

Bob was very hands-on when it came to the nation's sporting psyche. He had that chart-topping classic 'Advance Australia Fair' (known widely as the 'Girt' song) adopted as the national anthem.

The 'AAF' malarkey was originally intended to be sung at international fixtures where two great nations competed for 'the greatest prize of all in the greatest games of all'. Nowadays it gets a blast whenever three or more Australians are gathered looking for peace to disturb. Apparently, this power ballad in the right hands unites the nation and allows Australia to stand as one.

Bob determined the national sporting colours would be green and gold. In doing so he set a challenge that no fashion designer has successful tamed – i.e. making those difficult colours when applied to singlets, shorts, swimmers and tracksuit trousers look anything but hideous. The colour combination spawned an endless bagging of national sporting designs, no matter how they looked. Green and gold have never looked good except on the top step of the podium with a medal dangling around the winner's neck.

Bob was a keen racing man. He loved picking a winner. Like all punters he loved seeing his selection salute. He loved the Melbourne Cup. Gold and Black's win in 1984 was one of Bob's big wins early in the top job. The vision of him riding the conveyance down the long Flemington straight while camped on a comfy chair in the PM's office still brings a smile to the lips. It was one of his great rides.

Bob donned the silks and was riding in the stands the day Queen Elizabeth II lobbed at Thoroughbred Park in Canberra, ACT, to open 'The QE2 Pew', named, obviously, in her honour. This stand was a very modern facility fully equipped with handrails and women's toilets. In those days the Queen was always out and about on the sniff across the Commonwealth looking for ribbons to snip, pavlovas to sample and bouquets of flowers to collect from the kiddies.

The QE2 Pew opening was one of the great Bicentennial occasions of 1988. Not sure anyone remembers the other great occasions during that fabulous year that 'celebrated' 200 years of occupation. For many local monarchists, the opening of this trackside perch selected itself as the highlight of that fabulous decade, the eighties.

*It was another incredible ride from Bob with the Queen riding shotgun in the saddle next door.*

The feature race on the card was the QE2 Bicentennial Stakes. The Bart Cummings–trained Beau Zam scored. It was another incredible ride from Bob with the Queen riding shotgun in the saddle next door. She was obviously impressed by the PM's technique. Bob was a winner on the day and left the course grinning and with a groaning wallet, creating an unsightly bulge in the front of the trouser. Records don't show which horse the Queen dropped a packet on in the race with her name on it. Surely the hard-working committee could have organised a result that went her way!

Bob was a bloke of his time and rightly got a lot of applause for doing what he loved. But many Sport Institute and Australian Olympic officials believe the pressure of work prevented Bob from expressing himself to the fullest in the sporting arena.

Newspaper and television sport editors knew that Bob had the skills to tackle our great sun, sand and surf epic, the

Coolangatta Gold. This was an energy-sapping three-pronger set on the magnificent stretch of sand at the southern end of the Surfers Paradise holiday strip.

The 1984–85 version of the surfside stroll was a case of life imitating art as the event was created for and featured in the movie of the same name. The film focused on the adventures of a crew of iron men involved in the fictitious race.

Holidaymakers from around the world gathered for a sticky beak at the surf-and-sand action. Nothing pulls a crowd more than young, fit Australians doing really stupid and exhausting things and tagging the run-around as both sport and art.

The original Coolangatta Gold race had a simple yet complex structure. It was a run, a swim and a paddle. The slog began with an eleven-kilometre run from Surfers Paradise over Burleigh Heads to Tallebudgera Creek, barefoot in the scalding sands. Competitors cooled off with a wade across the croc-infested river followed by a short sprint before hitting the soup for a four-kilometre swim towards Currumbin. Once the bull sharks were left behind in the Pacific, the transition to a board leg happened at Bilinga. The paddle leg took the competition down to Coolangatta where they turned north and paddled the ski leg all the way back to Surfers Paradise. If competitors felt peckish during the race, they could nibble on the fish they caught from a baited hook that trailed from the back of the ski.

This layout was a deadset stinker! But Bob's fitness would have held up and his great knowledge of ALP back-room tactics in tight marginal seat contests would have given him a distinct advantage in the cut and thrust of competition. The Gold was made for a man with his attack, discipline, elbows and rat cunning.

Bob would have been a tight fit for Goldie action, but a bigger loss to the national treasure chest of memories, according to many pundits, was Bob's failure to get a CAMS-approved racing licence. This is not a piece of paper anyone can pick up online from a university in Ohio for fifteen dollars. This is a qualification that requires a stern automotive speed test. It asks serious questions and a demonstration that you have mastered real pedal-to-the-metal skills.

Mount Panorama and the Holden Dealer Team were a natural stage for Bob. If only Bob had had a chance to strut his stuff in an XU1 Torana in 1972 in the Hardie-Ferodo. It was a lost opportunity. What an example to set for kids of all ages! This was the year Peter Brock drove the whole race by himself. Revheads across the nation would have loved to have seen Bob accelerating down Conrod Straight, scraping the door handles off on the turns in the XU1 when it was his turn to relieve 'The King'.

With Bob in the fire-proof overalls, imagine the scenes on the victory dais after the chequered flag had been swung and the dust had settled. The crowd wants to see Bob. He does not disappoint. He steps up and, to the roars of the Generals' troops, does his thing with a litre or two of the sponsor's amber-coloured bitter in one gulp. The bloke still has it!

Of course, given Bob's style in the cut and thrust of the Big House in Canberra, many fight fans believe Bob would have been very handy turning out in the big shorts in the squared circle.

Maybe the world of international pro wrestling would have been a big enough arena for his talents. Imagine seeing him turn out and add top-shelf glamour to the ranks of the

World Wrestling Superstars. He would front in the green and gold rubberised budgie smugglers with built-in protection from any malicious mat mayhem squirrel-grippers.

He could top the card with a *nom de ring* that screamed authority. Imagine the branding possibilities if Bob had appeared in the WWF or WWE, fighting under the banner of 'The Vicious Tossil'.

Talk about giving politics back to the people and talking in a language all Australians understand!

*Talk about giving politics back to the people and talking in a language all Australians understand!*

Today, looking back across Bob's record of staggering success in an action-packed lifetime, a wrestling career is the yawning gap in that magnificent list of achievements.

Even if a solo career failed, he could have appeared in a tag team combination as The Original Silver Bodgie with a team partner from back in the day, like Outback Jack. It could have been The Fabulous Kangaroos all over again. An electrifying combination of Bob's brains and Jack's muscle. They would have been an unstoppable shoo-in for the International Heavyweight Tag Team Title.

Sadly, Bob chose different paths, but based on what we saw early on with that stunning metre of 'sconce' home brew, his green and gold work and his love of Australian winners, Bob's record speaks for itself. And that's even allowing for the trifecta of misses at Coolangatta, Bathurst and wrestling in Festival Hall on the WWF card. Bob selected himself as our greatest sporting political all-rounder. The title was Bob's and Bob's alone!

## The green and gold man: John Howard, PM 1996–2007

John Howard loved cricket. He rated being the captain of the Australian team as a more important and onerous position in the nation's affairs than being Prime Minister.

*He rated being the captain of the Australian team as a more important and onerous position in the nation's affairs than being Prime Minister.*

He loved watching cricket, even when it was the most cod ordinary and stupefyingly dull affair and everyone apart from him and his bodyguards had left.

There was no more enthusiastic starter in the Paddington shuffle than John. This was a curious sight at the Sydney Test held every New Year. SCG members, including John, queued before the gates opened to get a good seat in the Members' Stand to watch the day's play.

At opening time, the hordes were let in and set off at a steady pace. It is a local version of Pamplona's running of the bulls. If anyone tripped or slipped, there was no help until after the first wave had waddled by, snapping up the best seats on offer.

John was a very keen watcher of all sport, especially cricket and rugby union. In fact, he was taken by any sport with an international agenda like the Olympics, the World Football Cup, Kangaroo tours, the Bledisloe Cup or World Series Cricket – any international event that allowed him to slip into the green and gold tracksuit and watch from the boundary or the TV coverage any time, night or day.

He struggled when it came to saying anything sensible about these events. That did not matter, he was quoted anyway. And playing? Well, that was in the distant past by the time he became PM. But people who know about these things said the bloke had a terrific spin bowling action.

John represented Australia at the highest international level politically. He was dubbed the Man of Steel by the Bush administration after 9/11. But he had very few opportunities to demonstrate to the nation the Howard line and length. He never bothered an opening bat in the corridor of uncertainty or took the ball, once the shine had been knocked off it, and demonstrated his prowess with a spell of impossible-to-play reverse swings.

An opportunity came to see the Howard action up close at Camp Bradman. This was a secure, well-fortified facility set up by an Australian Defence Force medical team deployed to Pakistan to provide healthcare assistance to people affected by an earthquake in 2005. The earthquake devastated the area and killed more than 70,000 people.

Camp Bradman was 1200 metres above sea level, twenty kilometres northeast of Muzaffarabad on the Pakistani line of control.

The Australian first eleven, with John as skip, were to play a local side dolled up in bright red Lynyrd Skynyrd T-shirts with the bold slogan 'Support Southern rock' plastered across the front. The opposition saw themselves as a team and certainly looked the part. The team had a cause.

*The team had a cause. They were stepping out to promote the Southern rock concept across Asia.*

They were stepping out to promote the Southern rock concept across Asia.

The Skynyrd were a hard-rocking, country-flavoured, blues-based combo that knocked out five studio albums and one live set during a career that ran from 1964–1977. They stormed the charts with now long forgotten big hits like 'Sweet Home Alabama' and 'Free Bird'. There was no indication in press releases from the camp that PM Howard knew their music or had taken any interest in their career.

Lynyrd Skynyrd were part of a surge of music from the Southern states of America during the 1970s. This wave rumbled out of Macon, Georgia, and included outfits like the Allman Brothers, the Marshall Tucker Band, Charlie Daniels, Stillwater and Sea Level.

How the Skynyrd shirts ended up in the Neelum Valley was never adequately explained, given that none of these bands had ever toured Pakistan or knew bugger-all about cricket. In fact, Lynyrd Skynyrd's career was cut short by a tragic plane crash in 1977.

The appearance of the Pakistani team in the Skynyrd shirts is one of the great mysteries of international cricket. It has never been adequately explained by the ADF, the BCCI or Wisden. It was a development that still baffles our finest cricketing minds. Despite a six-month probe by both *Mojo* and *Rolling Stone*, music buffs and cricket tragics still scratch their heads.

John, as skipper of the ADF eleven, selected himself for an opening spell of spin. He was worried. He knew the altitude could play havoc with his technique. He measured out his run and as he steamed in from the Everest end, he tried to remember everything his coach at Canterbury Boys High, the chemistry teacher, Luke 'Wally' Stout, had drummed into him on hot afternoons bowling in the nets at the far end of the school oval. Wally stressed the importance of the delivery stride, getting side on, giving the ball air, letting the pitch do the work and disguising the slower ball. John had these Stout off-spin pointers front and centre in his opening spell. They swirled through his mind as he set the field.

John set the field out exactly as he had imagined it lying in his sleeping bag on a camp stretcher under ADF canvas.

The visiting PM knew he had a good opening spell of maybe three overs. If he kept a tight line and length and took a couple of early wickets the batting side could be rocked. He thought the middle order was rubbish. But our skip was unsure what his teammates would bring to the table.

He knew Senior Sergeant Trevor Ferret, crouching behind the stumps with the surgical gloves on, would be a safe pair of hands. He had seen Ferret in action during an Army v Navy clash. The Sarge was a top croucher.

John set a wide slips cordon knowing if he could get the ball to grip he could turn it away from the stumps in the corridor of uncertainty, catch an edge of the bat and then have the slips crew do the rest.

Lance Corporal Herman Dick from the Broke Cricket Club selected himself at first slip, Captain Victor Tool slotted in at second slip and Chief Medical Officer Lionel Stiff completed the slip cordon.

For the opening spell there was a short leg, a silly leg, a square leg, a mid-off and a mid-on. If the batting side got after him and took the long handle to his spin, John would drop the mid-off and mid-on back to the boundary.

ADF quartermaster Harry Knob was tapped to open from the Rawalpindi end. John knew 'Knobbie' could generate explosive pace. The Knob looked fit and set for a bag of wickets. Taking over after John from the Everest end was the just short of a length specialist, Sergeant 'Tiger' Tim Tackle.

The pill was not a regulation Kookaburra six stitcher but a locally made DIY construction. When our number one looked at it closely all he saw was an irregular shape, just a bunch of rubbish tied together with rubber bands. The irregular shape of the ball made a conventional grip extremely difficult. John asked his travelling press secretary Herbert 'Rocky' Tudge to make a note to send through a box of Kookaburra six stitches in the overnight bag as a gesture of good will from the Australian cricket community.

So while the DIY Jaffa left the hand beautifully throughout the spell, John's deliveries squirted off the pitch at weird angles, that is, if they lobbed on the pitch at all, which was a length of rolled dirt.

The field could not take advantage of the opportunities that came their way. It was set too deep. Skip's opening spell failed to ask questions of the Pakistani upper order. After a few overs from the Everest end he swapped and tried to bowl up the hill into the breeze from the Karachi pavilion end with even less success.

John's technique was classical and he could not adapt to local conditions. He struggled. But it was a spell never forgotten by anyone who was lucky to see it. And what a way to cement relations between our two great nations in this troubled part of the world. Many believe it was the highlight of John's career as he had the opportunity to combine his great loves: politics, cricket and representing Australia.

*Cricket diplomacy was at its height with John Howard as PM.*

Cricket diplomacy was at its height with John Howard as PM. He turned up in Afghanistan, Iraq and Pakistan throughout his long career in the top job. He often timed his trips to coincide with the Anzac Day Tests and the best of three ODIs which have become a regular feature of the post 'shock and awe' sporting landscape in the Middle East.

For many years John thought the future of Australian cricket lay in the refugee camps on the Afghan–Pakistani border. So many kids heard of his deeds in the Lynyrd Skynyrd Test and had time to perfect skills with homemade equipment that allowed them to blossom once they got their hands on some decent kit.

## He came, he saw, he stayed: Bob Menzies, PM 1939–41, 1949–66

Oddly enough our longest-serving Prime Minister, Bob Menzies, was a shooter. He shot with the Melbourne University Rifles during World War One. But training in this amateur outfit was sub-standard. This was partially due to lack of bullets, even though every bullet shot by Australians during the First and Second big shows was made in nearby Footscray.

He was a great supporter of the Carlton Football Club. The club welcomed his support, building a ramp at Princess Park off Anzac Parade to allow Menzies' Rolls Royce to glide up the incline into a prominent position so that the PM, now of advancing years, could sit in the front seat, see the match and honk the horn whenever the Carlton Blues (the team that never lets you down) slotted a major.

## He loved fish: Harold Holt, PM 1966–67

So many of our Prime Ministers were keen sporting people and it was not the most obvious sports that they excelled at.

Harold 'Gunner' Holt was our seventeenth Prime Minister. He had big shoes to fill as the first Australian to get a shufti inside The Lodge after years of occupation by Bob Menzies. Sadly, he had a very short time to enjoy the digs, from January 1966 until late in the following year.

Early in life, Harold discovered his passion for shooting. In May 1940, he joined the Australian Imperial Force. He was posted to the 2/4th Field Regiment where he rose to the rank of gunner. He did all this while still warming a seat in federal Parliament.

When an air crash in 1940 wiped out several cabinet ministers, young Harold was promoted into the Menzies cabinet where he became Minister for Labour and National Service. Consequently, he had to park his dry-land shooting passion, but this opened the door for his real sporting career.

Harold loved fish. He loved nothing better than eating a fish. He loved nothing better than shooting fish. These were the three great loves of his life. When he went, he was lucky enough to go out doing what he loved.

He had an encyclopaedic knowledge of fish and how they tasted. In fact, on one magic night of Australian television on Bob Dyer's *Pick a Box* quiz show, Gunner beat the resident champ Barry Jones by five points. He dropped only one point in his special subject of correctly identifying a fish from smell alone.

As he says in his autobiography (as told to *Age* fishing correspondent Cedric Snook):

> I have had a hook into everything. I know fish. It was an honest mistake. I put it down to tiredness. The pressure of work, imagine thinking the waft of tommy ruff was snapper? Honestly, who would make that mistake?

Incidentally, quizmaster Bob Dyer was a mad hook, line and sinker man. He spent his holidays camped on the back of a boat chasing big fish across the Pacific.

There was nothing Gunner Holt loved more than getting away from the cares of the office, togging up, getting wet and drawing a bead on a flathead that could feed a family of seven.

Whenever time permitted, he would drop everything, pull on the wetsuit, grab the speargun and plunge in.

He was probed by senior fishing correspondent 'Slugger' Doak for a pictorial in *The Australian* newspaper in mid-1967: 'Slugger, my dream is to snare a great white with a lucky shot, but it would be hell trying to get the bugger back on shore to prove to the knockers, and there are many, that I had done it.' But he noted in the spray his great weakness: 'Slugs, honestly, I just love spearing fish, any fish, it doesn't matter what the breed. If it swims and has fins, I will have a crack!'

One of his favourite locations for a shoot was Cheviot Beach near Portsea in Victoria. The beach is named after the *S.S. Cheviot*, which got into trouble, broke up and sank in terrible conditions in October 1887 with the loss of thirty-five lives. This grim detail suggests the beach is not the easiest place to relax and contemplate a sunny swim. It was a restricted area for some time, and Surf Life Saving Australia rated it as extremely hazardous, with plenty of heavy rips, especially as the tide drops.

Harold had a special pass that allowed him access, and even though it was remote from all the usual beachside services, Cheviot was his second home. Fast forward to 17 December 1967: on that fateful day, a carload of boat freaks headed towards Point Nepean to see nurseryman and fruit merchant Sir Alec Rose pass through The Rip at the entrance to Port Phillip Bay. Alec was at the helm of *Lively Lady*, a thirty-six-foot cutter, heading off to complete his round-the-world solo voyage.

On the way back from waving bon voyage to the mad fruiterer in charge of the quickly disappearing yacht, Harold persuaded his driver to stop at Cheviot Beach so he could have a dip before heading home for a well-earned lunch. The menu on that fate-filled day was the house speciality of beer-battered flathead, tartare sauce and those large-cut chips Harold loved, followed by a passionfruit and strawberry pavlova.

Given that it was rough, with a lumpy sea running, there was some reluctance from the crew about plunging in, but Harold could smell a big school of salmon lurking just beyond the white-water surge. He togged up and set off with a companion who, spooked by the conditions, stayed close to the shore, while 'Gung Ho' Harold tackled the beach he 'knew like the back of his hand'.

Suddenly, Harold was in trouble, caught in a rip. He disappeared from view. An eyewitness, Karen Carpenter, from Reservoir, who was holidaying nearby, blubbed to senior newsman Kevin Loaf from Channel Nine News in an exclusive:

> Ah no, Kevin, I had a perfect vantage point up on the cliffs, but it all happened so quickly. One minute Harold is grinning

> and waving at us up here and the next moment he is gone. Honestly, he disappeared like half a kilo of high-quality weed power flushed down a dunny when the Victorian cops are bashing on the door. Tragic! But what a way to go! It's a national tragedy, Kevin!

Her final words were: 'Sadly the sea did what the great whites couldn't!'

There were so many questions about Harold's end. Early QAnon theories alleged that Harold had faked his own death, knowing a Chinese submarine was on its way to pluck him from the soup. In fact, cliff-top observers claim they saw an unmarked submarine on the surface chugging west, past Inverloch towards Point Nepean, minutes before the PM went into the brine. The sub sighting lent credence to the view of the Chinese involvement in events. An extensive sea and beach search failed to find any trace of Harold Holt.

One of the great ironies of his life and his mysterious demise is that even though he disappeared in the drink there is a wonderful swimming pool named after him, located in the Melbourne suburb of Glen Iris. The Harold Holt Memorial Swimming Centre is a beautiful pool. It was under construction at the time of his death. Only in Australia is it possible to name a swimming complex after someone who has drowned. What a thought-provoking warning to those who may be slack in the surf. It is a powerful reminder that trouble always lurks wherever the surf meets the turf.

*Only in Australia is it possible to name a swimming complex after someone who has drowned.*

There are also five fishing reserves named after Harold, including ones at Point Nepean, Mud Islands and Pope's Eye.

The spearfishing PM made a significant contribution to Australian slang, as in the phrase 'doing a Harold' as in 'Holt' rhyming with 'bolt', meaning to nick off quickly, without leaving a trace.

## He chased his cheque doing what he loved: Bill Snedden, PM 1972–75

Bill was born in West Perth. He and two friends tried to join the navy at fifteen as under-aged recruits. The navy saw the troublesome treblesome coming and would not allow them up the gang plank, but the RAAF squawked, 'Why not have a crack at the sky, Bill!' two days after his eighteenth birthday.

As World War Two came to an end Bill was able to transition, getting an early step up in the hospitality industry tending bar in the officers' mess. Barman Snedden could whip up all the popular drinks, the Brooklyn, the Manhattan and the Diamantina cocktails.

In his playing days he was talented footballer and played a few games for the West Perth Football Club in the 1944 WANFL season: the Falcons' colours are red and blue, and their motto is 'Does your heart beat true?'

Bill must have a had good leg on him as he represented WA at the Australian Amateur Football Carnival in Melbourne in 1951. He left for the Carnival touching six feet and weighing thirteen stone ten in old speak. He did not bother the All-Australian selectors at the Carnival. There were other fish to fry.

Later that year he became president of the Young Liberals and began the long march towards a seat in federal Parliament.

Bill relocated to football central, Melbourne, where he practised law for a crust. In 1955 he had a successful tilt at the outer suburban seat of Bruce. He camped in Bruce until 1983. The seat was named after Stanley Bruce, 1st Viscount Bruce of Melbourne and the nation's eighth Prime Minister, who ran the big show from 1923 till 1929.

Once in Canberra Bill had a go at everything. He was Leader of the Opposition, Attorney General, Speaker of the House of Representatives, Leader of the Liberal Party and Treasurer.

As Speaker, he loved to frock up when working the point-of-order coalface. He was the last Speaker to go strolling in the traditional gear of the full-bottomed wig and gown. It was a rig that featured in the House of Commons. He was a total conservative and loved the dress-ups.

He became Opposition Leader after 'Tiberius with a telephone' Billy McMahon lost to Gough Whitlam in December 1972. The next election in 1974 was a double dissolution affair after the Senate and the Opposition led by Bill tried to block the Whitlam government's budget.

Bill stumbled and fell short when results came in, and his post-vote quote to all Australians was, 'While we didn't win, we didn't lose all. We just didn't get enough votes to win.' He could not admit failure. That was pure Snedden.

*He could not admit failure. That was pure Snedden.*

Bill was a supporter of the Melbourne Football Club, often turning up at training to demonstrate how he did it in his day – much to the amusement of the current players who treated him as a hopeless joke.

He served as a director of the Victorian Football League and was patron of the Professional Boxing Association of Australia. How did he find the time to cram it all in? They were different times with simpler responsibilities.

He had a good turn of phrase, once describing Vietnam Moratorium organisers as 'political bikies pack raping democracy'. It is hard to get the mind around the exact image in his head.

In fact, a colourful turn of phrase followed him out the door. On 27 June, hours after attending John Howard's campaign launch for the 1987 federal election, Bill checked into the Travelodge at Rushcutters Bay and checked out for the long goodbye in curious circumstances.

The newspapers of the day bellowed, 'Bill Died on the Job', and the 'Condom Was Loaded'. No further explanation is required. It was a great end to a sporting career. Bill, like Harold Holt, went out doing what he loved.

# THE OLYMPICS

*There are wonderful forgotten years where Australia made its mark in precious metal at the Big Show. They are worth a squiz!*

AFTER A 1500-YEAR PAUSE, the quest for golden success was suddenly back. The ancient Games concept had ground to a halt due to corruption, war, cheating, international indifference, pandemics, lack of interest and people having different things to do with their time. The whole concept had carked it and was lying on a cold slab, out for the count. For centuries, medical experts thought that the pose was a fair indication of death.

But in 1896, Baron Pierre de Coubertin, a French PE teacher, passed the cold marble slab and detected a flicker of a pulse in the lifeless body. He applied the electrodes to the nodes and turned on that gold medal juice. He brought the five-ringed beast back to the perpendicular with an ambitiously bigger card of events than featured in the original shebang run around the suburbs of Olympia in ancient Greece.

*The old agenda of war-related sports looked tired and quaint. The big parade had to be jazzed up and plugged into the power board of modern times.*

These modern Games offered many more chances for gold than the old, 'prehistoric', all-nude circus. The Baron realised times had changed, and to be taken seriously competitors had to compete in pants. The show needed a new-look line-up if it was to be relevant in the twentieth century. The old agenda of war-related sports looked tired and quaint. The big parade had to be jazzed up and plugged into the power board of modern times. After all, electric light was a real thing now.

Any thumbnail sketch of Australia's Olympic involvement in the first ten Olympiads of the modern era illuminates how crucial and central the Olympics are to the total package of Australia's sporting identity since the turn of the twentieth century. Australia has been to every modern Olympics since the burly, bearded Baron summoned the youth of the world to Athens in 1896 for the relaunch of the five-ringed competition.

Our sporting greats have graced every summer Games and every winter wonderland white-out, with the exceptions of 1924–32 and 1948. Although, and this still pains every right-thinking Australian, in 1908 and 1912, Australia competed with New Zealand in a combined team. What! Stewards, call for the screens!

Since the Baron got the ruckus underway twelve-and-a-half decades ago bellowing, 'On your blocks! Ready, steady, go!', Australian athletes have scooped up 169 gold, 178 silver and

215 bronze, totalling 562 (counting Tokyo's COVID-era games). This impressive haul of loot puts the lucky country in ninth place against all comers.

The star attraction of the medal tally is Australia's poolside effort of sixty-nine gold. Getting wet has produced a sustained and sensational streak. The team did not always win, but Down-Under splashers were knocking on the door more than most. Australia's tally in the pool is second only to that of the United States. When things looked bleak, Australian swimmers have been the hope of the side.

*Swimming is part of the national DNA. Is it any wonder we are champs of the damp?*

Australians live on a big island 'girt by sea' with the majority camped along a long sandy coastline. We cannot stay out of the soup even when the shark alarm is blaring. Swimming is part of the national DNA. Is it any wonder we are champs of the damp?

Women were late to the Olympic pool party, but they have put in and quickly made up for lost time. Australian swimmers have struck gold surging from the deep end to the shallow end and back faster than their opponents, a dribble of showboating dawdlers.

With such a long and sustained interest in going to the five-ringed rumpus overseas, it is no surprise that the Olympic cavalcade has washed up on Australian shores twice, once in 1956, when no other city in the world wanted the international school sports carnival, and in 2000, when Sydney staged 'the best Games ever'.

In recent coming attraction news, Australia has snared another chance to shine with the big golden thing lurking off to south-east Queensland and set to drop in 2032. A decision that gives confidence to those who worry about the future of the planet, that the international festival of leisure wear, lycra and poorly tailored tracksuits will be happening in Brisbane at the start of the third decade of the twenty-first century. Life on Earth as we know it will last till then. The battle it took to get the Tokyo Games to the starting line suggests the Olympics will survive anything.

Home ground advantage is a huge leg-up when the Games rumble into town. The green and gold crew came from the clouds for a fast-finishing third in Melbourne in 1956. Our swimmers snared eight of the thirteen gold medals up for grabs in the pool. In Sydney, the Fatso-powered Team Oi! Oi! Oi! blasted to the higher altitude with a be-on-me-next-time fourth.

From the current vantage point on top of the ten-metre diving board, the chances of a golden clean sweep in every event, apart from break-dancing, look very good in Brisbane. The Australian Olympic Committee would be mad if it did not go into the 2032 meet with winning every event as their simple ambition and mission statement.

Incidentally, the jury is out on the depth of break-dancing talent. Australia does not know if local funksters, as in b-boys and b-girls, have the footwork and chops to compete in the toprock, downrock, power moves and freeze caper at Olympic level.

Australia's Olympic story is a tale that needs its own book. Thankfully there are several already written by superb Australian authors.

*The Fairytale* is not a vehicle for an in-depth examination of our historical successes or a probe into our winning times. Others have done that with great enthusiasm and dedication.

## THE FAIRYTALE

The facts and figures of our Olympic tilts have been beautifully recorded in Bruce McAvaney's *Special*, a nine-volume set detailing every Australian Olympic performance from 1896 to the present day, and his award-winning *Away! My Olympics* is Bruce's hilarious behind-the-scenes tell-all personal diary of his Games experiences dating back to Helsinki in 1952.

To get an essence of the excellent handiwork available from this nation's top writers let's turn to Wally 'Fitzy' Goffage's bestseller *My Golden Trout*. On page eighty-nine he captures the moment of unexpected athletic success that is always tinged by both elation and terror.

It's the medal presentation for our coxless pair. But only the backend of the boat, 'Lonesome' Cyril Stiles, stood on the third step when the medals were being handed out after a personal best performance in Brazil 2016. Fitzy takes up the story in Lonesome's own words:

> No writer in the world can describe the alarming thrill of standing unexpectedly on the third step of the Olympic podium waiting for the medal presentation ceremony to begin. Failure is there for all to see and yet you feel as though you have won against tremendous odds.
>
> I did not think I could race, let alone podium. I came down with gastro last night, I had pulled the groin off the bone in the first twenty metres of the race. I spewed as we reached halfway. Then Brayden 'Snare' Drum caught a crab and was flung from the boat. I was now on my own. I had lengths to make up. I could not let Australia down. I went for it. When it was over, I looked at the scoreboard and our tub, *Australia 69*, had finished third. Go figure!

Sure, a couple of crews capsized, and two crews collided in lanes seven and eight. That doesn't happen often. I channelled Steve Bradbury and ploughed home as others tipped over.

The atmosphere for the medal presentation was electric. Knowing that you have beaten the best in the world, apart from those on the two steps above on the podium, is a tremendous thrill. But up there, there is no place to hide. Standing in the green and gold lycra, all you can think about is the flimsy stretched fabric between excitable flesh and the watching world. The emotions are running riot. Panic is suddenly lurking.

Without even thinking, the sloop begins to point north at the thought that one of the big names of international sporting glamour is coming down from the committee room with your medal in their hands.

Paranoia takes hold in a mind weakened by physical effort and the mid-race vomiting. Would the IOC send out one of the new breed of medal givers, like Princess Anne, Sporty Spice or stars of *Game of Thrones* like Brienne of Tarth or Missandei? It would be too much!

Your eyes dart around looking for a soft spot to collapse. If the worst was to happen, you could stack on a faint. But there was nowhere soft to land safely. It was rock hard concrete everywhere.

The sense of relief is enormous when you see one of the old Lausanne IOC crew like Prince Albert of Monaco, Lord Sebastian Coe or John Coates, the Aussie supremo, on the stroll, hobbling down the gangway with the three lumps of metal. That athletic trio of stars have stood on this very spot with the hand-out and know that just being on this spot can play havoc with emotional equilibrium.

In those beautifully crafted paragraphs, Fitzy sums up the turmoil and mixed emotions that always accompany an Olympic medal presentation.

But the dishing out of medals on the steps of the podium is the end of the process. Fresh starts and new beginnings are interesting because no one knows how the story will unfold, let alone end. The narrative is revealed with each step of the journey. That is the fabulous and compelling uncertainty of all sport. Let's take the long amble back through the fogs of time to the beginnings of the modern Olympic era.

The first ten Olympiads rapidly accelerated advances in Olympic competition and culture. Along with our medal success, the Australian Olympic Committee's contribution to the Baron's rumble off the track has been remarkable. Our administrators have shouldered the burden of supporting the Olympic ideals and principles. If this meant giving away soccer balls to an under-thirteen team in the Chang Mai region of Thailand or funding a go-kart track in the northern suburbs of Montevideo, or setting up appointments with Swiss dentists for the president of the Nigerian high jump community, then our frontline sporting diplomatic troops were up to the task.

But back to Athens in 1896: Australia's great success rests on the shoulders of one champ, Edwin 'Ted' Flack, aka 'The Lion of Athens'. Ted, the only Australian competitor, burst onto the international scene, rewriting the Olympic record book. Obviously, the old record book had been lost long ago and very few in the Athens organising committee were fluent in ancient Greek. The new record book, an A4-sized lightly lined school exercise book with the word 'Ted' hastily written on the cover, was picked up from the local newsagent on the morning of the meet.

Knowledgeable and award-winning athletic podcasters Vera Verushka and Trevor 'The Underpant' Staines argue in their weekly ninety-minute spray on Olympic issues, *The Golden Shower*:

> The Lion was the greatest Australian athlete of all time. He was the first modern Olympian and arguably our best GOAT ever. Look at the record. Ted did the lot. He won on the track in the 800 metres and the 1500 metres. He paused to settle the breathing before pulling on the Volley OCs and having a crack at the marathon. A day later he put the OCs on again and medalled in tennis. Who else is there? Who else is on the list?

The 1896 marathon was a run with a tale. At the thirty-two-kilometre pole, Ted was in the lead and running beautifully. His main rival at this point was the French middle-distance star and shooter, Albin Lermusiaux. The Lion's rival was no slouch, he had won the bronze medal in the 1500-metre scamper, but he found Ted's pace in the big one too hot and dropped off, leaving just the finishing tape between our hero and another finish in first place.

Tragedy struck the Flack tilt eight kilometres later. At the forty-kilometre mark Ted collapsed on the track. A French spectator stepped out of the crowd to help The Lion to his feet. This unsolicited intervention broke all the complex Olympic rules of the long stagger.

Ted did the only thing any right-thinking Australian would do. He flattened the Frenchman.

*Ted did the only thing any right-thinking Australian would do. He flattened the Frenchman.*

It was a lucky punch, but he was red-carded by officials, removed from the course and taken by horse-drawn carriage back to the main stadium where controversial Prince Nicholas, who was president of the shooting sub-committee and part-time organiser of the 1896 Games, gave him the once-over with the stethoscope. No harm done. Ted resumed the perpendicular and was able to take a seat in the stand and watch the finish of the race.

Later in the meet, Ted turned out for tennis, scoring a contested bronze. This created the first of many Olympic medal controversies. Olympic ding dongs can take centuries to sort out. There is no tiff in the world of sport like an Olympic rules ruckus. Finally, in 2008, Ted was given the nod for bronze from that first modern Olympic tennis medal hit-out. Sadly, Ted could not be there for the medal presentation as he had moved on to the Wimbledon in the sky in 1935.

As Edwin 'Teddy' Flack was our sole representative in Athens in 1896, he had to do the lot. Captain the team, carry the flag in the opening and closing ceremonies, run the water, wear the big hat as Australia's *chef de mission* and be a sporting ambassador for the yet-to-be-federated nation, as well as compete. It was a big ask!

*As Edwin 'Teddy' Flack was our sole representative in Athens in 1896, he had to do the lot.*

There was no Australian nation in 1896 as we understand it today. There were no national colours; the idea of green and gold was decades away up around the bend. Edwin ran in the colours of Melbourne Grammar, his old school – a lovely touch, cementing the concept of the Olympics as an international school sports carnival with gold, silver and bronze up for grabs.

The Athens Olympics was The Lion's only big international meet. After the long boat trip back to Australia he retired from the international sporting scene to breed cattle. There is a bronze statue of Ted in Berwick High Street. The Lion, rather belatedly, was ushered into the Australian Sporting Hall of Fame in 1985. This was a glittering night of nights for Flack freaks. The great and the sporting good finally acknowledged his extraordinary leonine prowess.

Three Australians made the trip to the 1900 Games in Paris: swimmer Fred Lane, sprinter Stanley Rowley and shooter Donald Mackintosh.

There was no government handout for the team, and athletes had to make their own way to Paris and cover the costs of transport, accommodation and competing.

The Olympic pool, that mine of precious metal for Australian swimmers over the decades, had not been invented in 1900. The concept of a body of chlorinated water, twenty-six degrees centigrade, fifty metres long, with eight lanes roped off, had not been imagined by the bright sparks in the world of wetness. 'Fearless' Freddie Lane got the poolside party started when he snared Australia's first aquatic triumph. Fred, like the rest of the Paris competitors, made do with the River Seine for his swims. That special stretch of water between the Courbevoie and the Asnières Bridges was Fred's sodden office.

He had been introduced to water sport at an early age. He was four years old when his brother pulled him from a near-death experience in Sydney Harbour. After his pre-school plunge from the wharf, young Fred realised he needed to learn to swim. He was soon finning along in the drink like a northern red snapper.

There were seven swimming events on the Paris card. Seventy-six starters turned up from twelve countries to take the plunge. The card featured the 200 free, 400 free, 1000 free, 200 back and the 200-metre team swim. As a final highlight there was the mystery event, the 200-metre obstacle race.

Fearless Fred won the 200 metres, beating the Hungarian superstar, Zoltán Halmay. It was a quick swim because Fred dropped into the tidal rip in the middle of the river. He cashed the cheque he wrote in the 200 free forty-five minutes later with another win in the 200-metre obstacle race.

The obstacle race was the bankside talking point of these Games. Twelve competitors from five nations fronted for the final. It was a hot field: some observers say the best wet hurdle and hindrance line-up ever. But the knockers point out it was only run once at Olympic level, so there is a certain amount of truth to this poolside observation.

Swimmers had to plough up the 200 metres of the Seine, climbing over a pole at the start and then over a line of rowing boats before swimming under another line of boats as the final obstacle. It was described in the Paris newspaper *Le Monde* by swimming correspondent Jean Paul Pigasse in these tart terms: 'The 200-metre obstacle wet-side wiff-waff is a "Knockout Olympic Style" event with a golden gewgaw on offer.'

The French team had a distinct home river advantage. The local crew did not have to travel far or adapt to foreign food, or put up with uncomfortable accommodation, or cope with changeable weather conditions. Fred put these snags to one side and came home in a time of 2.38.4. It was a personal best. Second home was the Austrian swimming sensation and 200-metre obstacle superstar, Otto Wahle.

This very popular event was dropped from the subsequent line-ups, as no one could see the important underwater action where the race was won and/or lost. The event screams for inclusion as a demonstration sport on the swim card for Paris 2024 and to hold its place for Brisbane 2032. In part as a homage to Fred Lane and those early pioneers, but also because today's television technology allows spectators to see all the brutal underwater action in living colour.

Stan Rowley from Australia's cherry capital, Young, scored a third in the track sprints. He had a great Games. Stan was a model of consistency, finishing third over sixty metres, third in the 100 metres, and yes, it was another bronze spot in the 200 metres.

Shooting for gold for Australia's Don Mackintosh featured a live pigeon shoot in Paris. It is still talked about when old Olympic heads gather and reminisce about past glories over a glass of gold medal–winning chardonnay. This glamour shoot blasted 300 birds from the sky. There were two categories, one charged twenty francs to enter and the other 200 francs.

The pigeons were released from traps in front of the shooters. Then it was bang away for a cash prize. It was a simple competition. In the first leg of the event a purse of 200 francs was up for grabs, approximately US$3.916 million in today's money. The big purse and the gold medal lured the world's best.

When the guns fell silent, feathers carpeted the spot where the podium (not yet part of the medal presentation celebrations) would be in future Games. In a lovely sporting gesture, the top four finishers agreed to split the purse. This was in the real spirit of the Games as the Baron imagined it in 1896. Athletes were encouraged to compete for prestige and glory, not money. He suggested they leave financial gain for the world championships and national competitions.

The live pigeon shoot was the only event in Olympic history in which animals were killed. For the sake of the squeamish, as in 99.89 per cent of the population, the organising committee declared the event a non-Olympic affair and shoe-horned the blaze-away into the cultural programme.

Shooting pigeons as an art ... well, there were issues with that tricky concept from the start. But it was a very Olympic solution. If it is not sport, it must be culture. A live bird shoot ban sensibly came into force in 1902. In St Louis (1904) and beyond, the flying feathered targets were all clay pigeons.

In the twenty-franc blow-off, Australian 'Deadeye' Donald Mackintosh came first, taking out twenty-two birds. Don was up against 166 other competitors from around the world. The lolly on offer explains the big numbers of the trigger happy.

Post-shoot, Donald was quizzed by *The Argus* shooting and duck hunting correspondent, Heiko F. Meins. The Walkley Award–winning Meins began by asking, 'Slugger, how do you feel now that you have bagged the gold?'

> ... Heiko, how do I feel? Heiko, I am over the moon. This is a dream come true. I felt very nervous coming into the shoot. But once I got in the trench, technique took over. Both the birds and the bullets came out beautifully today. You saw the numbers. I have never shot like that. I would like to look at the score card, but I reckon I hammered four with a single bang early. Never done that before.

Heiko asked, 'Slugger, I notice you were using a different trigger-pulling technique out there today?'

> As a shooter, Heiko, you know you get days like these. I was using that new Giorgio de Morandi breathing technique. I was pulling the trigger between heart beats. But Heiko, the results are in the book. I won. They can't take it away from me.

'Deadeye, how much do you put the win down to the gun you were using?'

> . . . Heiks, this is the new Lee Enfield. It's the same gun Digs will use in the Boer War in South Africa. It can really make a mess of a turkey. You can hardly find anything apart from feathers and lead once they are hit. The officials did a tremendous job tracking down the bird count today. People will knock the result, but the organisers did a great job. They produced a good quality of bird with plenty of get up and go.
>
> And you know, Heiko, I love Australia. I put in today for the great nation that Australia will become next year. I wanted to show kids that if they work hard, they can achieve golden dreams. My message to youngsters wanting to go all the way is: Don't shoot at the bird, shoot at where the bird is going to be. It is as simple as that.

In his Olympic wrap-up, Heiko reported that other contestants complained that 'Our Macca' went berserk over the three heats, banging away at anything that moved. They moaned, 'That Australian shooter went totally troppo. There was so much smoke, gun powder and feathers wafting about no one could see the pigeons!'

In the next event, the 200-franc entrance fee blow-off, Deadeye had a poor shoot. He only collected eighteen kills and tied for third.

While Donald scored in the twenty-franc shoot, the Committee reclassified both the Mackintosh events as non-Olympic. But in the mysterious way in which the Olympic officialdom works, in 1992, he was finally awarded Olympic gold and bronze medals for his efforts in Paris.

Deadeye was a product of Rockbank, now an outer suburb of Melbourne. He originally shot for the Bacchus Marsh Club, bursting onto the scene, stunning the club with an easy-on-the-eye style and blessed with a natural trigger-pulling ability. His career took off. He was soon in demand on the professional shooting circuit. He often shot three days a week, touring the lucrative European circuit where crowds of 100,000 would turn out to see the champ take a bead on a Black Orpington pullet, a pet budgie or an endangered South American condor. He shot on the pro live parrot circuit from 1896 until 1908. His trick shooting was a sensation. He could bag a budgie from 200 metres with his head in a paper bag and ping a parrot from the car park sitting in the back seat of a Benz. His accuracy was recognised when he was tapped as world champion.

*He could bag a budgie from 200 metres with his head in a paper bag and ping a parrot from the car park sitting in the back seat of a Benz.*

When Donald was not banging away, he relaxed from the intense pressure of international competition by writing poetry. The poet with a loaded pen, the artist with a shotgun: it is such an Australian image. Knowing that Deadeye was a whizz with words it is easy to see why officialdom relocated the pigeon shoot to the cultural programme.

Donald had to give the sport away when he lost sight in his shooting eye, but he had the poetry trade to fall back on. He published *Whooping Cough* ('The song of a one-eyed wombat as the bumper bar of the hearse approaches'). This award-winning volume of 230 poems was a popular seller between the World Wars, especially with the wilder, beret-and-maroon-velvet-jacket-wearing, bohemian smoking set that lurked in Melbourne's downtown laneways. A critic swore that 'All Deadeye's rhyming couplet work with the fountain pen was infused with the stench of cordite and the flutter of feathers'. That top review is from The Lively Loon in *Oriental Rugs* vol 6, July 1924.

Shooting is still a great Olympic staple. On the current card there are six different disciplines. The men bang away at targets, starting with the ten-metre air-pistol, then the ten-metre air rifle or slug gun, followed by the twenty-five-metre rapid fire pistol; by now the contestants are getting warm, and next up is the tricky fifty-metre, and the three positions event (standing, kneeling and prone). The big cannons are then unpacked for the shotgun skeet and bringing the golden bang-off home is the ever-popular shotgun trap.

It is the same card for women shooters. But the show does not stop there. Team events begin with the ten-metre air-rifle mixed, ten-metre air-pistol mixed, and finally the curtain comes down on the Olympic Festival of the Boom with the team shotgun trap.

An Olympic shoot is a great day out for the whole family. All these separate disciplines require different training, different techniques, different weapons, and most importantly, different bullets. What a card! No wonder the world licks its lips in anticipation of this golden Festival of Detonation every four years.

*An Olympic shoot is a great day out for the whole family.*

Continuing Deadeye's success, Patti Dench broke Australia's shooting medal drought for women when she banged her way to medal glory, picking up bronze for the twenty-five-metre air pistol at the 1984 Olympics in Los Angeles.

The Dench medal was in the bag years after Deadeye's success in 1900 Games. But to return to our tale, it was time for the St Louis Games of 1904, the Games of the third Olympiad.

These Games were originally awarded to Chicago. But a clash of dates with the 1904 Louisiana Purchase Exposition World Fair produced a big stink. The Baron de C. had to step into the ring of controversy with a packed peace pipe, strike a match and play Solomon. After passing the pipe around the circle, the Games tent was packed up and sent strolling down the highway from Chicago to St Louis. These were the first Games held outside Europe, but tensions created by the Russo-Japanese War meant that only sixty-two of the 651 athletes who took part came from outside North America: 645 men and six women turned up to have a crack at ninety-five gold medals in sixteen sports. To state the bleeding obvious, there was a huge Stateside home ground advantage.

Boxing made its Games debut, and Australia competed as a nation (without NZ). Basketball, hurling and baseball were the demonstration sports. When the action stopped and placings were decided, gold, silver and bronze medals were handed out for the first time.

Runners Corrie Gardner and Les 'Macca' McPherson made the long trip. The 'G train' placed sixth in the 110-metre hurdles and ninth in the long jump. Corrie was a well-known Australian Rules footballer, who pulled on the boots for Melbourne (forty-eight games) and Essendon (twelve). He played on the wing. He had a big tank. As a student at Melbourne Grammar, he was inspired to compete at the Olympics by a school visit from The Lion, Edwin Flack. When he lobbed in St Louis, he was surprised no accommodation had been arranged for him, so he had to camp out in a downtown park.

McPherson blew into Mound City and promptly withdrew from his event when he discovered the hurdles in the 400 metres were twelve inches lower than the ones he used in training. As he said in a letter back to his parents, 'Mum, it was a total joke. I could not believe they wanted me to compete in this Mickey Mouse event!'

In 2009 a bunch of Games nerds trawling through the record books discovered there was a third Australian on the St Louis team. Francis Gailey was Australian and not American, as was previously believed. Frank swam in the 220-, 440- and 880-yard finals without success, but he did Australia proud when he was placed third in the one-mile swim. He lived in San Francisco after the Games and was thought to be an American, hence the century of record-keeping confusion.

These were unusual Games, spread out over four months. There were ninety-one events, forty-nine of which were contested by American athletes only. The final medal tally reflected this domination, with the United States winning seventy-seven gold medals; the next best results were Cuba and Germany, who won four each.

After a cup of tea and a lie-down, the bags were packed for London in 1908. Actually, Rome was the chosen venue, but the Games were moved to London after Mount Vesuvius blew its stack in 1906. Bad luck has dogged the Olympic city selection process. After the big blow, Italy was stuck for a quid. The move was not easy. These Games were stretched: they lasted six months and four days, the longest of the modern era.

Australia and New Zealand sent a combined team of thirty athletes and came away from London with one gold, two silver and two bronze.

The gold was in rugby. Silver went to middleweight boxer Snowy Baker, who lost the big one in a controversial split decision.

Snow took off the gloves and backed up for his pet events wearing just the Speedos. He finished twenty-second in diving off the three-metre springboard. But Baker had a swim left in him. He plunged in, holding down a slot in the four-by-200 relay. Our team finished fourth.

Harry Kerr, the great walker with a twinkle in his toes, brought home bronze in the 3500-metre walk. The wizard of the wet, Frank Beaurepaire, flew to get second in the 400-metre free and backed up for third in the 1500 free. It was an excellent Games for the joint venture.

In 1912 the youth of the world packed their bags and shorts for Stockholm. The Olympic kerfuffle was gathering pace. The years were zipping by. It was time for the fifth Olympiad.

A total of 2408 competitors from twenty-eight countries competed in 102 events in fourteen sports. The Baron's wheeze was getting serious. It was in Stockholm that Australian women swimmers began a run of remarkable success. Women's swimming was included in the Games schedule for the first time.

*The story of Australian golden success begins with Fanny Durack, but right from the start there were battles with swimming officialdom.*

The story of Australian golden success begins with Fanny Durack, but right from the start there were battles with swimming officialdom. Before our swimmers clambered onto the blocks, even before they got on the boat, the NSW Ladies Swimming Association opposed women participating in the Games. Fanny and her great rival Mina Wylie were refused permission by the NSWLSA to compete at Stockholm. Eventually, after pressure and protests, including the burning of the Ashfield pool in a night of wild 'let them go' outrage, officialdom caved in. The girls were allowed to go, provided they paid all their expenses.

To raise money for the trip the swimmers and their supporters organised a lively campaign of fundraising. Bunnings-style barbecues, cake stalls, lucky envelopes, trivia nights, jazz concerts, lamington drives and can collections out the front of schools and town halls – all helped to pay their way.

The battle to get there and their heroic efforts in the Stockholm pool cemented a strong relationship between the swimming team and the Australian public.

The Stockholm Olympic pool was a fenced-off 100-metre section of the harbour. One hundred and twenty competitors from seventeen countries turned up to take the icy plunge for the precious metal. There were nine events, just two for women, the 100 metres and the four-by-100-metre relay.

At this point in the historic national timeline, Australia was a decade old. We were on the world stage – and winning. But 1912 was one of those years when the team made up the numbers by including New Zealanders. The AUS/NZ combined team came away from the Scandinavian Games with six medals: two gold, two silver and two bronze.

Our number one, Fanny Durack, was a remarkable swimmer. She won the 100-metre freestyle in Stockholm, and from that year until 1920 Fanny held the official world record for the glamour event. During that stretch of dominance, she also held records for the 200-metre free, the 220-yards free, the 500-metre free and the mile freestyle. That is some record.

The 1912 organising committee produced a very racy medal to be dished out to winners by the era's equivalents of Juan Antonio Samaranch and Jacques Rogge. The gold featured two very fit, nearly nude Nordic women, wearing nothing but see-through gauze, holding a laurel wreath above the victor, a bloke who is looking very casual indeed. The victor is not nearly nude; he is totally nude, as in the days of ancient Greece.

*The victor is not nearly nude; he is totally nude, as in the days of ancient Greece.*

After the sun set on Stockholm there was a pause in Olympic sport for World War One. In ancient times all hostilities ceased while the Games were held, but the chaos of the World War delayed the next summer Games, due in 1916. The next time the youth of the world gathered was in May 1920 in Antwerp.

Europe was still devastated when the athletes arrived. It was a time of chaos. The war created new nations. Some of these nations were banned from Olympic competition. Hungary, Germany, Austria, Bulgaria and the Ottoman Empire were blamed for starting the war. They were Axis powers – the enemy – and were told to ride the pine and sit 1920 out. Germany had to stay on the splinters until 1928.

Then as the guns fell silent, the Spanish flu, H1N1, exploded around the world. Estimates suggest it killed fifty million people. The circumstances were not unlike the complications created by COVID-19 for international sporting in 2020, in particular the Olympic Games in Tokyo that were postponed until 2021.

In the 1912 circumstances of chaos and plague, it was an enormous challenge to get to the Games, but thirteen Australians made it. Twelve men and one woman made the trip by slow boat and represented the young nation in four sports.

Albert I, King of the Belgians, declared the Games open. It was an impressive sporting competition, with 156 events in twenty-two sports. New additions to Olympic housekeeping included the Olympic oath and Olympic flag. The medal was another racy confection, again harking back to the ancient Games, featuring laurels, floating wreaths, nudity and fit athletic types soaring heroically into the sky.

An unusual feature of these summer Games was their inclusion of a week of winter sports. The programming committee had a brain explosion and collapsed winter and summer in the mind and on the track. They soon realised that this was a big mistake, and by 1924, the Winter Olympics were on their own, having a wild time in the winter wonderland of Chamonix.

The Antwerp winter card of competition had the usual line-up of speed events. Figure skating and ice hockey were included for the first time. The teams went round for gold in the Palais de Glace where there was a good depth of ice all year round.

Alfred Swahn, a seventy-two-year-old Swedish shooter, provided a genuine highlight when he finished second in the 100-metre running deer double shot. This bang-off involved shooters taking aim at moving targets 100 metres away. Since the Paris pigeon shooting debacle no animals were involved.

Alf, the Swedish number one, turned up for an Olympic shoot in 1908, 1912, 1920 and 1924. His swag of loot included nine medals: three gold, three silver and, you guessed it, three bronze. He was a success in the team running deer single shot, solo running deer single, running deer double and clay pigeons. Big Alfie should not be confused with his son Oscar, who was as good as the old man but had none of his elusive trigger-pulling, crowd-pleasing charisma.

The United States swimming champion, Duke Kahanamoku, returned for another dip and retained the 100-metre gold he had won in Stockholm before the war. The US team had a golden Games, their winning medal tally aided by a clean sweep in the pool. From the Australian perspective, forehead curtains have to be drawn over our Antwerp Games efforts. Our team came back with zip, nada, bugger-all. This short summary allows us to swerve on to better results. The tide was out in Antwerp but came rushing back in later years.

The Duke had time between his 100-metre gold successes to introduce surfing to Australia. On 9 January 1915 he paddled out to walk the plank and hang five at Freshwater Beach in Sydney. Nothing was quite the same ever again surfside around Australia.

Sadly Australia's 100-metre gold medallist and original superfish, Fanny Durack, was unable to take her place on the blocks when the field assembled for the 100-metres heats in Antwerp.

Before these Games, she was struck down by appendicitis and had to have an emergency operation. She was getting back on her feet and back in the pool when she was clobbered by typhoid fever and pneumonia.

Our diver, Lily Beaurepaire, Frank's sister, turned out in the ten-metre platform. It was our debut in the event. Lily just missed the finals. Walker and flag bearer George Parker came second in the 3000-metre walk; back in the pool our four-by-200 relay team of Beaurepaire, Hay, Herald and Stedman came second, and Frank B backed up in the 1500 metres, plugging home for bronze.

In 1924 the Olympics were back Seine-side in Paris. Thirty-four Australian athletes made the trip. Australia debuted in rowing. Our team of ten rowers included the legendary rowing eight, the Mighty Murray Cods. On the bus home, when the medals were tallied, the team had three gold, one silver and two bronze, equalling the haul from Stockholm in 1912.

This time in Paris our athletes struck gold with Nic Winter in the triple jump, Dick Eve brought home the golden prize in diving and in swimming, and the new kid on the blocks, 'Boy' Charlton, came first in the 1500 metres. With Boy and Frank Beaurepaire anchoring the squad, we scored silver in the four-by-200-metre relay. Charlton plugged home for third in the 400 free and Frank was third in the 1500. It was a great Games, with Australia finishing the medal tally in eleventh place.

The year 1924 was a time of great change. As indicated earlier, the Games were split into summer and winter Games. The Olympic flame, such a staple of the modern era, was lit for the duration in the cauldron of courage. Athletes competed with the Olympic motto 'faster, higher, stronger' tattooed on their foreheads for the first time. Not sure what they were doing before these instructions from the IOC that they had to get out there, put in and be quick.

In 1928 the big show put up the tent in Amsterdam. Fourteen men and four women made the Australian team. They ran out in six sports and returned with one gold, two silver and one bronze medal. These four gongs in the Cheese and Tulip Town Olympics placed Australia nineteenth in the overall competition.

Bobby Pearce won gold in the men's single sculls. Boy Charlton was back and came second in the 400 free and 1500 free. Dunc Gray scored a bronze on the Speedwell in the men's track cycling time trial.

It was an awkward time for Australia. The joint was running on the hurly burly of those twin economic prongs of boom and bust. The nation was at the bottom of a bust. Canberra could only afford to send ten athletes: the cost was 73 pounds and 57 pence per athlete, or approximately $111,857.12 in today's money. Eight athletes were so keen to be part of the big show that they paid their own way to get there.

The 1932 Games were held in the Great Depression in Los Angeles. There was not a lot of spare change for anything, let alone sport. Many countries simply did not have the cash in the kick to send a squad of starters.

There were several firsts at these Olympics. An Olympic village, built for the first time, was home to 1332 men and 126 women. And the three-step podium became part of the medal ceremony furniture. The low point of any Games, the Olympic mascot, appeared for the first time. The L.A. organising committee turned up with a Scottish terrier named Smoky. The sporting world groaned, and from then on the mascot moan became a regular part of the Olympic cultural programme in the weeks leading up to the first day of competition.

Nine men and four women made the trip of a lifetime to L.A. On the medal front Dunc Gray won Australia's first cycling gold. In a brilliant ride he clocked one minute thirteen seconds in the 1000-metre time trial. Bobby Pearce was back and won gold again in the single sculls. Clare Dennis picked up gold in the 200-metre breaststroke and Bonnie Mealing silver in the 100-metre backstroke. Eddie Scarf won bronze in the men's wrestling freestyle, light heavyweight. It was a good Games for Australia.

An art competition took place in conjunction with the sporting show. Medals were given in five categories: architecture, literature, music, painting and sculpture. Not sure how the Australian tilt went. James Quinn (one of Australia's great war artists) picked up the camel-hair brush, knocked the top off the Winsor & Newton tubes and represented Australia in the mixed painting category. There was no pigeon shooting on the cultural agenda.

## Art of the Olympics

*Letting the youth of the world know when and where to gather for the Games was not easy.*

From Athens 1896 until Sydney 2000 the media coverage and access to the Games was relatively limited. There was radio and television, not much cinema and very little advertising apart from the humble poster. In the early decades, language barriers and distance slowed communication. There was no multi-platform, in-your-face-and-everywhere social media that is such a part of the media landscape today.

The 1896 Games poster did not inspire: it featured an athlete kitted out in an odd ensemble, part national dress, part Lululemon exercise apparel, wreath in hand, standing around in the rubble of ancient Greece. But it was not long before Olympic posters began giving the youth something to think about.

The 1908 Paris poster bellowed, 'Saddle up or miss out!' It featured a suitably attired high jump champion using a revolutionary jumping technique developed by the altitude-seeking medico, Otto 'The Doc' Peltzer.

The Doc's high jump modus operandi was not without enormous personal risk for those going for gold. It required great commitment. The Doc trained high jumping athletes to run flat out backwards at the bar, plant the feet, take off and elevate into the sky, bum on.

The trick was to see clearing the obstacle in the mind's eye before the take-off, to visualise the whole body clearing the bar before touching down buttocks first in the sand pit on the far side. This internal seeing-is-believing was at the heart of the Peltzer technique.

The 1908 poster was an exception in that it focused on an Olympic gold medal sport. The high jump was the glamour event. Almost all the posters for the first dozen games of the modern era featured nearly nude blokes straining for glory. The laurel wreath of success dangled just out of the athletes' reach. The finest examples of the genre were run up for Stockholm in 1912 and Antwerp in 1920.

The 1912 poster featured a nude portrait of likeable Swedish team captain Sven Henriksen with the wedding tackle securely strapped to his left thigh by two strands of orange ribbon. No one is now sure of the competition Sven dropped the shorts for, but he has his eyes on Swedish gold as he twirls a weapon of war above his bonce.

Olle Hjortzberg, the well-respected 'flower and vase' man, had been approached by the committee to step outside his comfort zone and have a go at a Games poster. His riding instructions were to produce an image that caught the eye and let people know the Stockholm Olympics were on and everyone would be mad if they missed this fortnight of fabulous fun. Olle did not disappoint. He returned after three weeks alone in the studio with a very suggestive image that had the committee standing and saluting. This will be a must-see event, was his artistic message. Get your tickets early!

Eight years later, the mayor of the athletes' village, Soren Lassgard, posed for the award-winning artist Hallvard Holmen. Super-fit Soren is depicted nearly nude winding up for a fling of the discus in the direction of Antwerp Cathedral. Not sure why the cathedral should cop it, but that was Hallvard's vision. Mercifully, as the big bloke is about to let fly, a spectator's scarf has blown out of the crowd and given Soren's bed flute area and thighs a modicum of decency.

The early years were the salad days of Olympic lewd. In later decades the village, where the athletes camped during the fortnight of competition, was the home of the pants-around-the-ankles action. It became the centre of international romance and lust.

Times change and as the years tick over artistic and sporting sensibilities change as well. There were no-nearly nudes by the time the Games lob in Melbourne in 1956. By then, poster art had become much more abstract, echoing cultural changes in the art caper worldwide.

The eleventh Games of the modern era survived Hitler's Germany in 1936. The Berlin Olympics was the first to be televised and the radio coverage reached forty-one countries. These media innovations increased the profile and accessibility of the Games. Suddenly almost everyone, everywhere could see or hear the action.

One hundred and twenty-nine events were scheduled in the Games of the XI Olympiad. Among the twenty-five sports, basketball, canoeing and handball were added to the ranks.

The torch relay, now a big part of any Games build-up, took place for the first time. From Olympia, the torch was carried by hand to the main stadium in Berlin.

Thirty-two fit Australians braved the politics of Germany on the eve of World War Two and participated in twenty-six events in seven sports. Jack Metcalfe won our only medal, a bronze in the triple jump.

The Australian squad boasted three boxers: a fly, a welter and a light heavy. On the bikes, Tasman 'Tassie' Johnson was in the road race, and the time trial specialist Dunc Gray was back in the sprint, but they made the long trip without success. Off the diving board, Ron Masters took the plunge from the three-metre springboard and ten-metre platform but failed to impress the picky judging panel who did not know quality if it clobbered them in the face. In rowing, Australians lined up in three events – the single and double sculls and the eights – but after their heats there was nowhere for our rowers to go except home empty-handed.

It was slim pickings in the pool, too. Bill Kendall in the 100 freestyle and Percy Oliver in the 100 backstroke struggled, while Evelyn Lacey in the 100 and 400 freestyle, Kitty McKay in the 100 freestyle and Pat Norton in the 100 backstroke all failed to advance.

It was a similar story in the wrestling. Our big three, Dick Garrard lightweight, John O'Hara welterweight and Eddie Scarf light heavyweight, made the trip to Berlin. It was a hot competition and none of our grapplers advanced into the rounds where medals were on offer.

For obvious reasons, the XI Olympiad are the forgotten Games of our Olympic involvement.

*A look back over these early decades of the modern Olympics illuminates the evolution of the international school sports carnival. It is an incredible organisational feat.*

A look back over these early decades of the modern Olympics illuminates the evolution of the international school sports carnival. It is an incredible organisational feat. Look where the five-ringed circus lobbed in 2016. In Rio the twenty-eight sports contested featured forty-one separate disciplines, which generated 812 gold medals. It had become a Very Big Thing. The 'faster, higher, stronger' fortnight added five additional sports for Tokyo. Will the committee ever decide it is big enough?

## War, what is it good for?

Absolutely nothing apart from the Olympics. So many of the sports at the 'peaceful' Games have an origin in warfare.

The Baron's modern Games additions had a distinctly military flavour. Shot-put is based on the cannon ball. There were no cannons in ancient times. The cannon concept was put together by the Chinese in the twelfth century. The big ball blast was adopted as a weapon of choice in the thirteenth century. Early balls were rounded stone, but by the seventeenth century they were cast from iron.

Artillery troops on the front line needed to be quick on their feet between lighting the blue paper and blowing away the enemy. The highly trained grunts manning the cannon needed a steady supply of big round ammo. Hurling the cannon balls from the horse-drawn cart up to the gun emplacement became a specialised skill.

The delivery of the deadly iron orb by the heave routine has given the world one of the great Olympic sports. Is there anything more arousing than seeing big muscular people in national-coloured leisure wear enter the circle of chuck, take a deep breath, skip across the ring and put everything from the taut thighs and bulging buttocks up through the torso and into a gold medal–winning heave of the shot?

The shot-put was won in 1896 by Robert Garret, who tipped out the Golden Greek, Miltiadis Gouskos, with a throw of 11.22 metres. It was an Olympic record. Today's top heavers, both men and women, are throwing twice that distance. But records are only there to be broken. Women began throwing for gold in 1948. Imagine the stars of the lost years between 1896 and 1948 when women could not step into the ring and enjoy the camaraderie and competition that blokes had enjoyed for decades.

The shot-put is a sport that talks to all Australians once every four years. On that special afternoon of intense exertion and electrifying competition, Australians are the world experts on all facets of the big fling.

Australians instinctively know exactly where the feet have to be planted for a winning gold medal heave. Every schoolkid knows how much power has to be generated by the toes and hips, in the skip across the circle of brawn before the shot is fired skywards into the Olympic record book.

The nation knows there cannot be a big pause after entering the ring before the fling. Any pause allows nerves of failure to agitate. On release, the big hoist is often accompanied by a blood-curdling scream that can scare the stadium crowd, creating blood-dripping drama until it's grins all round as another Olympic record is broken.

In the build-up to the 2021 Tokyo Olympics Ryan Crouser threw the 7.26-kilogram (16-pound) mass of metal to a new world record of 23.37 metres. He broke a longstanding world record by 25 centimetres. That is some heave!

The discus was originally a weapon used by ancients to clobber opponents in the far distance. It is one of the ancient disciplines that gets a guernsey in the modern Games. The balletic twirl by the competitor inside the cage of contest generates energy that travels down the arm and into the discus, which is sent on its way to golden glory or silver or bronze or potato.

In 1896, men danced the delicate twirl for a hurl. Women began throwing in 1928. It's a sport where it is important to let a big one go, early. Throw down a gauntlet. Get on the board with a fat PB. Then watch the field sputter in the wake as they play catch-up!

*In 1896, men danced the delicate twirl for a hurl. Women began throwing in 1928.*

The hammer throw was introduced into the Olympic Games in 1900, possibly from a suggestion by the USOC champion, John Flanagan. The sport has competitive roots that can be traced back for centuries to warriors in Ireland. On the day of judgement in Paris 1900, Big John won gold, Truxtun Hare silver, and Josiah McCraken was third. It was an all-American podium finish (that is, if the podium had been invented at that point). American athletes had a big advantage. They could study the hammer throw at universities across America. This Stateside tossing trio had bugger-all to beat, as there were only five competitors.

Training, diet, visualisation and completing a PhD in hammer history and technique put Flanagan in the box seat for more golden success. He stepped into the ring of toss and won hammer gold at the next three Olympics. Not sure why any other throwers made the trip.

The hammer throw was an exclusively male event for decades. It is only in recent times that the IOC has reinvented itself as an equal opportunity employer. Women finally contested the hammer in the Sydney 2000 Olympics for the first time. Kamila Skolimowska from Poland won gold with an Olympic record throw of 71.16 metres.

The hammer talks to a new generation through the Marvel Comics character Thor. He was an ancient winner with a big and powerful hammer, associated with thunder and lightning, trees and strength. He is part of the pagan parade of Germanic heroes and a big figure in the Old Norse myths. Today Thor is strutting his stuff on the silver screen in Marvel superhero movies, starting in 2011 with *Thor*, which has spawned three sequels. The central character is played by Australian fitness freak, hammer thrower and actor Chris Hemsworth. From what he has shown on the silver screen, Chris would be no slouch in the Olympic hammer event.

The Thor big screen experience points to a future direction for Olympic sport. An avalanche of interest, money and technology is being tipped into e-sports, threatening to consign many of the traditional Olympic sporting competitions to the trashcan of history.

Sadly, those ancient war sports, the pole vault and javelin, will need YouTube cartoon heroes to make them popular with a generation of athletes keen to compete from the couch at the highest level. No one in the IOC is quite sure how to make hip again those very old-school wartime classics, the 10,000-metre walk and the 3000-metre steeple chase.

Wars today are being fought by troops camped on a stool behind a computer screen in a double garage in the deserts of Utah or the frozen wastes of Siberia. A mouse is used to activate weapon systems on unmanned platforms in constant circulation above the enemy.

*When hand-eye coordination, finger-tip keyboard skills and rapid joystick activity are the athletic tools of war today, how long before they become the basis of Olympic competition?*

Remote-controlled drones and weapon systems lurking on ships kilometres offshore are the future of combat. Humans are often far away from the front line and in a future fracas they need never go near the business end of a bomb again.

Is it any wonder that e-sports are taking over? When hand–eye coordination, finger-tip keyboard skills and rapid joystick activity are the athletic tools of war today, how long before they become the basis of Olympic competition?

If all else fails, there will always be drone racing and competitive hacking. These are sports that can be practised in the bedroom, in pyjamas with ugg boots on, enabling the sports stars of tomorrow to win gold without leaving home.

In a desperate bid to remain relevant to the modern generation, the IOC included kite surfing, surfing, skateboarding and break-dancing on the Tokyo card. These 'wild' sports are seen by the inhabitants of head office as happening, groovy, cool sporting pursuits. But will they bellow 'Olympics' to the younger set?

## The Tug of War

*Could it make a timely comeback in Brisbane 2032?*

What a great sport. But like pigeon shooting it was there and then suddenly it disappeared!

The Olympic Games are subject to pressure from sporting organisations that desperately want their sport included at Olympic level. The argument is that if running and swimming are in, why is our sport excluded? Sports fall in and out of favour and fashion with the IOC, which is tasked to juggle the fortnight of competition and make it fit the ever-expanding budget and the television schedule.

There are obviously certain must haves! The inferno would not be the Olympics if events like track and pool events of the

100 metres, 200 metres, 400 metres and the marathon were dumped. But lesser events and sports without great clout come and go with the regularity of the tides.

The 1900 Games saw the introduction of the tug of war. This crowd favourite was part of team events until the Antwerp Games in 1920. The terms and conditions varied. In 1900 there were six in a team, in 1904 five turned out, and for the last three Games it was an eight-a-side competition. If the images from those Olympics can be believed, the T.O.W. pulled a crowd of knowledgeable tug freaks, who knew exactly what they were looking at and were ecstatic at the heat this level of competition generated.

There is an incredible photographic record of the 1900 competition snapped by the great Minsk-based Russian sports photographer, Wolfgang F. Krupskaya. 'The Wolf' was the only photographer who actually took photos while representing and pulling in the quest for gold.

In 1900 a mixed Scandinavian team put away a team from France in the final. In 1904 it was a clean sweep to America, in 1908 Britain swept the medals. In 1912 only two teams turned up. The Stockholm Police, great tuggers, took on the thin blue line of the London Police in the final, and the Swedish synchronised pullers were victorious. It was a disappointing turnout as a number of countries entered but failed to appear on the day.

But in 1920 it was a different story. The event captured the public's imagination. Forty teams from five nations turned up. It was a golden finale to the event, with Great Britain taking the gold, Netherlands the silver and Belgium the bronze. This great crowd-pleaser was dropped due to issues concerning nationalities of teams, betting irregularities and illegal equipment, like studded boots, being used by the pullers.

Not sure what was happening with the T.O.W. scene in Australia during this golden age of Olympic tugging. Records in the sporting archives of the Australian War Memorial in Canberra indicate there was a lively interstate tug-of-war competition from the 1890s that climaxed with a very popular State of Origin, best-of-three pulls staged every July. Origin tugs were dominated by powerful teams including the South Fremantle Winches, the Oxford Street Drag (based in Sydney), and the Southside Slims from the Wonthaggi area in Victoria. The interstate pulls drew enormous crowds. On one July night at the Adelaide Oval, when snow fell on Mount Lofty, 57,987 people turned out to see an Origin victory to the Willunga Wrench.

It appears that, unfortunately, the message never got through to the Australian tug-of-war community that the yank and strain was on the Olympic card in that magnificent twenty-year stretch of red-hot competition when this event was considered central to every successful Olympic fortnight.

# RUGBY LEAGUE

*'Simply the Best', the Greatest Game of All.*
*Does anything more need to be said? Hell yeah!*

THE GAME OF RUGBY league erupted in the north of England in 1895. A few years later, big slabs of Australia fell under the new code's charismatic spell.

The game was revolutionary in concept when it broke away from rugby union. The sticking point was money. No surprises there!

The union wanted the players to turn out and cop a whack around the bonce and a boot up the date for free. Ultimately all it offered, apart from life-threatening injuries and a permanent wobbly boot in later life, was unlimited travel options, while the league offered to pay players for roughly the same experience. To the casual observer the main difference was that the league required teams of thirteen players prepared to cop it, not fifteen.

In 1908 the bell rang at Birchgrove Oval and with a loud tinkle the league was underway in the lucky country.

The Australian sporting landscape pivoted and was never the same again. NSW-based clubs, there at the dawn of creation, were Glebe, Newtown, Western Suburbs, South Sydney, Balmain, Eastern Suburbs, Newcastle and Cumberland. From these humble beginnings, the league has grown into a multi-billion-dollar industry.

The origins of the sport, dubbed the Greatest Game of All (G.G.A.) have been well documented in journals like the now-dead *Rugby League Week* (The Bible) and *The Big League*, and ute-loads of books about the G.G.A., including the international sports book of the year in 2019 *From Biter to Bubbler: A History of Rugby League Fun* by Ray 'The Penalty Puller' Bietz. The romance of the game is front and centre in *Married at First Sight to a Rugby League Player* by Madison F. Bump, *I Left the Light On* (an intimate personal history of rugby league) by C.A. Carpet, the harrowing, controversial and very funny *I Was a Prop in a Winger's Body!* by Andrew 'The Ferret' Frizell and *Hanging on the Edge* (rugby league's great wingers from 1908 to 2021) by Andrew 'Lightning' Bolt.

These great reads capture the history, the excitement and the drama of the code. In the Library of League, top of the top ten is *The Book of Feuds*, which focuses on the controversial and weirdly frosty relationship between the South Sydney Rabbitohs and the Eastern Suburbs Roosters. The Greatest Rabbit, former Gladiator Russell Crowe, reads a chapter or two of *The Feuds* before every hutch and fowl-house clash. This winds the coachwood-and myrtle–clad Bunnies right up. Russell gets them in the groove ready to run out and savage an uncooked Chook.

These tell-all exposés of the great games, the incredible tries, the injuries requiring the ambulance, the outrageous refereeing howlers, the ridiculous send-offs and the greatest players record the development of the code over ten decades.

What is not stressed in this avalanche of print, which has required the destruction of a rainforest or two, is the simple statement of fact that no sport in the world has a greater redemptive power woven into its DNA than Australian rugby league.

*This humble barge-and-charge code makes those masters of reclaiming souls, the Catholic Church, look like amateurs in the spiritual restoration caper.*

This humble barge-and-charge code makes those masters of reclaiming souls, the Catholic Church, look like amateurs in the spiritual restoration caper. This is why Australians are drawn to the game as players, officials, referees, spectators and punters. Redemption is a simple lark. League lovers witness the odious on-field crimes. They hear the whistle blow. They see the send-off. They hear the penalty handed down by the tribunal Monday night. They see the offenders doing time. Then these evil doers are welcomed back to the game. The remorseful and the rueful are cleansed of all sins. The contrite, in club colours, will be given an even greater welcome if they score under the black dot in the first attacking play of their comeback match.

Rugby league crime lurks in every eighty minutes. Players exert themselves on the very edge of their physical, mental and spiritual capabilities. The sport involves stretching every fibre, every sinew, every muscle the player has in all directions. And it asks the hard questions of their very soul. That is the code's great charm.

League is a game of obsessive passion and biblical lust. The head and the heart pull players in opposite directions. They want to do the right thing for the team, but ...

*League is a game of obsessive passion and biblical lust. The head and the heart pull players in opposite directions.*

> Bloody hell! There is a bloke in the opposition's jumper coming at me with the ball. I have to hit the clown, so he stays hit! I will whack the Steeden free of that tight grasp. The try line is wide open. I will score. People will love me! Thighs don't fail me now! But hang on a minute ... the bloke is my best mate! I went to school with him. Too bad! Whack! Whammo! Kapow!

The plan is executed perfectly. The opposing player is clobbered and put into the half-dream room on the outer reaches of the planet Coosbane, unsure who he is, or where he is, and unable to list any of Cold Chisel's top ten hits.

Out in the middle the try is called back. The bunker rules the tackle was head high. 'Thighs don't fail me now' is sent off for twenty minutes in the sin bin. The schoolmate is loaded into the back of the ambulance on his way to the nearest hospital.

The clobbered player comes to in a hospital bed with a lot of tubes going in and out. No surprise to see the schoolmate who did the whacking, still in the shorts, jumper and boots, blow in bedside as the first visitor in the intensive care unit. He greets the injured mate with an ice-cold beer and a grin from ear to ear. Never mind that he has to pour the amber nectar

*The bell might have rung in 1908 but the one great league leap forward was the creation of the State of Origin concept in 1980.*

down the mate's bed-ridden throat. That is mateship and that in a nutshell is the enduring beauty and the mad mystique of rugby league.

The bell might have rung in 1908 but the one great league leap forward was the creation of the State of Origin concept in 1980. It was such a basic idea: the best players from Queensland dolled up in Meninga Maroon should pack down against the best from NSW in Backdoor Benny Elias Blue.

As this novel idea cleared the guttering, the code's custodians were dragged kicking and screaming to the sideline card table for an interstate parley. Once all parties embraced the idea, they suddenly loved it. They loved the income from the crowds who wanted to be there for every thump, bump and dump, and the rivers of gold that flowed from those all-important and very lucrative television rights. The loot from television came in elephant dollars stacked in the back of the code's Toyota ute.

The original concept has evolved into a three-verse ode championing world peace through brutality, international harmony through unforgettable violence, and reconciliation through eighty minutes of war with football boots on.

State of Origin has become one of the great rivalries in the World of Sport. It is the pinnacle of the rugby league caper on this planet. It is far more important than weekly home-and-away matches and the annual Grand Final, and wildly more significant than any Test match, in which Australia is matched against a side from the easy-to-beat basket.

The Origin three-pronger has always been an excellent opportunity for branding. Everybody wants a piece of the shirt and short ensemble to carry their company's name into combat. Historically it has been a Battle of the Brews: XXXX, north of the Tweed, and various beer brands in NSW.

There is plenty of disruption in this interstate tale of tipples. The complex roguery of the Origin beer history requires in-depth PhD research. It does not stop with jumper and shorts. There are on-ground signage rights and arcane pourage rights (as in what beer can be served while the game is on in the venue and indeed pubs around the country that take the TV coverage). This is all grist to a promotional mill. These beer brouhahas can often end in the courts before a panel of beaks. All of it provides free advertising for those three nights on the Origin calendar.

The great motivating theme of the rumpus was generated before teams from Queensland became part of the National Rugby League competition. In the bad old days, whenever the Queensland v NSW fixture loomed on the agenda, the Sydney-based clubs, which had nicked all the good players north of the Tweed, claimed these champions should now play for NSW. This drove the Maroon-clad, Cane Toad community nuts. All their good players were wearing the colour of their fierce rivals, the blue-rinsed Cockroaches that infested Sydney.

The simple genius at the dawn of State of Origin's creation was to select teams from the players based on where they began their careers in the junior grades. It did not matter where they played in the home-and-away club competition. This certainly levelled the playing field.

This simplicity was never as simple as it seemed. The brains trust think-tanks in Queensland and NSW endlessly chew the fat over whether a player is actually a Blue or a Maroon. At the dawn of time, players were either Cockroaches or Cane Toads, and proud of it. The system should have provided certainty. But the very simplicity of the system generated long-lasting, arm-wrestling arguments based on disputes about who, what, where, when and how old.

Back in those fogs of time that cloud so much sporting history, mascots dressed as Cane Toads and Cockroaches rampaged up and down the sidelines of early Origin matches. Sideline battles between the mascots were often as entertaining as the on-field struggle for state domination. The grotesque vermin battles were eventually 'Morteined' as too many serious fights broke out among the ranks of the rancid, drawing attention away from the league combat happening metres away.

*Sideline battles between the mascots were often as entertaining as the on-field struggle for state domination.*

A curious feature emerged early in this two-state war. The NSW Blues selectors often listed a much better side on paper than their opponents, but Queensland could never be discounted. Since the start, the NSW team has had a genius for under-estimating the Queensland side. The Maroons regularly pull off an upset result when the odds and injuries were stacked against them. These life-affirming wins were based on the famous Maroon heart and desperation. The team often surprised, playing with huge heartfelt pride. This was particularly true of matches played at the cemetery of Lang Park, now Suncorp Stadium.

Origin matches are simply the best game of rugby league because the best players are playing. The original match in 1980 had its doubters. Pundits said it would not be taken seriously. But in the first Origin, when Mick Cronin, playing in blue, was thumped by Parramatta teammate and, for the night, Maroon skipper, Arthur Beetson, there were grins all round in the stands. The committee realised the concept would work. Being Maroon was suddenly the most important thing in the rugby league world if you were not Blue. Maroonism is a state of mind, something the heart can only feel. But it is something Queensland builds a team on.

*Maroonism is a state of mind, something the heart can only feel. But it is something Queensland builds a team on.*

That elusive ingredient of spirit often swerves around the Blues. The NSW supporters wear bright blue plastic wigs to show their support. But a Blues wig is no match for the beating heart of Queensland.

It is an odd sport that requires players to pack down on the weekend with teammates who will be their mortal enemies at Origin level mid-week. On Wednesday night, players who hate each other's guts at the weekend club level have to put those animosities aside to play together for their state. This takes some skill physically, intellectually and emotionally. But only the best and most adaptable are tapped for the higher calling. Becoming a Maroon or a Blue is the pinnacle of world league and the highlight of any player's career.

Origin is a wild risk-taking ride. It is a potent mix as it is a mate v mate, state v state, hate v hate and date v date occasion. Excitable players clash head-on, geed up by the partisan supporters in the biggest rugby league crowds on the planet. Both sides share an irrational hatred of the opposition and where they come from three nights a year. Understandably, the Origin cauldron is the place where league legends emerge.

Origin time illuminates an old truth that many rugby league players freely admit to: 'If we did not have rugby league in our lives, we would be in jail.' The code provides an outlet for young adults who don't fit in or have an anti-authority chip on their shoulder or just want to be idiots. With so many jail inmates familiar with the rules of rugby league, jails are now running courses in rugby league refereeing. Many ex-inmates now control matches across Australia every weekend. They are doing an excellent job with the whistle. When it comes to penalties, no one knows rugby league crime like a rugby league player who has spent several years on the inside thinking about where they went wrong. Remember, the possibilities of mayhem during eighty minutes of controlled violence are virtually limitless.

*When it comes to penalties, no one knows rugby league crime like a rugby league player who has spent several years on the inside thinking about where they went wrong.*

The rules of the game are always being pushed to the outer edges of common sense by bright sparks in the wrestling departments of all clubs. The new COVID league rules are going through a period of weekly changes in emphasis and application. Changes that were unimagined by the creators of the code. Referees have to take on board new emphasis and nuance of interpretation from head office. The nuance is sent round by email on Thursday morning, before the top-of-the-table clash between two teams who could be there in the big dance. It is a game of many moving parts.

The trouble for officials has always been that as soon as one particular life-threatening tackle is outlawed another creative invention is unleashed from the club's wrestling coach's playbook. This new outrageous stretching of the rules has one purpose. That is adding significant damage to the young Wagga High School product Ezra 'Ace' Hensby who is turning out in his third game for the Dragons. Ace has been described by the Nine *Wide World of Sport* commentary team as 'a try-scoring machine' and a certainty for the Kangaroos. The opposition wrestling coach hopes the kid will be on the sideline after the second scrum.

Tackling technique has evolved with every passing minute since 1908. A great deal of pain has been inflicted by the tick tock, the crusher, the squirrel grip, the hip drop, the shoulder charge, the head high, the bounce and the sleeper hold in which players were literally put to sleep in a tackle.

The sleeper hold featured in the repertoire of the great American wrestler Mark Lewin. Mark wrestled in Australia during a golden age of local mat men. He pulled on the trunks, climbed between the ropes and grappled using the *noms de undies* The Purple Haze and Skippy Jackson in the late 1960s. His signature grip, the startling sleeper hold,

*A great deal of pain has been inflicted by the tick tock, the crusher, the squirrel grip, the hip drop, the shoulder charge, the head high, the bounce and the sleeper hold in which players were literally put to sleep in a tackle.*

put many an opponent out for the count. It was featured weekly in Channel Nine's *World Championship Wrestling* (1964–78). This black-and-white must-see TV experience was a highlight of the channel's *Wide World of Sport*. It was hosted by the voice of the atomic drop, Jack Little.

The 'sleeper' has been banned by rugby league for wasting too much time. An opponent was often out for twenty minutes at a time. The great Western Suburbs league legend Tommy Raudonikis missed a whole second half of a semi-final when an opposing prop put him under in the crucial minutes leading up to half-time. Play was held up as the trainers and doctors dragged Tommy into the sheds. By the time the limp, prone package was brought around by the club medicos with a sprinkle of Fuji dust, the game was over.

As the offending prop, Randy 'Besser Block' Bruce, said when a guest speaker at the opening of Lithgow's Watsford Oval, International Centre of Rugby League Excellence in May 2017:

> Everyone asks about the semi-final hit on Tommy. I tried a hat full of tricks on the little bugger during the first half, the grope, the squirrel, the atomic drop and the head-high coat hanger. I gave him a nip in the third scrum of the match and eventually I planted a simple punch to the jaw, but Tommy kept coming back for more. In desperation, as half-time approached, I went in with the sleeper. I was half-hearted. I wasn't sure I could actually put the blighter away.
>
> But I got him exactly in the sweet spot. I rate it as my best tackle ever. I knew he was gone as soon as I applied the pressure. I turned off his power at the mains and blew the

> nearby substation in the process. And no surprises, after the win Tommy was the first to buy a beer in the Kennel Club Bar. That was the sort of bloke he was!

The rugby league wrestling coaches never forgot the impact of those great *World Championship Wrestling* holds. Today these senior rugby league mat men see the human body as a canvas on which inflicting pain can be taken to a whole new James Bond villainish level. Tackling has become so hotly contested that the rugby league head office now offers tackle clinics in the off-season on how to put a player away correctly. Although in recent seasons it is difficult to tell if anyone attends these summer schools.

The brutality of the game and the heroic deeds of players have created legends. There have been many very dangerous moments in the history of league up to and including death. The unpredictable violence leaves many Australians scratching their heads, wondering whether the code actually has a future in its current form. No matter how often they change the rules, it's still a collision sport of enormous ferocity. It will never be table tennis.

# Part 2

# HEROES

# 'AUSSIE JOE' BUGNER: THE NAME SAYS IT ALL

*The madness begins early and rumbles on over twelve magnificent rounds with a heavyweight belt on the line.*

THE 'SWEET SCIENCE' IS one of Australia's oldest European sports. The first recorded stink in Sydney took place on 8 January 1814. Two well-credentialled convicts, 'Pummelling' Johnny Parton and Charles 'Soapy' Sefton, pulled on the gloves for this original Down-Under ding-dong.

The bout was illegal, so the style of hype and promotion that normally accompanies a heavyweight clash in today's boxing circus was simply not possible. This was an underground, under-the-radar event. It was a fight club happening long before a fight club was considered normal.

Even though no one knew about it, this was a big occasion and a large crowd gathered to see what the prize fighters had cooked up. The gloved two had set themselves to go the distance. Australia's first title bout was decided over fifty-six rounds. The boys punched themselves to a standstill. After two days in the ring the fighters were still keen to swing on, but the crowd was drifting away and there was a big undercard of age divisions still to go. The referee, Earl 'The Fog' Gust, did the sensible thing and declared a winner. The hand The Fog held aloft was the bloodied fist of Pummelling Parton.

The colony was an early adopter of sport. This heavyweight bout was staged four years after the first horse races were run on the exciting Hyde Park layout. A race meeting that set free the great Australian tradition of the punt.

*Pummelling was a very fine tradie, ticketed in the break-and-enter crafts.*

Pummelling Parton (aka John Berringer) was part of the convict cohort on the *Fortune,* which blew into Sydney in June 1813. Pummelling was a very fine tradie, ticketed in the break-and-enter crafts. He was originally sentenced to death, but the judge allowed the southpaw to swerve around the big sleep and booked him a passage on a boat set for a long sea voyage. The judge made an example of Parton as he did for hundreds of others who came before him for stealing a loaf of sourdough or blowing their nose in public. He commuted the death sentence on many occasions to transportation to NSW for life.

The colony was lucky to get Parton. He was a trash-talker with that 'What are you looking at?', 'Want to step outside and go on with it?' style of brutal patter. He had a collection of stock lines and insults for all occasions.

His opponent on the day, Soapy Sefton, aka 'Stinky', aka 'Nobs', aka 'Putrid', aka 'Sluggo', appeared before a Liverpool judge who booked him into a hammock on the *Fortune*. He was a second-storey man and found guilty of nicking stuff. He liked lifting promissory notes and, well, anything else that could be lifted. Soapy just loved lifting. He was sentenced for the big drop by his Honour Justice Cedric Slime, known around the lively Liverpool court scene of the era as the 'one-way ticket' man. His Honour loved gallows humour, often offering the wretched crim in the dock a choice of the rope, the lash or the long, slow goodbye. It was pick-a-box justice!

Both Parton and Sefton had plenty of time to cook up the first fight wheeze on the *Fortune*. They got to know each other's technique as they made the long, slow trip to the penal colony of NSW.

This great bout – some critics say it was the original and best – began a rich tradition of people trying to make the transition from other sports and other trades to boxing.

The history of Australian boxing is a saga of great moments of vigorous action followed by big gaps where nothing much went on. Fight game critics and punchers on the sniff for a bout were always declaring it cactus or about to drop off the twig. Just when the nation thought the whole dust-up caper was slipping into the cold, hard ground, another champ with a good left-right combination, another trainer with ideas about losing weight or another promoter with a ute-load of money would get a bee in their bonnet about reviving the shebang and begin breathing new life into the lifeless corpse. It is a recognised truism of the fight caper that everyone is just one fight, one punch, one bout away from retirement; likewise, the whole wheeze.

*It is a recognised truism of the fight caper that everyone is just one fight, one punch, one bout away from retirement; likewise, the whole wheeze.*

So many great names have been associated with the thump-and-count-to-ten profession. The Marrickville Mauler, Jeff Fenech, the Russian-born Sydney-based former world champion, powerhouse Kostya Tszyu, the featherweight Johnny Famechon, the five-time world champion Lester Ellis, the heavyweight, cruiserweight, light heavyweight and middle weight Tony Mundine and his son Anthony 'The Man' Mundine, also no stranger to the light middleweight, middleweight, super middleweight and cruiserweight divisions. The Man had the trade of rugby league before he pulled the gloves on. There were others called up to the ring like Rocky and Lucky Gattellari, Jimmy Carruthers, Spike Cheney and the Waters boys to name a few of the local fight heroes.

Lionel 'Slim' Rose was a world champion bantamweight and the first Aboriginal boxer to win a world title and be named Australian of the Year. What a record! Slim pulled on the shorts for fifty-three bouts, forty-two wins (twelve by KO) and featured in eleven losses. Lionel won his first professional bout at the age of sixteen outpointing Mario Magriss. In February 1968 he defeated Fighting Harada over fifteen rounds in Tokyo for the world championship. The win catapulted the youngster from Warragul, Victoria, to national fame. At a reception at the Melbourne Town Hall in 1968, 100,000 fight-mad Victorians turned up to greet the champ. He put Melbourne on the world stage.

Lionel had a musical career after farewelling the ring. His chart-topping song 'I Thank You' became an unofficial national anthem. These two great champs, Lionel and Harada, were reunited as part of the 1991 VFL Grand Final festivities at Waverley before the bounce. It was a great get for the VFL.

The fighters joined singer Angry Anderson in the centre square. There was talk of a rematch, as in Rose v Harrada 2, before the bounce, but mercifully sanity prevailed.

Recent Australian ringside adventures include Mundine v Green encounters followed by the fight of the century between Queensland powerhouse Jeff Horn, a primary schoolteacher, and Filipino senator Manny Pacquaio, in 2017. The visiting senator had never fought a well-tutored schoolteacher. He had no idea how to handle a fit, determined Brisbane-based chalkie, and it was no wonder the punching senator was found wanting.

Peering into the distant past there's a long line of greats lured into the ring for a swing by the prospect of putting away a pug for a plump purse. These were different times, when money was much harder to come by, and punching an opponent in the head was a great way to earn a year's income. Greats emerged like Les Darcy, the middleweight who held the heavyweight belt, the all-rounder Snowy Baker, Dave Sands, the boxer with 'the educated left hand', and the featherweight 'Young' Griffo, who never aged – he was always 'Young'.

All Australian blokes of a certain vintage think they have one punch in them. Of course, concussion and resulting brain damage are greater concerns today than they were when all sport was groping around in the dark wondering why the big stars of yesteryear often went wobbly in later life. This simple idea that a punching was not recommended by the wellness industry was yet to dawn on the majority of the sporting community.

*All Australian blokes of a certain vintage think they have one punch in them.*

Curiosity and charity bouts between the stars of the football codes, Australian Rules and rugby league in particular, now plug the widening gaps on the fight night calendar. Footballing boxers like Cronulla Shark Paul 'The Stool' Gallen, former AFL Saint and Swan Barry 'Noodles' Hall and Sonny Bill Williams have intrigued match-makers and fight fans love the added battle of the codes dimension to the rumble.

Fighting footballing 'mates' call each other out on television footy shows like *100% Footy* and *Sports World* where it is easy to get the 'I hate you, you big pillow!' vibe going. The pre-fight weigh-in war of words is traditional fodder for the tabloid press. The build-up to fight night features articles on how great the fighters look at training and how great the players were in their footy days, when they were fifteen years younger.

Then the fighting footballers without much training are in the ring swinging at each other, raising money for research into how the brain is affected by big knocks and punches to the head. Critics moan about joke footballer bouts 'demeaning the sport'. This latest outrage of the ordinary proves boxing is cactus and society does not give a fig about the sweet science anymore. But the fight game somehow staggers on, and in no time at all the Olympics are on again and Australia is sending our best team ever.

IN THE LONG HISTORY of Australian boxing one name stands out from the historic ringside ruck! That name is Joe Bugner, aka 'Aussie Joe' Bugner, aka 'Atomic' Joe, aka 'Vigneron' Joe.

Joe was a great role model for younger generations. Anyone just out of school, with a rock-solid melon, looking to get into a go-ahead sport with opportunities to travel and a big pay day attached, could do a lot worse than embrace the Bugner legacy.

'The Teenage Tornado', Joe Bugner was born in Hungary. 'The Tornado' tag was ironic as Joe was a slow mover who did everything with deliberation. The family fled to England in the mid-1950s when the Russian tanks turned up in Budapest uninvited and declared the party over. He was a large kid and willing. As a teenager he excelled at sport, becoming the British national discus champion in 1964. After cleaning up the competition in the age divisions of rotate and release, he began an action-packed journey through sport, which eventually brought him to the fight game.

In the ring, Joe had a defensive style. He was exceptionally cautious, but ring watchers agreed the kid without much footwork looked durable. Like most boxers, Bugner did not like smelling the glove, let alone tasting it. But his record speaks for itself. He stepped into the squared circle eighty-three times for sixty-nine wins, of which forty-three were knockouts. He drew once, and the maths suggest he lost thirteen times.

*Like most boxers, Bugner did not like smelling the glove, let alone tasting it.*

His big break was in March 1971. The bout that established Joe as 'the next big thing' was the fight against the champ, Henry Cooper. This was a highly anticipated bout between age and youth. It was a contest as old as the fight game itself. The ding-dong was postponed for a year until Joe turned twenty-one. By then two belts were on the line, the British Commonwealth and European heavyweight titles.

Henry wielded a big punch, known as 'Henry's Hammer', but Joe triumphed. The Tornado won by one quarter of a point over fifteen rounds. Joe found a way to score with a left jab, keeping his opponent at bay. Henry took the fight up to Joe but could not land the lights-out blow with the ball pein in his fist.

The incredible closeness of the margin got fight fans talking. A quarter-point victory is something to hang a pair of big shorts on. On the night there was just one official scoring, the charismatic Harry Gibbs. No one could count like 'Left Hook' Harry. He often scored a fight based on the audience reaction to every punch.

Harry described the never-repeated decision to Eddie 'Slow' Charlton, fight correspondent for the *Sunday Times*, who asked the ref, 'Hookie, was it your best?':

> Yeah, no. Slow, that was my best! I will never be that accurate again. I was always good at counting at school, but that scoreline was special. Sure, Joe did bugger-all, but the sweet sound of leather does not lie. You hear every whack to bonce and body in the ring. As you know, a judge always feels a fight. Often, I get home more bruised than the brawlers.
>
> But a quarter of a point – it's a helluva a margin. I am not sure how I did it. And I have replayed every punch over and over in my mind.
>
> The fight made Joe, but it made me as well. Everyone knew I could score after that twelve rounder. People in the street stopped me, shook my hand and mumbled, 'Harry, love your work, when is your next fight?' I never looked back!

It was a controversial decision. People still argue about it. Even fight fans who had no interest in the bout nor seen the replay have an opinion. Joe could not keep the momentum going, he lost both titles in his next bout against Jack Bodell. Atomic Joe put this down to inexperience and the unkind suggestion in certain sections of the media that the win over Cooper's hammer was a Gibbs-inspired fluke.

But 'The Tooting Tornado' was on his way. The big heavyweight names of the era, Joe Frazier and Muhammad Ali, were lurking. Everyone wanted to know him. The Bugner dance card was suddenly chock-a-block.

Joe took on Muhammed Ali and did enough to earn the respect of both the picky public and the hard-to-please big-headed boxing media. Many knowledgeable fight fans judged his next rumble with Joe Frazier, in July 1973, as the best of his career. Bugner was flattened by a stunning left hook in the eleventh by the other Joe in the ring. But The Tottenham Tornado got back on his feet and finished the round. At the death, Bugner had done a bit, but not enough and dipped out by a couple of punches in a points decision.

After these two heavyweight losses, The Twickenham Tornado won eight in a row and challenged Ali to another tango. This time it was a world title affair. In June 1975 Bugner and Ali fought in Kuala Lumpur's heat and humidity. Ali easily won a lopsided rumpus. Bugner kept his strictly defensive posture going throughout the fight in the blistering tropical heat of the outdoor venue.

Late in the first act of his long career he lost interest and walked away from the game he loved. But a mere ten days later he knew it was a big mistake and announced his first major comeback. Through the next two decades, like a sporting addict, Joe had trouble staying away from the thrill of the fight and just one more night centre stage in the shorts under the bright lights. He knew that a lucky punch at the right time could give him another shot at the world heavyweight title. He knew boxing was a game of millimetres and ticks on the clock.

> *Through the next two decades, like a sporting addict, Joe had trouble staying away from the thrill of the fight and just one more night centre stage in the shorts under the bright lights.*

He was in this very challenging retiring and comeback phase of his career when he moved to Australia in 1986. He was a genuine government pin-up boy for the great Australian multicultural programme. He loved Australia. His name and record still opened doors. He still saw a ring and wanted a fight. This time he slipped through the ropes as 'Aussie' Joe Bugner. The new handle let all fight fans know where he stood on the migration issue and who he now supported. He wanted to give something back to the nation that welcomed him with open arms. His rebadging talked to fans who might have thought he was just another freeloading blow-in. Not sure if there were other Joe Bugners knocking about the circuit elsewhere, but this Joe had the big point of difference: he was the only Aussie Joe.

He appeared ringside in a green and gold dressing gown. These are not easy colours for a designer to work with, but the ensemble was tarted up with a cascade of wattle draped across the shoulders and a sprig or two of real wattle tacked to the breast pocket.

He fought on through a forgotten litany of great and lesser names until a big night in October 1987 when he returned to London and fought Frank Bruno at White Hart Lane. Now thirty-seven years old, Joe entered the ring as 'the most unpopular man in British sport'.

Frank was a complex opponent. To get a feel for the canvas and stay sharp, Frank Bruno erected a boxing ring in his backyard. As the bout approached, Frank did not want ring rust to creep into his game, so the champ began sleeping in the ring outside under the stars for days before the bout. When Frank's ring days were over, he retrained and had a successful career as a panto dame. His Widow Twankey in *Aladdin* brought all the skills from the squared circle to the 'Oh, yes it is!' stage at Christmas.

Joe lost to Widow-T-to-be. This night of nights for glove freaks was followed by another pause for Joe along the winding road before inevitably another comeback turned up when he swerved around the next bend.

But even after the White Hart Lane debacle he could not stay away, and he fought on during the 1990s. By now the world had lost interest in his limited ring style. It was a masterstroke of movement that he only progressed forwards and backwards in straight lines as though his feet were strapped to a skateboard. Many opponents worked out a fight strategy as they had a fair idea of where Joe would be headed next at any point in the bout and aimed the punches at the spot he was travelling to, not where he was.

He pushed on until his brain finally got the message through to his body that enough was enough. He was gone for good in 1999, just as a new century dawned, at the very young age of forty-eight. Many wished the OAP of the ring had pushed on into the twenty-first century.

Did Australia see the best of Joe? That is a hard question. Joe understood that boxing was about 79.9 per cent show business

*His only failing was he could not let a stink go by without wanting to lace on a glove and be part of it.*

and 15 per cent brawn and bashing, which left 5.1 per cent of the brain still working. Australia got to see a man in his prime with something to say. His only failing was he could not let a stink go by without wanting to lace on a glove and be part of it. He went everywhere prepared. He travelled with the shorts and gloves in the boot of the car with the hands taped, ready to stride into the bright lights and take a pummelling from an opponent and a torrent of abuse and shouts of derision from his fans.

Joe, like many great sporting identities, could do the lot. Through the marketing power of the name Bugner he suddenly had a blossoming career as a winemaker. Joe and partner Marlene began working grapes in the Cessnock area, knocking up Marlene Hermitage and Joseph Chardonnay. These were two great attacking wines that could go the distance. Joe's wines were marketed under the St Merovingian brand. St Merovingian is the patron saint of boxers-turned-winemakers, among other things.

Joe was very hands-on, involved in every facet of the process. He pruned the vines, drove the tractor, had magic hands with the secateurs, picked the grapes, trod the vat, rammed the corks in and was the brains in the marketing department.

The range, sadly, did not find a foothold in the tricky Australian wine market. The operation stumbled, losing a vat full of loot in the process. But he tipped that bottling know-how into his next venture, producing a range of mineral waters marketed with the phrase 'Once sipped never forgotten' on every bottle.

But Joe had always been keen to expand into other areas. He knew an act was needed to promote fights and so with his ring craft it was a short skip to starring in internationally produced feature films. His career took off to great acclaim with Bud Spencer and Terence Hill's Italian classic *Io Sto Con Gli Ippopotami* (*I'm for the Hippopotamus*), in which he played the challenging role of Ormond.

Joe worked with the Bud and Terence team during the 1980s. They showed their young fighting apprentice the cinema ropes. There was a lot to learn, how to hit a mark, where to stand, how not to look at the camera, how to be tough (that was easy for Joe) and that great skill of how to deliver a line while robbing it of all meaning.

Joe cashed the cheque he wrote as Ormond when he packed down in *Buddy Goes West* as the evil Sheriff Bronson. These early films were from the boutique funny Spaghetti Western school of film-making. As he gained confidence and found a fan base, Joe attempted more serious works, tackling *Sher Mountain Killings Mystery*, in which he played the career-defining role as the Ranger. *Street Fighter* saw him playing the heavy again as Bison's Torturer, and he brought it all home when he appeared as Claw Miller in *Fatal Bond*, an Australian erotic thriller. Excited film-goers were so moved by his performance that on occasions they began hurling their underwear at the screen. This was a great vehicle, but unless anyone was looking in the wrong place no one seems to have watched it. His career on the big screen had a final act when he played Fingers McGee in the award-winning *Bad Behaviour* in 2010.

After thrilling several generations on the big screen and in the big ring, Joe got another lucky break behind the information desk at Boondall Tools on the Gold Coast. He was a sensation advising hardware types where the four-inch roofing nails, the cross-cut saw and the bags of cement were located in the vast store.

Bugner's career needs its own book. In fact, it has one: *Joe Bugner, My Story*, told over twelve rounds. He was built to be a stayer and that was the street where he plied his trade. He ended a long and varied career simply telling people where to go. It was a great success.

# THE CAPTAIN OF THE TEAM

*Scott 'It's Not a Race' Morrison is the first cab off the rank.*

THE THIRTIETH PRIME MINISTER of Australia, Scott 'I Don't Hold the Hose' Morrison, is no stranger to the Canberra cultural bubble of sport and its intense political ramifications.

Rugby league is his go-to sport for entertainment and relaxation. As soon as he was tapped for the top job in Canberra, the Sutherland Shire product, out of the Bronte hub, was out on the school oval demonstrating his rugby league credentials. He has a genuine knack for the six-tackle caper that made him a tight fit for The Lodge.

There he was, having staggered back from the Governor-General's big house at Yarralumla, with the commission to run the joint still wet in his pocket, straight into the shorts and boots, running the ball up, laying on a fend, pumping a dummy, before stepping to the left and going over to score against a plucky Under 13 side from Kirrawee Primary School, school motto 'Our Best Always'.

The Kirrawee Destroyers were no easy beats. They made it tricky for 'Smoko' and in doing so made the new PM look good. Cameras from all free-to-air channels and major news outlets were on hand to record the The Hose's footwork and his incredible ball security.

Knowledgeable observers at Channel Nine and Fox Footy thought 'Bus Tickets' had the skills to go all the way in the greatest game of all. The burning issue along the east coast of the nation, as 'JobKeeper' Joe made his run for the top job was: is this bloke rugby league literate? That stiff stumper was answered convincingly in a lively twenty minutes of power and passion against the stars of tomorrow.

Desperate Australians relaxed, secure in the knowledge that, at last, rugby league would be represented at the highest level in the nation's affairs. A collective sigh of relief was expelled by a grateful nation, knowing that the new man in The Lodge had a firm grasp of the fundamentals.

*A collective sigh of relief was expelled by a grateful nation, knowing that the new man in The Lodge had a firm grasp of the fundamentals.*

He could do the lot. The gouge, the crusher, the don't argue, the hip drop, the tick tock, finding a gap, bursting through, breaking the line before getting the ball down over the line under the black dot – 'The Jab of Hope' man had it all. That effort he put in against the kids confirmed to the knockers, and there were many, that 'Vaccines' was ready for the top job.

It was an impressive hit-out against the kids from Kirrawee. The Australian coach, Mal Meninga, knew he could run

'Captain Smoke' off the bench for fifteen minutes of game time if the Kangaroos needed an injection of pace in the back row against the PNG Kumuls. If a tricky Test match was hanging in the balance, 'Sooty' was genuine dry powder.

Not long after snaring the keys to The Lodge in a tight three-way tussle with 'Spud' Dutton and 'Blinga' Bishop, 'Super Soot' got a chance to sample the cut and thrust of international rugby league when he ran the water for the green and gold in a Kangaroos v Fiji clash that coincided with a high-powered South Pacific summit on climate change.

What a week for the recently installed PM! He climaxed seven days of selling the dump to the Pacific Islands on rising sea levels and offering the low-lying atoll and island nations more frequent hurricanes and warmer seas by getting the water job in the first Test.

But the sporting prowess of the 'Six Again Hombre' did not stop with rugby league. He cashed the cheque he wrote with league when he reached for the tennis racquet and new balls.

He made a young number one representative from the Shire's tennis club look a complete idiot when he took him on over three hard-fought points at the Ken Rosewall Tennis Centre in Mortdale. The kid was never the same afterwards, especially when 'The Trumpette' sent him packing with a Bernard Tomic X-rated spray.

Scott 'Handshakes' Morrison was always up for a kick of footy, a hit of tennis or a swim in a clapped-out pool during a meet-and-greet listening tour around the nation. In campaign mode, he recorded his great swims in the pools of Australia on social media, encouraging voters who dialled up his deep end posts to take the plunge and do a few lengths.

*Scott 'Handshakes' Morrison was always up for a kick of footy, a hit of tennis or a swim in a clapped-out pool during a meet-and-greet listening tour around the nation.*

Discussing 'Announcements' Morrison's hands-on style, many tertiary-educated observers have made the obvious observation that the 'Where the Bloody Hell Are You?' bloke is our first PM to be totally inspired by television, advertising in particular.

With his background in marketing, it was only natural that he modelled his approach to the top job on the can-do style, no-job-is-too-big, local stars of television.

Australia's reality TV is the best in the world. Shows like *MasterChef*, *The Bachelor* and *Australia's Got Talent* are the envy of the reality TV industry. They are must-see appointment viewing at the Morrison-supervised screen-time when the team are at home in The Lodge.

The family gathers on the lounge before the credits. Phones are put away. There were cheers for *MasterChef* stars like Reynold, Poh and Callum when they wore the apron. There were louder cheers when the contestants plated up and nervously strolled up to the top table trio with their free-range vegan lamb chops, in a hummus and prune jus and deconstructed passionfruit pavlova, all Eton-messed on the same plate. Magic!

This nation is so blessed to have a talented bench of dolled-up wise heads who can adjudicate the passion on the plate while the nervy chefs step back, awaiting that sobering, career-defining decision.

The Morrison clan loved everything that Pete, Manu, Jock, Melissa and the man with the fork in hand and the cravat at the neck, Mattie Preston, have had to say in their meticulous judgements. Like all Australians, the Morrison clan were a family of fanatics lapping up the cut and thrust of cutlery in competition.

'Bonk Ban' Scott's real hero from this potpourri of Australian reality television culture was another Scott; can the man from *The Block*, Scott Cam, take a step forward? So taken was Handshakes by *The Block* superstar in action with the spirit level that Canberra Scott opened the taxpayers' Prada handbag, plucked several thousand very large and hurled the folding into the back of *Block* Scottie's idling Toyota V8 Landcruiser. The lolly lobbed in the boot alongside a bag of Portland cement and a Paslode cordless nail gun from Total Tools in Taren Point.

In return, 'Shocked and Appalled' Morrison tasked Scott Cam to encourage all school leavers to become tradies. This was not a big ask. 'Toolie' Scott was to tour music festivals, craft beer shows and school formals with a powerful message about how much fun and what a great earn slogging away with a hammer, chisel and a cross-cut saw can be. The ambitious plan was to have 94.9 per cent of all school leavers enrolled in a trade by 2027. A move that would create 65,440 jobs.

Inspired by the YouTube vision of Cam's end-of-year sprays at school breakups, lecture notes from Scott's series 'Wood: What is it Good For?' and the stunning drama of the dovetail joint, PM Scott decided to strap on the tool bag and give it a go at home.

In 2020, the PM had time on his hands as COVID-19 travel protocols prevented him from fleeing back to holiday hotspots that featured sun, surf, deck chairs and burgers. Hawaii's loss was Kirribilli's gain as Scott has overseen substantial renovations around the harbourside Lodge since the moving vans dropped off their load.

He has knocked up a fowl run in the backyard. It is very professional, with twenty-four laying boxes and a built-in self-feeding and watering system. The fowl-house construction meant that the whole Morrison clan can slip away and get their feet up for at least three weeks before the chooks run out of food pellets and water. All he has to do before laying rubber to a NSW holiday hotspot is to notify the office manager at the PMO to swing by and collect the eggs.

*During his rise to the top, many media critics thought 'Phillips Head' Morrison was headed for a career in television.*

During his rise to the top, many media critics thought 'Phillips Head' Morrison was headed for a career in television. The closest he got to this ambition were the regular appearances in the Parliament House courtyard where he made a number of significant announcements. Through the early months of his reign, with his hands gripping the nation's levers, he developed a professional polish standing behind the lectern and delivering a skilled spray with that trademark wicked smirk.

'Flash' Scott had a rare skill. He could make those long, intricate announcements he dropped earlier that month, at the same lectern, seem totally fresh and wonderfully original. When he laid them on the public again, the press gallery responded enthusiastically as though they were hearing these repeated sprays for the first time. He was that good!

But Scott's real television inspiration was not *Hey, Hey!* or the inspirational handiwork of Captain Wood, Scott Cam, it was that very popular long-running TV show of the nineties, *Home Improvement.*

This was a vehicle for comic Tim Allen as a suburban dad, who was always todger deep in DIY scrapes around the house. In his working life Tim presented the show within the show, *Tool Time with Tim the Toolman Taylor.*

Tim the Toolman was a master of adding his special mayhem to the on-going domestic chaos. When it all became too much, Tim escaped to the double garage attached to the house for a fiddle with a red 1933 Ford Roadster's donk. He sought a certain Zen-like grace by laying a set of socket spanners on the never completed 350 cubic inch power pack.

The running gag in *Tool Time*, was, well, fairly obvious: Tim was unable to complete the simplest of tasks, like banging in a nail or finding the right screwdriver. He had to be rescued from DIY disaster by his trusty colleague, Al Borland. Al understood tools and how they worked, unlike Tim, who was a complete amateur. When 'Toolman' was not running amok in the studio, he was searching out power tools with even more buzz.

The great Sooty Morrison lifestyle themes were all there. The 'Have a Go' man's go-to position is tradie focused. A lingering shop at Bunnings was always a terrific day out for Scott. People with four-by-four dual-cab utes and big V8 motors with something to say about tyre pressures were his favourite people.

If there was taxpayer loot to be dished out to revive a struggling national economy, the instant response from 'Jabs' was to shovel a load of cash in the direction of extensive home improvements. When tapped for the throne he believed Australia was short of carports, second stories, en suites, third bathrooms, pergolas and granny flats. In fact, it was short of everything a pandemic-hit nation needed 'to get back to normal'. Swinging a claw hammer, digging a trench and taking aim at some plywood sheets with a nail gun were obviously the right ways to get back on track for thinking Australians.

In Scott's world, federal tax relief must always target the nation's cash-strapped tradies first. The rest of the nation can get in the queue, shut up and wait. If the LNP party room was forced to consider a handout and leg-up to the long-suffering, almost forgotten and desperate arts community, then this government largesse had to have a total tradie bias.

'Road Maps to Recovery' Morrison was keen to dish out chunks of cash to lure Hollywood heavyweights Down Under to cook up Marvel- and DC Comic-based projects in our world-class studios. A large wedge of loot encouraged big-name blow-ins to knock up heavily subsidised action movies instead of taking on local productions tackling great Aussie tales like *The Brendan Fevola Story* and *Eddie McGuire's Lost Weekend*.

The foreign action features, destined for the cinema-mad Chinese market, are comic book–inspired capers or space epics involving battles between good and evil, calling for acrobatics performed in front of a green screen and a lot of time spent in post-production.

As Sooty said to 'Grumpy' Cecil Sloop in an extensive profile for *Show and Shine: The Election Special*, two days after being tapped by his party room colleagues for the top job:

> Grumps, I love the Arts. I often go to the movies. Sure, I was limited by COVID protocols, but I went twice last year. Admittedly I saw *Spider-Man: Homecoming* twice. I loved it. I even got the Spider-Man socks for Christmas.

Cecil, I have the Love Machine at home so naturally I am a tool man. There is nothing I like more than laying a shifting spanner or a Phillips head screwdriver on a problem.

Missus Soot has a never-ending list of jobs tacked to the fridge at home and it is getting longer and longer. The list is tacked to the fridge with a couple of Maui island life souvenir fridge magnets. What with China on the turn and the continual power/energy rumpus in the party room, I just don't have the time. But give me a set of Stillsons and a blocked S bend and I am in heaven.

Cec, I don't mind admitting it, I have modelled myself on 'Toolman' Taylor, who like me has all the answers even if they are wrong. Tools are king in my cabinet!

Now duck out to the truck, sonny Jim, grab the footprints and bring the gum boots. We cannot knock off until this Fowlerware is fixed. The lumpy, brown stuff will go everywhere when she blows.

Sunday is always the big day in the Morrison household. It's a day when the two great stabilising prongs of 'Have a Go's life swing into focus. There's an early clap-along with all the gang down at the Palace of Prayer, often with a couple of tunes from the Demon Souls of Bundeena. 'Appalled' is up and about and moving when the Souls flick open the Slayer songbook and launch into those big 'hell to pay' biblical hits.

But the highlight of the day is an afternoon of rugby league at Shark Park née Endeavour Field and a top-of-the-table clash featuring his team, Cronulla Sharks. The Sharks are the biggest noise in the sport-mad Sutherland Shire. But there was always so much to do before the league kick-off.

Ah, the Shire, it is a special place. That is why 'The Coalman' Scott lives there. Only special Sydneysiders are allowed to drop anchor along its sandy shores and enticing rivers. Once in the Shire, many Australians spend their whole lives camped in comfort without heading north to the wintery wild lands beyond Tom Ugly's Bridge.

Unless you live there, the Shire is a very difficult concept to get your head around. This fabulous patch of southern Sydney has its own unique outlook. A heady atmosphere in the joint proclaims, 'Listen pal, we belong here! You don't! Now you know what a road is, why don't you use it!'

Top of the Shire agenda are home DIY renovations, air-conditioning, cars (especially V8 utes), real estate prices, boats with twin outboards, specials at Bunnings and how bloody crowded the beaches are becoming, and it's getting worse every year!

The genius of the man they call 'Smoky' was to drag these suburban issues centre stage and place them at the top of the national political hit parade during the 2019 election.

After the sing-a-long clap and a loosening of the larynx on the holy hits, the PM, with the portfolio of tradies, drops in to Caringbah Bunnings to sniff the specials and hopefully bail up the knowledgeable staff for a twenty-minute chat about the speed and stamina of the new range of Makita battery-powered angle grinders.

He might pick up a Black and Decker Workmate, which he really needs, now that he is strapping on the nail bag again, a pack of double power points for the laundry and enough wood to build a cubby for the kids. That is why the bloke drives a ute!

'On the Bus' runs a four-door, dual-cab Ranger Wildtrak, five-cylinder, 3.2-litre turbo diesel. A twin pack of supersized tradie cupboards are bolted to the back tray and are stacked with the latest hardware. Up front there is plenty of room for the seldom seen, but oft referred to, 'Jen and the girls'.

At the 2019 federal election, the ute and ute technology featured heavily on the hustings. Post-election university surveys suggested the Liberal Party's visible commitment to the ute may have got 'The Sootster' over the line.

Raves from the 'COVID app' man and Employment Minister Cash suggested that the Labor Party were coming hard for Australia's utes and four-wheel-drive wagons. 'The Curry for the Country' minister's rave was, 'If Labor got up, Albo and his lot of mad loony socialist greenies were going to force all Australians to drive electric vehicles. Imagine our nation without the heady aroma of diesel.'

Minister Cash is easily spotted on the campaign trail. She is a committed wearer of captivating, high-waisted loon pants in beige and appeared at many campaign rallies, arm in arm, with Captain Smoke.

They attacked Labor's all-electric, no-petrol policies, saying this mad idea was an assault on Australian values, Australian interests, the Australian way of life and Australian wildlife.

'Under Labor, the weekend, as we understand it today, would be history!' bellowed Minister Cash. 'The electric car has bugger-all power and so little prod forward that it couldn't pull the skin off a rice custard, let alone a boat on a trailer with twin Evinrudes tacked on the back.' It was a powerful argument. The nation was suddenly terrified.

Many real Australians decided they could not take the risk and slept in their dual cabs armed with a shanghai, ball bearings and slug guns in case Albo's 'No Petrol' stormtroopers came sneaking about in the night looking for the keys.

But the nation was mercifully saved from this horrible fate on election day with the words, 'How good is Australia?', and everything returned to normal. Climate change was back in its box and we could steam ahead planning that base load generating coal-fired power station with confidence.

With 'Sharkman' safe in The Lodge, Sundays were once again great. After a hard morning on the sing-song and a top shop at hardware central, 'Under the Bus' often felt peckish. He swung the ute into Engadine Macca's car park for a double burger with the lot and a side of fries.

This Golden Arches, the saintly jewel of junk food in the Shire, is the PM's spiritual trough. The hard-working team behind the counter always have a curried chicken burger and lettuce on tap in case 'The Values Bloke' turns up in the drive-thru with Minister Cash travelling shotgun. This Golden M location is now a very popular stopping-off point on the 'PM Morrison: This is your Life!' Bus Tour. It's a thirty-minute pause for the ravenous patrons.

Before heading out to Shark Park on Captain Cook Drive, 'Take the Knee' Morrison dresses for an afternoon of relaxation. It is an afternoon of rugby league, a few beers with the mates and bellowing inanities at the Sharks and those idiotic league-lovers who support the opposition. It requires dressing down in well-travelled and well-stained Country Road or R.M. Williams gear.

He has a special cupboard of rural-inspired clobber in the double garage at home, Kirribilli and The Lodge. In his working life, Captain Soot may be booked to open a school fete in Orange, a drainage canal in Ceduna or a Wagyu beef feedlot in Longreach. His PR people know the news cameras will be there and the last thing they want is the big bloke to stand out like a city goose. The cupboard of clobber, like Superman's phone box, allows him to slip in and emerge minutes later looking the part.

The 'No Jab No Job' master's role often calls for glib emotion and fake sincerity, as seen on the post-inferno Handshakes Tour of early 2020. He knows looking the part will enable him to deliver all important rural and regional emotion with total conviction and pitched with perfect tone.

The washed-out baby-vomit-coloured chino daks with the dropped crotch and the alluring smidgen of plumber's smile anchors the ensemble. The faded denim shirt that looks as though he has wrestled his way into it screams, 'Look out rugby league!' That's the look those pesky PR people want.

*His love of league is well documented. In early pandemic times, 'Gold Standard' famously declared, after locking down the nation and confining everyone to their homes for a month, that he was off to the footy on Sunday.*

His love of league is well documented. In early pandemic times, 'Gold Standard' famously declared, after locking down the nation and confining everyone to their homes for a month, that he was off to the footy on Sunday. This was meant to relax the nation, suggesting business as usual, until the trailing press pack pointed out that 'No Tick No Jab' would be there by himself as everyone else was indoors. A wise media head up the back of the bus suggested that 'National Anthems' going to the footy when the rest of the country was stuck inside was not the best look for a senior politician.

But that is the smirker's mindset. Off to Aloha-land when the joint is burning down, off to the footy when the nation is locked inside.

As Scott said to Quentin 'Clanger' Wilkins in an in-depth cover story for the final edition of *Rugby League Week*:

> I love the whole vibe connected with Cronulla. I love the Shire and I love the Sharks lifestyle. Clangs, as a five-year-old kid, I saw myself slotting into the back row. I modelled my game on Sludge Rodgers, the original and the best, I billed myself Sludge 3.
>
> I set myself the goal of 107-plus games, I had even prepared a speech when I was tapped for a Dally M. Of course, it wasn't to be, marketing came calling and then the Party knocked on my door. They bellowed, 'We want you, Toolman.'

With changes in rugby league scheduling, due to the demands of television, matches are scheduled for five nights a week. The PM yearns for a simpler time when the rugby league nation could be sure that the Sharks were doing their thing 3 pm on Sundays. This was an era when he, along with the tradie world, could down tools with confidence. It was a golden age of certainty. The world knew the Sharks would never win the

Premiership but everything else was as it should be. This all changed in 2016 when the Sharks did the impossible and won the flag. The Shire is still celebrating.

If it is on the cool side with a southerly blowing, 'Curry King' Scott rolls out to Shark Park in the vintage Cronulla jumper circa 1990. It's the glamorous Brewer's Draught and Aussie Duct sponsored affair in Col Eadie white, Tommy Bishop blue and Gavin Miller black. Up top, jammed on the bonce, is a beanie signed by all the players from the 1986 side. The gear is broken in with sauce and beer dribbles down the front. At the footy, 'A Jab by Xmas for all' Morrison is a regular bloke who bellows, 'Go Sharkies!' with as much mad fervour as any other committed Sharks supporter.

The catering at Shark Park suits the PM's tastes. Whenever the ref blows his whistle, the crash of big powerful units in shorts assaults the ears and that heady Dencorub tang wafts into the stands, Handshakes and everyone is on their feet raving, and suddenly they are starving.

Luckily there is a pop-up food and beverage outlet five metres from where 'Every Aussie Home by Christmas' PM parks the bot. The truck offers a limited range of exciting Australian cuisine, four varieties of pie, including the very popular curried beef and offal, hotdogs, thirty-centimetre sausage rolls and litres of beer. There is a great range of genuine big-volume, Aussie-brewed beers on offer and not a 'busted-arse' Yak-style craft brew in sight.

Foreign ministers know that visiting dignitaries are in very safe hands when 'The Jabmeister' suggests an afternoon at Shark Park.

*Heads of state will never be embarrassed when they turn up to sample the culture or the cuisine, such is the variety of food options at Shark Park.*

Heads of state will never be embarrassed when they turn up to sample the culture or the cuisine, such is the variety of food options at Shark Park. The PM likes to grab a fistful of pie before kick-off. In the first stanza, he will sink the molars into a one-hander with a great flaky pastry casing. Like most Australians, 'Anthems' Morrison likes a pie case that can hold a good depth of beef and gravy without dribbling over a crusty rim and down the front of the Country Road denim shirt. He wants something to shove into the cake hole in celebration once a young Shark in his first game busts the line and runs fifty metres to score. The last thing a league fan wants in a moment of triumph over a top-of-the-table outfit like the hated Manly Sea Eagles is to discover the pie has gone wobbly and dumped the contents all over the front of his daks.

Statesmen and women, especially foreign ministers, who know bugger-all about rugby league, are stunned by the Shark Park atmosphere. They are reluctant to leave, wandering back to their official cars gobsmacked by the skill of the players, the excitable crowd and the local cuisine.

More importantly, guests leave loving the greatest game of all. Especially if the thoughtful catering staff have waddled out of the kitchen, at half-time, with a cup of tea, a tray of scones and a Shark Park special: double-dipped, creamed lamingtons.

## The world's best on the world stage

*Lift the gaze and savour the international perspective on our leaders.*

Overseas perception is often very different to our own. It will surprise no one that in a round-up of late mail, in the dying days of that fabulous Trump administration 2016–20, that 'Man of Steel 2.0' Morrison was tapped for the highest military honour the Americans can dish out, the Legion of Merit. This is right up with the Aussie Knights and Dames wheeze that former PM Tony Abbott hurled at the upper reaches of Australian society with a special one-off made available to HRH Prince Philip. Remember the Man of Steel, the original and the best, was former PM John Howard.

This Merit bauble is strung around the neck of anyone for exceptionally meritorious conduct in the performance of outstanding services and achievements.

As Australians we are too close to the action to really see what the 'G7plus' man has been up to on the world stage. The American view is that our Sooty is a Sergeant Slaughter type ready to rush in, all guns blazing, whenever there is an international dumpster fire threatening to get out of control. 'The Sarge' summed up the medal with these few words: 'It is not all about me. This gong, which I rate alongside the Dally Ms, is something all Australians can take pride in. Go Sharkies!'

Sadly, the exacting COVID protocols of late 2020 prevented a glittering presentation of this great gong for his international achievement. FLOTUS Melania was booked to do the honour of hooking the bauble around 'Get a Go's neck on the lawn in front of the White House, beneath a flyover of USAF Hornets trailing green and gold smoke as the twenty-one gun salute was blown off in the Rose Garden, before the 'Rhiannon' gang, Fleetwood Mac, swung into a selection of Aussie classics, including the GWS Giants club song, 'What's My Team?' by the Hoodoo Gurus, John Farnham's 'Sadie the Cleaning Lady' and Cold Chisel's 'Ita', featuring the Nathan Cleary TikTok dancers, finishing up with the Sharks song, ' Up, Up Cronulla!' Fleetwood Mac were a good get for the ceremony as Tina Arena was booked at Tradies in Gymea.

Morning tea was to be served on the White House South Lawn after festivities. It was a traditional Aussie spread of sliders, party pies, chips, chocolate cake, lamingtons, Margaret River chardonnay and a selection of West End or XXXX beer.

A pity we never got to see Melania pour the tea.

# RUGBY LEAGUE IS WAR

*The game is only happy when it has a cause.
It is even happier when it is something that
it is not - that is, trench warfare!*

THE GAME IS OFTEN referred to as war with boots on. At celebratory and commemorative occasions through the year, hacks, TV shows and the wide world of digital media cannot resist the comparison between the heroic deeds of Australians during our great wartime conflicts in far-off places and the fearless feats of players on the rugby league paddock.

Headline writers in hard-working sports departments knock up copy that includes wartime references like 'the opening minutes will feature a salvo of bombs' and 'after a traditional softening-up period the battle between these two sides settled down into a war of attrition in the trenches'. This enduring media line and length suggests that in both war and league there are horrendous injuries.

The Grand Final is a high-stakes battle ground, and players know that trouble lurks with every step. But for the NRL

Grand Final media build-up, it is always important to produce a dramatic despatch from the front line with a forensic focus on facial rearrangement stories.

A recent NRL pre–big watusi spray featured an extensive player profile suggesting that Josh Mansour, the Penrith Panthers winger, would waddle out into the rugby league big polka knowing it may be the last thing he ever does. That is the best promotion league can get. A fit, young Australian prepared to die on the biggest battlefield in the greatest game of all.

Josh sustained terrible facial injuries playing against the Titans in 2018. The surgeon who picked up the pieces of his skull and stitched them back into place declared that in his entire career, he had only treated a dozen patients as smashed up as Josh. The injuries to the bonce the doc's sickly twelve received were the result of head-on car prangs and IED bomb blasts in war.

Josh's scone demolition suggested that rugby league was now a far tougher experience than the front line of war. The Grand Final foxtrot was elevated to the status of one of Australia's great modern campaigns in Iraq or Afghanistan. This is exactly what the rugby league cheer squad had always known. A comment from the Head of Army confirmed what the league had been saying for decades.

The doc, once he had found all the pieces, postponed Josh's trip to surgery for two weeks to allow the swelling to go down. When the highly skilled team got to work under the bright lights in the operating theatre, they were on the job for seven hours. The scrubbed team put Josh's head back together with three plates and eighteen screws. It was a very fine jigsawing display on the bonce in bone from the world's best practitioners.

In the recovery stage the doc who applied the bandaids and bolts worried that any further knocks to the plucky Panther's melon playing league could spell curtains. It was a fine line. If the worst happened, the medical staff could be calling for the screens in the first half and signalling the long goodbye at the final hooter. The medicos stressed that rugby league could cost Josh his life. Luckily, on the day there was no need for the screens.

In 2010 the rugby league playing ranks were bolstered when burly British prop Sam Burgess began a rampaging run in the Rabbitohs jumper. Sam was the senior member of a quartet of Burgess brothers who played in fur in the flag-winning season of 2014.

In the big mambo that year the bad news arrived express delivery for Sam. The Big Burgess bopper was caught out of position for the kick-off and suddenly the ball was headed straight for him.

It was the first hit-up in the brouhaha and it was all down to Sam. What was he supposed to do? What he did became rugby league folklore. It was carved into the rock of Grand Final heroics. He ran back with the Steeden tucked under the arm. Ball security was all he could think about. Opposition prop Bulldog James Graham (one half of the polar bear front row combo), who was also willing to die for the league, saw him coming and did not miss. It was a clash of hard nuts, a sickening collision of cement forehead on tough-as-teak cheek.

*It was a clash of hard nuts, a sickening collision of cement forehead on tough-as-teak cheek.*

Sam copped a shattering whack to the noodle, instantly fracturing his eye socket and jaw.

He was in a 'fair bit of trouble'. Nothing new for Sam; he played on, punching out a best-on-ground performance.

League lovers wondered how he did it. People began to talk. After six years of silence on the incident Sam opened up about the night of nut in the popular league podcast *Head Damage Hurts* hosted by Zoster 'Big Knox' Fox. The England international began a five-hour deep dive quietly enough:

> Knoxie, it was the sort of clash that happens five times in every game. Jimmy 'Ice Block' Graham came up out of the Bulldogs line, I didn't see him until after the whack. He was a crumpled in a heap at my feet. But he caught me right on the soft spot of the socket. It was A-grade nut work.
>
> But Knoxie. I know you played the game. Many top players would have been proud of his quality handiwork. I certainly applauded it. I knew how good it was and I was on the receiving end!
>
> During a long league career, I have been hit by elbows, knees, foreheads, wrists, adjustable spanners, rifle butts and ball pein hammers while playing, but this was something very special. I can't remember a thing about it. And remember James's work was unforgettable! They don't call him 'The Tungsten Tow Bar' for nothing.
>
> Now Zoster, you have met that Rabbits medico Doc 'Jangles' Sprague. He is quick on his feet. He did not hang about. He got me into the rooms, but I was too revved to listen to anything sensible like a diagnosis. I said, 'Jangles, I need to get out there. I need to feel the game! I have to be on the sideline! I need to talk to coach Madge Maguire. Tell me, am I OK? Can I play?' I look back now and find that behaviour embarrassing.

Jangles is a gentle giant. He has a very calm bedside manner. He swung the stethoscope and gave me two pieces of advice. At this stage nerves were getting the better of me; I don't mind telling you, I was shit scared. Stains were everywhere. Rabbits don't get many chances to win a Figtree Foxtrot. This might have been my only go!

'Sam, if you go back on and take another Tow Bar whack to your scone, you could lose your sight.' Obviously, I ignored that advice. After all, I play rugby league.

The other advice, and this surprised me, was don't blow your nose. This was easier to deal with: for the rest of the Redfern rhumba, if I felt a blow coming up from the lower depths, I swallowed the phlegm and moved on, unless I could use it to the Rabbits' advantage.

Remember these were days when no one cared about concussions or damage to the brain or a lifetime of not knowing who you were or what you were eating. I ran back to the sideline. I decided to take my chances. Whenever I took the ball up and hit the Bulldogs line or had to defend, I was clobbered by their second rowers in hard defensive tackles. I could feel the bones in my face bouncing around.

My eyesight on the side of the initial smack was affected. It was weird at the start. I managed the pain with mind control, focusing on the colourful history of Rabbitohs v Roosters feuds and how important a cooked chicken sponsorship is to any player signing with a new club. Ideas like that can keep the pain at bay for days.

At one stage our try-scoring winger Lote T. plunged over for a try in the corner. I was Johnny-on-the-spot for the try-time celebrations. Rabbits came from everywhere. I gave T a hug. At the same time our superstar Greg Inglis jumped on my back and his skull whacked into the back of my loaf, which in turn collided with Lote's crumpet in a chain reaction.

It was just one of those things that happen in footy after you have put the ball down for four points.

The rough and tumble of the celebration clinches hit right on the fracture on the busted side of my nut. But the force from behind wedged the jaw, the cheek bone and eye socket back together. It was a miracle!

Knoxie, my face was a four-thousand piece jigsaw puzzle of the Opera House. Lote's try was called back and disallowed, but at least the scone up top felt a whole lot better. After the post-try pile-on, the loose bones in my lamington did not bounce around as much. They were sort of jammed into place.

But K-man, the Bulldogs obviously had a chat at half-time. In the second half scrums, the Dogs' front row had a red-hot go at adding to the damage upstairs. I stayed calm. I could see what they were up to. The Rabbits stuck together, pushed the score out to 30 to 6 and snared both the chocolates and cheese.

Sam finished the match, winning the 2014 Clive Churchill Medal for best on the park, and the South Sydney Rabbitohs grabbed their first flag in forty-three years.

The Rabbitoh head clash brought back memories of other great big square dance efforts, including Souths great John Sattler and Knights champion Andrew Johns overcoming a broken jaw and punctured lungs respectively to triumph in the final. In playing on and triumphing over adversity, these greats encouraged hundreds of young Australians to think about sticking their head into a scrum and playing rugby league.

The code today is far more worried about health and safety issues, especially the effects of concussion in later life once a player has said the long goodbye and retired. In Johnny Sattler's day the understanding of concussion was primitive. The main tool in the medico's concussion sideline black bag were three challenging questions:

*In playing on and triumphing over adversity, these greats encouraged hundreds of young Australians to think about sticking their head into a scrum and playing rugby league.*

What's your name?
What are you doing?
Who is Australia's Prime Minister?

If a player got two out of three right, they were passed fit and rushed back into the match to have another go.

Today there are evolving Head Injury Assessment (HIA) protocols, which probe the nuts and bolts of those tricky circuits in the brain box. Concussed players come off and wait twenty minutes. They are assessed by a fully qualified professional in club colours using the latest sophisticated HIA tools. Doctors assess the players' ability to know what is going on before allowing a return to the paddock for the next fortnight.

Given the game has been slack, since that bell was rung in 1908, about the damage to players with head-high contact, big legal issues and great payouts are lurking for players whose lives have been ruined by being allowed to play on when caution and rest would have been a far better course of action.

There have been many gruesome injuries in the history of rugby league and there have been deaths while playing the game. But 2019 university surveys across all states revealed that among right-thinking Australians, if they were stuck in the trenches during a ferocious battle overseas, nine out of ten would want a ticketed rugby league front-rower or hooker alongside them. When probed further in focus groups, the survey's respondents all said they wanted rugby league players there for their emotional, physical and spiritual safety.

With the Australia–China relationship on the rocks once again and all the talk about war between the two great nations, a platoon of registered rugby league players ready to do on the battlefield what they do on the weekends could be just the ticket Australia needs to swing the odds in our favour. The players certainly would not let us down.

## Rugby league promotion: The sound of success!

Since 1908, promotion of the game has been crucial to its success. The game has fended off attacks from the AFL, the world game and its archenemy, rugby union, since its birth.

The perpetual flame of league controversy consumes a lot of fuel. Hullabaloo, scandal and gossip have been the fuel on the fire. It is a fire that requires continuous stoking. It is so easy, in the off-season, when racing, cricket and tennis capture the sporting headlines and monopolise media space, to forget that rugby league, the greatest game of all, is played from the middle of March to the first weekend in October.

*The perpetual flame of league controversy consumes a lot of fuel.*

Supporters during the long hot summer are desperate for any snippet of league news or any chitchat about the players' harmless holiday high jinks. Hopefully the high-jinks news can be accompanied by nude happy snaps taken with a very long lens from behind a sandhill two beaches away. The bulk of off-season sensational coverage, social media pile-ons and tabloid front pages are created by the players. Registered players have traditionally come to the aid of the game at this tricky holiday time before the pre-season kicks off and the mind of the nation focuses once again on the looming league season. They are prepared to get their hands dirty and do the heavy promotional lifting. They get no thanks for keeping the caper in the summer media spotlight. Their invention of space-filling copy is only limited by the players having imaginations.

In the modern media landscape, there are many ways to attract attention, whether it's trolling, TikTok posts, inappropriate Twitter comments, online spats, WAGs getting involved, an exchange of rancid emails, or contemporary Fans Only sites where football stars are snapped at home nude in front of the mirror. Then there are tried-and-true japes, like urinating on a restaurant window in full view of diners inside or falling asleep at the wheel of a car as it rolls across an intersection at 3.30 am or snapped doing a bubbler, as in a drink from a leak. These are always good for a front page and followed by a week of unexamined public outrage.

Pun-filled headlines shout the latest offences. The fallout continues for months. There is a follow-on parade of players in suits on the courthouse steps as the off-season legal cases titillate. Appearances before beaks keep the roaring bushfires of league promotion alight.

The public is easily outraged. Mad Monday scandals often linger throughout the whole of the cricket season. Having been off the turps for the whole season, many stars are desperate to make up for lost time – with sensational results. Mercifully, full-on riots fuelled by excessive consumption of alcohol have been largely consigned to club best and fairest nights and retold in the pages of tell-all footy biographies.

Bonding over a few beers with mates rounds off the season that has just been cracked, boxed and buried. A few jars in October can clear the way for the battles looming when the new season rises over the horizon. As well as beers, Mad Monday often involves nudity and dressing as women and babies – oldies but goodies. Most of the Australian public are tolerant of these end-of-year rituals. Many sensitive patrons will do the right thing and vacate the club premises or the local league watering hole once the club secretary has announced on the in-house PA:

> Ladies and gentlemen, Wally Cistern, Club Secretary here, now a large number of rugby league players, celebrating the end of the season, are now on the premises. Patrons would be wise to finish up their beers and leave without using the club's toilets! Portable toilets are available for use in the car park. Thanks very much.

Things in league-land can go seriously silly and stupid. The rugby league crime space is groaning with legendary characters and bizarre criminal enterprise. Characters who have cooked up pranks and larks over a few too many beers. The league has its hands full worrying about how to police wilder, wilful wrong-doing.

The league's task in this area would be improved if an authority figure, like a serving state police commissioner, was added to the Rugby League Board. With the commission representative attending every meeting, the distance between rugby league crime, rugby league penalty and jail (as a last resort) would be substantially reduced. The legal process has to be transparent so the ultimate goal, that of rugby league redemption, can be achieved as quickly as possible. With the commish in place at board level the game could reduce the whole process to a few hours.

The range of league criminality that the commissioner would pass judgement on is extraordinary. For instance, not every player can bring the date-hunting skills that the great rugby league amateur proctologist John Hopoate brought to the table. Hoppa's was a unique contribution to the G.G.A. He created a tackle that required just one finger. It was all his own work, a simple routine that generated worldwide attention for the league. How could anyone except a representative from the highest level of our law enforcement community assess and pass judgement on such a complex case?

There is an upside to league crime: kids everywhere love going to the games to see the player who was in the headlines all week. The player who was caught iPhone filming a love tryst in a public toilet cubicle or stuck outside the motel room in the nude at 3.20 am, simply because he was busting for a slash and thought the door he was opening was the door to the bathroom and not the door of his motel unit. Suddenly he found himself naked outside in the corridor with people staring. That is a very easy mistake to make. It could happen to anyone after they had put away a slab of beer and a bottle of vintage Corio rum at a lively post-match function. Remember, winning a rugby league

*Remember, winning a rugby league Grand Final or Origin decider can reduce the ability of the mind to operate within society's normal rhythms and inhibitions.*

Grand Final or Origin decider can reduce the ability of the mind to operate within society's normal rhythms and inhibitions. What sobering challenges these cases would be for any police supremo who is more used to dealing with people speeding while talking on their mobile phones.

Player-generated promotion of the code has saved the game billions over the years. There is no master plan. It is a spontaneous expression of how much fun and satisfaction playing rugby league generates. The playing publicists don't get nearly enough credit for all their work.

Origin bonding camps were a source of publicity leading up to game one of any series. What could possibly go wrong? The team went to a five-star well-being retreat in the bush. The programme featured two weeks of living off the land with mates. They were given a Swiss army knife, a kilo of butter and a slab of the sponsor's finest every day and sent on their way. When they gathered on the logs round the campfire at night, it was rugby league stories and tactics from dusk until dawn.

Sure, some players got lost, one or two fell into the campfire. They were fished out, hosed off and helicoptered to hospital. It was a tricky day when the horses were brought in for three days of riding. Whenever front-rowers who had never thrown a leg over in their lives clambered on board the Birdsville Express or the flighty Foxy Princess there was trouble. Falls occurred due to ineptitude in the saddle and horse fear. Cracked ribs ruled players out of the run-on side for game one. The injured had to sit on the sideline with a busted leg in plaster. It was annoying but was great promotion.

Finally, we come to the Freddie's State of Origin revolution. Brad 'Freddie' Fittler is one of the game's great thinkers, right up there with Canberra coach Ricky Stuart, aka 'The Angry Ant', aka 'Sticky', aka 'Carlos Smearson'. Brad has overseen a revolution in the very soul of the game. Freddie has so many ideas running riot in the top paddock. His bare-foot earthing, shambling around the football field without boots on, has changed how Australia sees the game. Not sure what it does; maybe in some way it focuses the mind on the battle ahead. The pyramid work, the Hogs for the Homeless runs, the Metallica soundtrack in the rooms so as no one can hear what Brad has to say – all contribute to the new-look NSW culture of success. The jury is still out on whether the Fittler revolution works. His thesis is, 'Blokes, be the best you can be!'

It shows again there is nothing rugby league players cannot do. In a time when the arts, across Australia, are struggling due to government indifference, it is great to see rugby league players keeping the flickering flame of fashion, art and the performing arts alive. Every player seems to have been working on a great range of fashion. Underpants are a speciality. Canberra prop Josh Papalii recently released his own special hand-painted briefs featuring an image of

*In a time when the arts, across Australia, are struggling due to government indifference, it is great to see rugby league players keeping the flickering flame of fashion, art and the performing arts alive.*

him ankle-tapping tearaway Titan half Jamal Fogarty. Talk about setting new standards in post-hooter bedroom apparel! Imagine the other half clocking Josh-branded Y-fronts gracing the groin when the trousers hit the planks and thinking, 'This is a person I need to get close to!'

So many great Australians with a connection to rugby league have moved on from league promotional activities to performance-based careers. With superstars like Russell Crowe heavily involved with South Sydney, so many great performers have emerged from the Rabbits' playing ranks. Actors Ian Roberts and the four Burgess brothers recently thrilled jaded league lovers needing a new fashion horizon with the B4 fashion range of T-shirts, shorts and shoes.

Brother George, a keen actor, could tackle Shakespeare's *Hamlet*. The man in tights with two minds about whether to become a South Sydney Rabbit or a Sydney Rooster? Drop anchor in the hutch or the fowl-house? Is it fur or feathers? Sure, it is a contemporary interpretation of the five acts about the past and future. But the play is a timeless classic with central themes that are pure rugby league – and will prepare all the players for war.

# TONY ABBOTT: THE PUNCHING PRIME MINISTER

*We were lucky to see him in action with the gloves on in the ring and on the spray in the Big House. Unlike others, this bloke held the hose.*

TONY ABBOTT HAD SWAGGER, in the way he moved. He could swagger sitting down. He had kids everywhere shouting, 'Hey Tony, where's your hat?' and 'Tex, who's holding the horse?' He always waddled into a room as though he had just parked the hayburner alongside a hitching rail instead of arriving in a Comcar Holden Commodore.

Tony 'Kid Cyclone' Abbott was our Punching Prime Minister (2013–15). The Kid had an explosive speck of dynamite in each hand. He packed a trash-talking lip that flattened opponents at weigh-ins. His adversaries in heavyweight title flare-ups were often nervy and cactus before they clambered through the ropes and the referee touched the gloves and bellowed, 'BOX!'

Ringside critics claimed his best unload was a solid right that came up from the feet into the fist. He reputedly put this scintillating whack through a partition in the SRC offices at Sydney University after losing a narrow vote. He claimed afterwards to the student newspaper's senior fight correspondent, Bruce 'Kevin' Sheedy, in his award-winning, weekly column 'On the Ropes':

> Yeah, no Kevin, it was a Warringah special. As you know I've modelled myself on Les Darcy. I trained hard for the election result. I did a lot of skipping, bag work, ran fifty kilometres a day and ate a dozen raw eggs for breakfast. But that punch, it was beautiful to watch. It was beautiful to throw. I saw that knuckle sandwich in my mind's eye long before I let it go. Feet in the correct position. It came from the arse, up the back, down the arm, into the clenched paw of steel and straight through the lime-coloured gyprock behind the front desk. I could have smashed the whole wall to smithereens if I'd connected with a supporting stud.

Incidentally, Kevin was handy in the ring. In 1958, he won a University of Sydney Heavyweight belt with a TKO decision, after going seven rounds with Robert Hughes. This was a couple of years before 'Bauhaus' Bob packed his bags, went to New York and took up art criticism.

Kid Cyclone had a rowdy style, not classical but vigorous. He loved winning with a cheap shot. He would strike a sagging opponent when everyone else was looking at the ringside celebrities. Tony was feared for his work in close, in the clinches. After a barrage of short jabs and with the opponent going backwards, 'The Kid'

*Tony was feared for his work in close, in the clinches.*

stepped away and unleashed a barrage of heavy body hits. Once Tony had mastered this in/out technique he used it to great effect whether he was fighting for a regional title in the ring or in a tightly contested preselection battle in the back room of national politics. He loved operating in that tight space where he could smell the gastric reflux of an opponent's breakfast.

As a youngster, Tony scored a boxing Blue at Oxford. The details of his opponents on the way through to the big bauble are lost in the mists of time. A number of challengers were up-and-comers from the Cherwell-side campus. But he soon lifted the gaze and took on a sorry array of pillows in the large shorts from Cambridge University who were unable to go with the vim of The Kid over twelve three-minute rounds.

Tony always fought as a heavyweight. Although to look at him these days it is hard to tell if size mattered when he began his meteoric rise through the University sweet science ranks. He fought as a heavy so he could take on all comers, no matter what they weighed.

Knowledgeable ringside observers who hung out at fight central in the front bar at the Prince Patrick Hotel in North Melbourne said The Kid could have gone all the way to a major Australian title if only he stopped fiddling about with religion and politics. The thinking of the front bar was that these two distractions ended a very promising career in the squared circle.

The bout that had the Prince Patrick drinkers licking their lips in anticipation was the dream bout of Kid Cyclone Abbott v Aussie Joe Bugner.

This clash of these two heavies was the fight that never happened. A punch-starved nation was cruelly denied this intellect v brawn rumble of the decade. The well-credentialled

*A punch-starved nation was cruelly denied this intellect v brawn rumble of the decade.*

Bugner had gone the distance with Mohammed Ali and was not in his prime when he returned to the ring for a fifth act. But Joe could still hold up an opponent over ten rounds hoping to get lucky with a points decision or have his wilting opponent stumble onto his formidable left hook. When he got the timing right, Joe's left hook packed enough TNT to knock an opponent out cold, leaving him on the canvas with claret oozing from the upper lip – a sight that always thrilled ringside fight fans.

Tony was keen. But by this crucial stage of Joe's career sanity had intervened. He moved on, tempted away from the ring by the alluring worlds of show business and hardware merchandise.

Kid Cyclone came to a similar conclusion, and with the fight years disappearing into the rear-vision mirror and the church looking elsewhere for talent he put away the gloves and went on to success taking his ringcraft style of politics to the rough house of Canberra. Where he rose to the very top of the tree.

Tony never forgot his sporting roots. While in Canberra he was always ready to pull on the shorts and make up the numbers in an intra-parliamentary rugby hit-out or plug a gap in lane seven in a politician v press swim meet.

He gave many days to his sporting charity work, especially his annual Pollie Pedal ride around rural and regional marginal seats. He was happy to throw a leg over the Trek Domane road bike for fitness, fellowship and fundraising.

On the Pedal, Tony rode the back roads on a listening tour of the nation where he bumped into his people, that elusive onion-munching community who believed 'climate change was crap' and 'experts were wrong'. These were his Australians, the ones who loved his radical Aussie Dames and Knights concept.

The Pollie Pedal was an old-fashioned idea that had elements of trail-blazing across the golden west of America. Blokes on the road forming a peloton in brightly coloured lycra wearing the clunky shoes. Out in the wild blue yonder for days at a time in all weathers with rest breaks every forty minutes for a catch-up with the nation's affairs and a chat with voters. For lunch, they would stop at a friendly pie shop for a chicken, mango and leek special, or a pork and fennel sausage roll with tomato sauce. Nothing fancy, nothing that screamed MKR's Manu or Pete Evans.

What is not to like? With the wind in the hair and weekday worries shelved for the duration of the ride.

Tony would give Team Abbott a motivational spray round the campfire at night, once the day's ride had been put to bed. He covered the big issues of men's health, saddle soreness, tyre pressures and what's for dinner, often finishing his spray with the heart-felt plea using the skills he had learnt in the pulpit. Tony returned to this theme on many occasions:

> Yeah, no! Blokes, we are pushing our Treadleys around the joint for all Australians. Everyone thinks of politicians as a bunch of losers. But we can put something back with this ride, and who knows, when they dump us at the next election, we may all be out of a job and need a leg up and a leg over. Ha ha ha!
>
> I believe the Pedalling Posse shows the nation that politicians are not just windbags who camp around the Canberra billabong, hanging out for a free feed, talking about bugger-all and doing even less. Yeah, no we are ordinary, fit Australians ready to do their fair share of heavy lifting.

After his spray, Tony would often open the Slim Dusty Song Book and get a sing-a-long going with songs like 'A Pub with no Beer' and 'Duncan', as the logs blazed away until the dawn light signalled it was time for bed.

It was incredible fun. The weather was often appalling, but after a hard day's ride into the headwind and sleet, when the blokes gathered around the burning logs at night ... well, the stories and the songs made it all worthwhile! And while the Pedal did raise money for charities, it appears that The Kid was one of the few on the bikes who claimed expenses.

In his political career Tony had a couple of vocal tics that served him well. He always said 'NO!' to begin any Q and A. He was the master of the 'ignore, deny and pretend' approach no matter what the topic or question. Once he got going, he loved filling space with repetition. This appeared to allow for thinking time. Although what followed showed no evidence of thought.

In an interview with a probing hack from a current affairs programme like the ABC's *7.30*, or with a top journalist in the News Limited stable, The Kid always repeated everything he said. It was a rule of threes. If something was worth saying, it was worth repeating twice more. If he found a line resonated with him, he didn't let it go until it was literally sonic manure devoid of meaning.

He said this recently to Ingrid Fineline during an interview for a *Sunday Times* profile:

> Politics is a pretty simple game. Ingrid, to be honest, I think I may have said 'Climate change is crap!' about 4.74 million times and 'Who needs experts!' at least 3.97 million times. It's a winning technique. You can't go wrong as long you say it

with absolute conviction. Repetition indicates you have said something really important!

When Tony was back home in the Warringah electorate he was a very visible part of the community, holding down a prominent position in the Rural Fire Service. He loved holding a hose, and no one on the truck could burst into a blazing building like Tony. The Fire Service always came off second best.

He was a member of the Queenscliff Surf Life Saving Club where those never-forgotten Kid Cyclone skills came to the fore in a senior flags contest on the sand. He was seen paddling out on the longboard looking for an early morning and was often a starter on the front of the grid in any local marathon or triathlon event.

In fact, Tony was up to his buttocks in any event that called for the budgie smugglers to be worn. He arrived at the start line in those hard-to-fit smugglers that were two sizes too small. It was gear that pulled the ogling crowd.

Who can forget his tilt at the House of Representatives in the election of 2019? On the hustings Tony was never short of ideas to pull votes. After years representing the seat now, he knew his electorate and its needs. For his final countdown he ran on an attractive 'More Dunnies for Manly' ticket.

Tony had noticed in years of patrolling the beach, whether on official SLSC duties or crewing the RFS fire truck, or running marathons or triathlons, that there were very few places to take a leak, drop a load or slip into the smugglers along that fabulous stretch of Manly beaches.

With his great knack of focusing on the real issues affecting real people, he thought that by standing up for more dunnies that the electors would do the right thing and send him back to Canberra for another term in the big house.

His dunny policy was old school. Appealing to the older voter. A quote from his campaign flyers said it all:

> There would be one door for Men and one door for Women. None of the same-sex latrine gibberish in God's own country, thanks very much, Tiger!

Tony's bold and innovative dunny platform planned a toilet every fifty metres along the Manly Corso and 400 metres between dump locations from Manly Wharf to Palm Beach. His toilet-led recovery plan, which was fully costed by Treasury, promised to create 6102 jobs in the construction phase and work for twenty-seven full-time cleaners once up and open for business. The scheme, dubbed Snowy 3.0, sadly did not capture the electorate's imagination and the man who had given so much to Australia was suddenly flushed from the national stage.

Tony still had something to offer. He found willing employers in the post-Brexit British trade landscape where government ministers loved his ideas on trade and climate. He hooked up with old mates, the former Foreign Minister and party animal, Alexander Downer, and the former Attorney General and Sports Minister with an interest in accommodation for ballet students, George Brandis.

As the sun sets on the pandemic years, The Kid is still young and has always kept himself in great shape. It is not too late for a three-round comeback bout with one of Australia's fighting footballers, like former All Black Sonny Bill Williams or the former Bronco and now Warrior Matthew 'the Toast of

New York' Lodge, or one of the nation's recently retired ring warriors like Anthony Mundine or Danny Green. Any one of them would give Tony a taste of what he has been missing. No need to put a title on the line. Promote the bout as a fun filled knock-about between mates for charity. There is a boxing donkey circuit that is providing meaningful bouts that would welcome Tony with open arms

*As the sun sets on the pandemic years, The Kid is still young and has always kept himself in great shape. It is not too late for a three-round comeback bout.*

Once Kid Cyclone squeezes between the ropes, lands that first uppercut and realises all the old skills are still there, who knows where a third act of the Abbott career could end. After all, the fight game is full of oldies and OAPs looking for a change of employment in retirement. At least it would be more satisfying than his last sporting venture, teaching seniors how to surf.

# JACK BRABHAM: THE BEST OF THE LOT

*Not bad for a kid from Hurstville who learnt to drive aged twelve.*

JACK BRABHAM IS ONE of the greats of Australian sporting history. He was rightly dubbed the Don Bradman of speed in 1964 by a panel of government-appointed experts tasked with nominating those in the next generation who had achieved Don-like importance. The big raps did not stop there. Jack was knighted for his services to the speed shriek in 1979. On the Grand Prix circuit he snared fourteen wins, was on pole thirteen times and placed on the podium on thirty-one occasions.

Jack dominated racing at the highest level from the 1955 through to his last hit out in anger in the 1970 Mexican Grand Prix. He was World Champion three times, in 1959, 1960 and 1966. In fact, in 1966, Jack Brabham was Australian of the Year, won the World Drivers' Championship and Constructors' Championship, and his name was on the biggest manufacturer of racing cars in the world. But how did he get there?

Many biographers have suggested Jack learnt to drive by applying for lessons he found advertised on the back of a *Phantom* comic. After just one lesson he gave it away as a complete waste of time. He got a start driving competitively in a midget, then hill climbing, and then progressed onto the dirt track speedway circuit. The dirt was a crowd puller.

Beginning at the Parramatta Speedway, he was soon stepping up to the big time at the Royale Speedway at the Sydney Showground in Moore Park, often racing several nights a week. The Royale attracted crowds of 40,000 and promoters would bring in international and interstate stars to get a 'US versus Aussies' vibe going at the box office. Jack did the early hard yards in dirt to avoid the alternative – an unwanted career as a green-grocer. Trucking fruit and vegetables was his other option but there was no future in that for a young man with a lead foot.

In 1955 Jack thrilled the world with his performance in the Australian Grand Prix at a tricky, purpose-built, motor-racing layout outside Port Wakefield. This was the twenty-sixth edition of the Aussie GP frolic and it brought that sleepy town lurking at the top of St Vincent's Gulf in South Australia to life for an October long weekend in which the cars, humans, dust and burnt rubber danced an attractive salsa.

The Port Wakefield Thunderdome, built in 1953, was the first track laid in Australia after World War Two. The SA government had banned racing on the state's public roads. The loss of life in off-track race carnage was bothering the elders of Adelaide. There were too many funerals

> *There were too many funerals clogging up the cathedrals in the City of Churches.*

clogging up the cathedrals in the City of Churches. Legislation confined car racing to specialised tracks and not roads used by the public.

The Thunderdome was opened by the Queen in 1954. People still talk about the day Elizabeth II lobbed into town with a big pair of Royal scissors looking for a ribbon to snip.

Her Majesty's speech, now in the National Film and Sound Archive, gives an idea of how much fun the Royals can be when away from the bright light of official duty:

> My Husband and I love motor sport. Whenever we can, the whole family gets a weekend away at Balmoral. We go fanging around the estate in a Land Rover HUE 166. The Scottish maintenance staff are brilliant. They have dropped a V8 into the front end of the 166. It goes like a Blue Streak rocket. We love giving the deer and the highland cattle a rear end Royal touch up. Prince Charles is a whizz on the bovine bumper bar bump.
>
> Now I know it has taken many hours of hard work by the committee under the guidance of Thunderdome Chairman 'Bongo' Bruce Dongers to bring this magnificent facility to fruition.
>
> I leave you with these words bellowed by my sister, Princess Margaret, from the back of the Royal Roller last month on her way to an all-nighter with The Rolling Stones, 'Go you good thing!'
>
> Speed on Australia! I now declare this magnificent racing complex open!
>
> Now where is that gin and tonic and make mine a double! And once the committee clears the track, my husband and I will take a spin. Bye now!

The original Port layout was a boutique affair set out in the scrub a kilometre east of the Port CBD. It was a mere 2.09 kilometres long in an era when tracks were usually three and four times that length.

In its heyday this magnificent semi-desert circuit had it all. The field was flagged away in Repco Straight. This stretch ended with a right-hand kink before a sharp left into the challenging Tyresoles hair-pin turn. Then it was full bore sprint down to Kallin Corner. This grim right-hander required power and skill to keep the car on the road. Once that shambles was tucked away in the rear-vision mirror, it was a flat-out burn down the 600 metres of Thompson Motors Straight. Turn five was the magnificent Dunlop Corner, then the last turn at Stonyfell. This was a tricky grief-maker that brought the start/finish line into sight. It required timing when hitting the skids and pouring on the power once the car was freed from the corner's grip. This was where the crowd liked to gather, knowing there would be incredible shunt action.

The stars of the age, like Brabham, Rex Hunt and Doug White, could knock the shebang over in a couple of ticks over a minute. The crowd just got used to the field being gone when suddenly it was back. Talk about trackside excitement!

At one stage the very go-ahead planning committee suggested putting in a turning roundabout at Stonyfell. This brilliant design concept would allow cars to race in both directions on the same roadway. The Port Wakefield facility would have a point of difference from every track in the world.

But as so often in motor sport, the local racing authority, the South Australian government and the Confederation of Australian Motor Sport were clueless when it came to creating a genuine spectacle that would encourage the South Australian public to drive from Adelaide for a unique motor racing experience.

In 1955, after eighty exciting laps of the circuit, Jack brought car six, the Cooper T40 Bristol, home in 1 hour 26 minutes and 44.43 seconds.

The podium finish had Jack on the top step, Reg Hunt lobbed into the silver slot, and Doug White left covered in the disappointment of bronze.

But many international commentators believe that Jack's Port Wakefield Grand Prix drive was his best in a stunning career chock-a-block full of gems. Two thousand pounds were up for grabs on the Labour Day long weekend. It was a big purse. In today's money about $15.7 million.

*But many international commentators believe that Jack's Port Wakefield Grand Prix drive was his best in a stunning career chock-a-block full of gems.*

This was the weekend when Jack, who was always on the tooth before, during and after a drive, pioneered the art of using the heat generated by the high-revving Cooper Bristol power pack to cook meat.

After a few experiments during qualifying, he wrapped half-a-dozen crumbed lamb cutlets and four Pontiac potatoes in Alfoil and placed them on the hottest section of the engine block.

Whenever he pitted for petrol, a tyre change or just because he was bored, the pit crew, after doing the regular checks, rotated his lunch on the engine block to ensure an even heat cooked the meat on what became known as the Brabham hotplate.

Jack timed his run home to perfection, so the lamb cutlets and potatoes were ready to plate with seasonal greens as soon as he pulled into the pits after his victory lap.

There was no great science in the Brabham approach to 'V8' cuisine. He realised after a few experimental engine block bakes that he could cook anything under the bonnet of the Bristol.

Jack never kept accurate records of his F1 oven work but, talking to very satisfied older hands to establish the breadth of his mobile bake, it appears the Cooper Climax maestro cooked on every track he drove at during his long career.

There is photographic evidence that in Grand Prix years he smoked sausages, did legs of lamb, rolled pork roasts with apple sauce and even pulled passionfruit-iced sponge cakes and apple crumble out of the four on the floor motoring microwave. He usually cooked what was locally available, whether it was Coffin Bay scallops, freshly shot kangaroo tail from Wilpena Pound, emu rump from Broken Hill or Mallacoota crayfish.

He sought out condiments like salt bush and wild rosemary from the nearby scrub to season the bake.

At pre-race press conferences Jack was often pestered not with questions about the car and its performance capabilities but with cuisine stumpers

> *At pre-race press conferences Jack was often pestered not with questions about the car and its performance capabilities but with cuisine stumpers tossed up by journalists and feature writers from housekeeping magazines.*

tossed up by journalists and feature writers from housekeeping magazines like *Women's Weekly* and *Woman's Day* and kitchen stars of the era like Margaret Fulton and Charmaine Solomon. Everyone wanted tips that ordinary Australians could apply on their daily commute or weekend away in the FC Holden or Ford Futura ute.

Racing fans were always delighted when Jack turned up as they knew a few lucky ones would get a feed. Schoolkids whenever they got a glimpse of Jack would sing out, 'Hey Jack, what have you got cooking? How about cooking something up for me?' And the big man never disappointed; he always had a droll, funny reply.

His cookbook, *Donk Finger: The Engine Heat and Red Meat Revolution,* sold 375,000 copies. It was voted Self-Help Book of the Year in 1965. It revolutionised the car-cooking concept across Australia. The central thesis of *Donk Finger* is that there is an art to matching meat and motors.

The producers of *MasterChef* are working on a motor meat special series for 2023. Thirteen episodes, where all cooking is done under the bonnet of a Holden car. It is part travelogue, part mechanical instruction, but mainly it is all meat and heat.

Recently, with greater environmental concern, there has been a massive revival of interest in the *Donk Finger* concept. Motorists are rightly concerned about not wasting the heat the car motor generates. There are now several online car cooking courses available and podcasts tackling the history and techniques of the craze.

After Jack's tradition-shattering drive in 1955, there was a spirited application to run the 1961 Grand Prix back at the headquarters of South Australian motor sport, but national authorities stepped in and claimed the venue was totally inadequate.

The main danger at Port was race cars colliding with box thorn bushes and other floral debris uprooted in nearby paddocks and hurled onto the track by the stiff, hot, northerly breeze.

However, the safety committee swerved past the mobile obstacles and highlighted a lack of women's toilets and no handrails in the non-existent stands as the main complaints for taking the big one away from this petite circuit. The authorities in head office then decided to relocate the whole shebang to a new track at Mallala. This layout was much closer to the Athens of the South, but the magic stayed behind in Port Wakefield.

Today this central piece of Australian automotive history has fallen into disrepair. The circuit is waiting to be rediscovered by a new generation of speed freaks, much in the manner that the rediscovery in 2020 of the Don Bradman concrete pitch in Bowral has reignited an interest in the original Don and everything he achieved in the baggy green.

Sadly, after 1961, when the circuit was mothballed, it quickly faded back into the scrub and salt bush, taking all that Grand Prix glamour and romance with it.

In 2005, to commemorate the great drives at Port, Jack recorded a podcast with *Modern Motor*'s Lester 'Flathead' Stim. Jack reminisced over twelve episodes about the Thunderdome days of motor racing and the conception of *Donk Finger* cooking at Port Wakefield.

There were many more winning drives ahead for Jack: 1955 was just the beginning. There was the knighthood and an OBE to collect. Perth, WA, went silly and named a whole suburb after him. The suburb had no speed limits in homage to the great man. In the end, Jack kept driving competitively until his late seventies, remarking to Carla Zampatti at the launch of the Ford Laser, 'Carla, driving is the only thing that prevents me from getting old!'

# Part 3

# LEGACY

# HORSE RACING

*As the top jockey said, 'If I win by a centimetre or lose by a centimetre, punters will have no idea if I am trying!'*

LET'S BEGIN AT THE end of time – that is, now. It is a very big end. It is The Everest. This fifteen-million-dollar sprint is the ultimate test of horse, chemistry and human. It is the big pinnacle in world racing, hence the name. It is the richest equine contest on this or any other planet. This is the highest vantage point from which to survey the long landscape and troubled terrain of Australian racing. It is an end that deserves a chapter because it tells the nation a lot about where it is heading, on and off the track.

Horse racing began in Australia around the end of the 1700s. The whips were cracking within hours of Europeans dropping anchor in Port Jackson. The new chums agreed in unison: 'What this joint really needs, to be taken seriously as a nation, is the repetitive rumble of galloping hooves, an eight-race card in town on Saturday with a rural and regional Cup every other Sunday!'

The joint came alive once a Cup field was assembled at the 1600-metre pole. It blossomed once the bookies started shouting the odds in the stands and shifty-looking colourful racing identities were spotted tipping the cobalt-flavoured go-fast into the favourite's chaff bucket.

In 1790 there were no champion thoroughbred horses skulking around in the colony's stables. There were no stables as the racing industry understands them today. All the available horse flesh was gainfully employed working, pulling ploughs, dragging coaches and delivering mail. But on weekends these hayburners were good enough to race. Even in the most modest field there is always a winner.

The European blow-ins fresh off the boat soon formed clubs, raised funds and marked out a course with the witches' hats of their era. With their efforts the racing industry was up and running.

Thoroughbreds did not turn up in the block of land girt by sea until the early 1800s. With the well-bred horses appearing on the tracks, trainers, jockeys, socialites in hats, the fashion-on-the-field types, busted-arse punters and the well-upholstered bookies all followed. Suddenly everything was tickety-boo. Racing became a thing.

The crowds came because there was bugger-all else to do in the early days of the invasion. The crowds looked at the horses in the mounting enclosure, made informed assessments, got set with the bookies, watched the race and took their place in the payout queue. In between races they could pick up a pie and a beer and watch the fashions on the field.

*The crowds came because there was bugger-all else to do in the early days of the invasion.*

Racing was a civilised, cultural, well-organised, well-attended and well-dressed pursuit. The rules of racing did not prevent race-goers from getting on the turps and taking a swing at anyone who wanted to go on with it. The bouts quickly moved to the car park (or where the Members' car park would eventually be), where there was plenty of room to go on with it. But the punching punters were soon told to 'take it off course'. A precaution so that this great sport was not tarnished by the stupidity of patrons.

The heart of Australian racing from the 1860s was Melbourne. Every spring a month-long carnival of the conveyance clustered around a number of gruelling energy-sapping distance races. These staying tests sorted out the great champions of the age.

The carnival began with the Caulfield Cup, run, unsurprisingly, at Caulfield, over 1.5 miles (now 2400 metres). It was first run in 1879 for very modest prize money. Today they run around the same track and distance for five million dollars. The next cab off the spring carnival rank was the WS Cox Plate, run at Moonee Valley over 2040 metres. This weight-for-age affair, first run in 1922, is considered by purists to be the race of the carnival. The Victoria Derby, first run at Flemington in 1855 also over 1.5 miles (now rounded up to 2500 metres), for three-year-olds under set-weight conditions, is now worth a few million. The Derby is the big race on a day of group one features, arguably the greatest day of racing on the Australian turf calendar. The Melbourne Cup was first run in 1861 at the height of the Victorian gold boom when 'Marvellous Melbourne' was loaded. This handicap for all comers is now worth an ice-cold eight million.

From the jump, racing has featured colourfully clad jockeys on top of four galloping hooves roaring around the track, looking for a rails run or scouting wide for the better going. Most Australians have a fair idea of the caper even if they are not the slightest bit interested in the sport.

These distant staying races appealed to old-school punters who graced Australia's tracks and horse thinking for decades. The Victoria Racing Club, which held the spring carnival reins for decades, is not an organisation interested in change. They liked what happened last year and like even more what will happen this year.

They ran the show for horses, connections and personalities. They promoted Melbourne as a destination for big punters who waded into the betting ring and snatched up value before bookies could wind the price down. Back in the day, it was old-school betting with real money, as in notes. On-course punters often pulled serious money out of the hip pocket of a well-cut double-breasted suit.

One only has to think of the late Channel Nine boss Kerry Packer, 'Late Mail' Dale Ouest, Frank Duval (aka 'The Hong Kong Tiger'), Perce Galea (aka 'The Prince of Punters'), The Fish Creek Fireball (aka 'Terrified Chia Chant'), Hollywood George Edser, Truxton Anasta (aka 'The Muswellbrook Meteor') and the 'Pride of Parramatta Road', 'Fast' Eddie Hayson. This was the lucky country. It was the envy of the world.

These older punters provided a familiar certainty about the pattern of events, and the whole process ran along neatly and soberly for years. Sure the wheeze swerved around the

*These older punters provided a familiar certainty about the pattern of events, and the whole process ran along neatly and soberly for years.*

potholes in the road of progress, the stars changed, the horses came and went, as horses do, the jockeys clung on and fell off. But who could imagine real, lasting, significant change?

The Melbourne Cup was always run over 3200 metres. Two miles of memories, drama, courage, heroics, disappointments. Fortunes were spent getting a horse to the starting line. There were big wins and even bigger losses. Since 1860 generations of Australians have filed away memories of great horses, incredible jockeys, dramatic finishes, terrible falls and dud horses that are still running. Most right-thinking Australians can list favourites in every category.

The race kept going through the great catastrophes of the nation's history. All through World War One, Diggers' spirits were buoyed by knowing that in 1914 Kingsburgh, owned by L.K.S. Mackinnon, won at 20 to 1. In 1915 Patrobas saluted. The horse was owned by Mrs Edith Widdis, the first woman to own a Cup winner. Sasanof missed the race record by half a second in 1916. The race was delayed by torrential rain until the Saturday after Cup Day. It must have been some dump of water to postpone the stopping of the nation.

Westcourt broke through after a string of second placings in big races in 1917. Finally in 1918, as the war ground to a halt, the great Night Watch saluted at 12 to 1, carrying ten stone, about sixty-three kilograms. That is a lot of lead.

The years of World War Two did not slow the big race. In 1940, when our troops were fighting overseas, Old Rowley saluted at 100 to 1. Skipton won in 1941. The prize money was now a staggering £7,700. A year later, Colonus won by seven lengths, a record margin. It was a one-horse affair in front of a small crowd that could be counted on one hand. Times were very bad in 1943, but Dark Felt did what his dad, Spearfelt, did when he won the Cup in 1926. In 1944 it was Sirius the favourite who won, from barrier to box. The big punters swooped in the last hour of betting and the horse did not disappoint. In 1945 the South Australian mare Rainbird dashed to the front in the straight; the prize money now stood at £10,200. The horse carried a mere forty-eight kilograms to victory. Average weight for a winner was around 54.5 kilograms. Not even world war could cancel the big event.

*The hats, the frocks, the fashions on the field, the over-indulgence, wearing stupid shoes with high heels on grass, getting pissed, riding the wheelie bin and having to be led home - all part of the big occasion.*

The hats, the frocks, the fashions on the field, the over-indulgence, wearing stupid shoes with high heels on grass, getting pissed, riding the wheelie bin and having to be led home – all part of the big occasion. The great day out trackside on Cup Day is made all the more memorable if you can't remember a thing about it once you wake up the following day around 3 pm.

It is hard to pick a standout from the 150-plus Melbourne Cups that have brought the nation to a complete standstill. They are all great. But for the sake of the plot, let's spin the dial on the clock face of kismet and see where the fickle finger falls. Woah! The digit of doom has lobbed on the year 1965! This was a year of tumultuous change.

The Bart Cummings–trained Light Fingers won the big one, scoring by the barest of margins. The horse was originally called Close Embrace, but this was considered far too racy for conventional Melbourne. The VRC committee said 'Close Embrace' was off the charts of acceptability. It was on a slippery slope of smut that would give racing a bad name and attract the wrong crowd. The sort of crew who wore leather jackets, studs for earrings and strolled about wearing brothel creepers in the mounting enclosure. Everyone knew someone in that badass pack! The name had to be changed. No one knows how Light Fingers became an acceptable substitute.

The main form guide race to the Melbourne Cup, the 1965 Caulfield Cup, was won by a Queensland horse, Bore Head, with South Australian Ziema second, Craftsman third and Matloch fourth. Light Fingers was scratched from the race.

Then it was on to Flemington. All the Caulfield Cup place-getters were backing up for another tilt at the treasure. Matloch, Sail Away, Craftsman, Strauss and Ziema were all well in the market. Bore Head was attempting the cups double, a difficult and rarely pulled-off feat.

A young Bruce McAvaney aired the first of his famous phantom calls on radio 3DB on the morning of the race. Bruce's great role model at the station was the senior race caller, the Accurate One, Bill Collins. As part of his coverage of the race on Cup morning, Bill gave young Bruce the opportunity of a lifetime.

Bruce's call of the imaginary race was won by The Dip with Zinga Lee second, there was a fall in which Tobin Bronze took out Light Fingers and Ziema at the point of the turn. As Bruce called it, Tobin Bronze came wide and cannoned into the other two horses. All three horses fell. There was an inquiry into the incident. In the Stewards' Room, after weight was declared, the stewards outed Tobin Bronze's rider for twenty-seven meetings. That is how Bruce saw it.

That afternoon during the Cup, as anticipated in Bruce's early morning phantom call, Bore Head, Matloch and River Seine all collided and tumbled out of the race. In the straight, Ziema pulled away and was headed for a win. But 'The Professor of the Persuader', Roy Higgins, got very busy on Light Fingers at the Clocktower. The horse responded to The Prof's vigour and in a beautifully judged ride, Fingers saluted by the barest of margins. Ziema missed the big prize by a bob of the head.

Seventy-five thousand, five hundred and eighty-one race-goers witnessed this race of high drama. Trainer Bart Cummings quinellaed the event. This sensational win was the start of Bart's incredible run of success – a winning streak that earned him the title 'The Cups King'.

Oddly enough, Light Fingers was the companion horse to Ziema, who was a bit of a ratbag and needed a familiar equine friend to settle the race-day nerves.

As for The Professor, he became a champion jockey. Higgins rode 2312 winners, snaring the Victorian Jockeys' Premiership eleven times. In doing so he collected two Cox Plates, five VRC Oaks, four Victoria Derbys, two Sydney Cups and the Golden Slipper twice. He battled weight his entire career and when he finished was happy 'just to be a little fat man'.

Light Fingers was sired by French import Le Filou, who went on to sire the 1969 Cup favourite Big Philou. This was another conveyance that carried the Bart polish. Sadly for Philou freaks, the horse was nobbled with laxatives before the big race. It would have been a tragedy for the image of the Cup if the horse had run leaving a lumpy brown trail for 3200 metres around Flemington. In the wash-up, The Prof claimed the horse was a certainty. The 1969 Cup was won by Rain Lover, who had saluted the previous year. Rain Lover was the first horse to win the race in successive years since the original champ Archer.

Back in 1965, as Light Fingers was winning, many fashionable Melbourne racegoers were looking elsewhere.

They were looking out for the supermodel of the era, Jean Shrimpton. On Derby Day, two days before the big race, Jean arrived in the bird cage with no gloves, no hat, no stockings and a 'What are you looking at?' grin. With a single appearance Jean changed Melbourne's fashion trajectory. The mini skirt had arrived. It was 'now' time! It was a pivotal moment in race day attire.

It was easy to outrage the Melbourne fashion establishment. The Shrimp knocked them sideways into the rose bushes along the running rail. The skirt was a 'scandal', the Flemington fashion arbiters bellowed. It is hard to imagine today but the supermodel was given a couple of days to get her act together. All eyes were on the Cup Day Shrimpton ensemble. Under pressure from her sponsors, she turned up in the conventional clothes, accepted by the fashion police. She wore a grey three-piece suit, carrying a brown handbag to lug home the winnings.

The VRC committee got their money's worth as at least 50,000 outraged fashion experts turned up on Cup Day prepared to be insulted by Jean's choice of frock. After all this time, in the context of Flemington fashions, the 1965 Shrimpton look still seems startling and weirdly modern. She stunned her critics with her departing words, 'I feel Melbourne isn't ready for me yet. It seems years behind London.'

For decades, there has been a Melbourne carnival vibe for the whole of Cup week. Kicking off with Derby Day, there is a parade of past Cup winners and stars on the Monday.

A holiday on Tuesday for the big one. Wednesday is a breather, and everyone gets out of town for the Kyneton Cup. Thursday, it's all back to Flemington for Oaks Day, and the carnival winds down with a Family Day on the Saturday. It is a week-long extravaganza generated by the madness of the horse.

The Cup carnival has often needed promotional help. They started to use big names in the build-up in 1907 when opera singer Dame Nellie Melba turned up between her comebacks to let fly with an aria or two before the jump. Since the Melba success, the VRC organising committee has worked flat out to attract the stars.

These stars give the big day international cachet. It is an easy gig for them. They do not have to do much. It is not as though the celebs have to throw a leg over a conveyance and kick it clear at the top of the straight to score with the grandstand on their back. They would never be asked to do any heavy lifting, like being part of a celebrity shooter programme. They would be well away from the action if the worst happened on the turn out of the straight onto the river side and a horse went down and the stewards called for the screens.

*All they have to do is look good, have a tip and talk about the brilliance of the on-field fashion.*

All they have to do is look good, have a tip and talk about the brilliance of the on-field fashion. Glib generalised comments for the media about being excited to be in Melbourne and a vague, tenuous connection to the world of the horse (as in seeing *National Velvet* on TV as a child) would be welcome. Most importantly, if the international star could plug for Melbourne in spring, that would be a bonus.

These overseas stars value-add on the nightly news, providing that all-important international perspective for the race. In a heaving race crowd of 100,000-plus trying to get a bet on and a beer before the jump, who would know if the big names were there or not?

No international artiste in their right mind, who understood the racing gambol, would turn up to a handicap for all comers like the Melbourne Cup; nevertheless, the committee has done extremely well over the decades. The roll call of the who's who of international entertainment is impressive, even if it left many punters scratching their heads and asking, 'Who? No really, who?'

Spring carnival stars are often big names on the wane or with a product to promote. Their most important asset is their availability on the day and their ability to organise their schedule to be in Melbourne on the first Tuesday in November.

Here are a few highlights from the long list who added their glamour to the Cup. When Princess Diana and Prince Charles rocked up in 1985, they had a lively hour or two before the Cup with Fosters supremo John Elliott in the VRC committee rooms.

The loveable, horse-mad, handbag-making sisters Paris and Nicky Hilton lobbed in 2003 – one dressed for the beach, the other dressed for bed. It was startling point of difference. Paris made a beeline for Australian Idol star Rob 'Millsy' Mills and the rest is back seat history. In 2005 Heather Graham was here to promote her latest movie *The Guru*. She was overwhelmed by the experience and Australian race-day hospitality. How *The Guru* promotion went at the box office is anyone's guess.

The unusual pairing of Snoop Dog and Jennifer Hawkins graced the mounting enclosure in 2008. The A-list duo thrilled frock lovers and rappers. That's a hard demographic to work on the same day.

Mötley Crüe man Tommy Lee arrived in 2009. He did not disappoint. He got on the turps as soon as he saw the bar. After the first he did not stop. He broke every VRC fashion rule, wearing a jumper made of dog hair. In 2010 the spin twins Liz Hurley and Shane Warne thrilled the marquee stretch.

*The O.C.* star Mischa Barton was trackside in 2012. Mischa had been going to the races since she was a kid. She was determined to have a good day and promised to bet on an Irish horse. Not sure how she went on the punt. That year, eighteen of the field of twenty-four were bred outside Australia and New Zealand. Mischa may have been paralysed by choice. But if stuck, in a strange place surrounded by strangers, it is probably as good a system as any. Horse Spice, Geri Halliwell, was back in 2013 casting a practised eye over the field in the saddling enclosure.

In 2014, Victoria's Secret supermodel Gigi Hadid had a lot of fun wearing a hat that was a working scale model of the Malabar sewage treatment works.

This cavalcade of celebrities came to a shuddering halt in 2019 when chart-topping superstar and Grammy-winner Taylor Swift created a big hullabaloo. When Taylor looked at her diary and said, 'Yes! Count me in!', it was cheers all round in the committee room. The Moët was cracked and poured. Job done! But then Taylor fiddled with the phone moments later and saw massive social media blow-back on the decision. It was only then that Swifty found out what the Melbourne Cup involved: horses and whips. The singer soon backed out of the barriers and took shelter in the nearest Chris Waller horse float, declaring herself a scratching from the event.

Taylor learnt that many of her supporters around the planet loved horses, hated horse racing and, suddenly, because of her temporary public pro-racing stance, were thinking twice about buying her tunes in the future. Many moved Taylor from the 'like' into the 'hate' column on their feeds.

BY THE TIME FASHION, hats, shoes, champagne, canapés for lunch and star-spotting are ticked off the agenda, stabbing a winner in any spring carnival race, let alone the big one, is almost tangential to a great day out for the 100,000 who lob trackside. Most people would consider stabbing a winner a fluke, snagging the Cup quinella to be one of those miracles Scott Morrison is always banging on about and jagging a nation-stopping trifecta a reward for dishonesty.

That is the racing and social landscape into which the richest sprint race in the world, The Everest, charges with all horns blazing and saddle bags groaning. The Randwick event packs a load of disruptive race day baggage. This fifteen-million-dollar sprint appeals to the OMG mob having a punt with their phone betting apps. These punters who swerve around the bricks and mortar TAB shops know all about quaddies, trebles, parlays and all the multis. The search for value on the multiple phone betting sites is admirable and all-consuming. This Everest is targeted at the FOMO crowd, who simply do not want to miss out. They did not! The Everest has quickly jumped to second slot on the national punting numbers chart.

*This Everest is targeted at the FOMO crowd, who simply do not want to miss out.*

When the political money crew talk about the importance

to the economy of the racing industry, it's the big events that have caught their eye. Millions are tipped into the pot of national turnover via these two big races, the Cup and the E. The jaw drops and the brain refuses to engage with these numbers, such is their bulk.

The Everest is a calculated jab in the Melbourne eye by NSW racing. This desperate attempt to steal the glamour and cash of that great racing institution, the Melbourne Cup Carnival, appears to be working. Never mind the fact that historically Melbourne Cup Day is the best attended day on the Sydney turf calendar. That is one of life's little trackside ironies.

## The Everest: The dream, the drama and the disruption!

The Everest is a race. It looks just the same as other races on the calendar. Horses jump and run. Jockeys do their best. The crowd cheers. Money changes hands. But it is a fright of the fresh, a blast of the now, a shock of the new. The old-and-in-the-way Caulfield Cup, worth five million, is still run on the third Saturday in October. Once the Cup is done and dusted, an hour later a race in Sydney is run worth fifteen million. The race will take approximately one minute and ten seconds. That is disruption! It is a ball-tearing sprint over 1200 metres for all comers. The starters have all paid a price to take their place. It is the biggest cheese on the Australian turf calendar.

This is a tale of two cities, a story as old as European settlement. The money in Melbourne spring racing is anchored around the Cup's carnival and the card of racing on either side of the Melbourne Cup.

The modern axis of Australian racing is always a Melbourne/Sydney tug of war. The Everest is the biggest piece of ammunition

*The modern axis of Australian racing is always a Melbourne/Sydney tug of war.*

in the Sydney cannon. According to the NSW racing brains trust, the youth of the nation love The Everest. It was designed to get them to go crazy with a fist full of dollars.

The Melbourne mansion of racing was so well built that it appeared dynamite proof. Many racegoers thought it would last forever, even beyond the coming ice age. For years the stumper that occupied the brightest minds of racing administration in NSW was: How can we blow the Victorian edifice up?

How could Sydney put a bomb under the four days of Melbourne's spring carnival and blow it away completely? This was a war, and the total demolition concept was advanced by desperate individuals. They were not afraid to drag governments and racing organisations kicking and screaming over the line to achieve their goal.

The other big stumper disturbing sleep and occupying the committee's late-night chinwags was, how can we create a race that had millions in prize money and pay bugger-all for it?

The hard-working Australian Turf Club working group, under the stewardship of Peter V'landys, more recently dubbed the 'Man of Feathers' after his achievements with the NRL, agreed the race would have to be a cracker. It would have to be spectacular and pack a skerrick of the stupid.

Prior to the steep climb of The Everest, the big Sydney race on the turf calendar was the Golden Slipper. This race for two-year-olds over 1200 metres was a relative newcomer in the stable of great Australian races. It debuted in 1957 and is now worth a paltry $3.5 million. This prize money figure no longer encourages a horse, let alone an equine tutor to get out of bed.

The new event capitalised on this point of difference between the two cities. The Melbourne spring carnival was crammed with staying events; the new race focused on the Sydney racing long suit: speed.

The stumbling block was funding. How is this race designed to give Melbourne the shits paid for? Funding the race was always going to produce an outcry from concerned woke citizens who do not identify with the bashing of horses down the straight as sport, even if there is an humongous purse dangling from the winning post.

Then came the breakthrough that really mattered. Why not get everyone who is interested in entering the cough-and-spit sprint to pay for it? The Everest generates a slab of the prize money based on buying and trading twelve slots. This was an equine user-pays breakthrough.

The cream on top of the big mountain of cake: the twelve barrier slots in the race could be bought and traded. This was something new. This icing on the race cake meant that at every step of the process someone had to pay through the nose.

Do the maths. Twelve wealthy individuals, cashed-up partnerships or racing enterprises, shell out minimum $600,000 a year for a slot. All owners have a lifetime option on a slot. The carrot that dangles, well, the first four past the post all snare a million or more for slot holders. Even the horse that smelled the field all the way gets a collect. In the 2020 Everest the last horse collected $450,000.

Money attracts big players and big names, like blowflies to a stable stall in summer after the champ has taken a mid-morning dump. Everest intrigue and the money runs all year behind the scenes. It stirs the publicity pot, but at the pointy end the race itself is over in the time it takes to breathe in and out five times. It has only been run a few times, but according to the grind of racing's publicity machine The Everest is the future. And it is here now!

*Money attracts big players and big names, like blowflies to a stable stall in summer after the champ has taken a mid-morning dump.*

Race promoters know this race is what the younger set want in an afternoon track side. They have noted the collapse of the Big Day Out music concept and figure watching a race with a glass in hand is a great option. Never mind that to the untrained eye The Everest looks exactly like every other race run in Australia every day of the year except Good Friday and Christmas Day.

The racing think tank in a light-bulb moment realised young, fit Australians do not want to be part of anything that smells of geriatric boomer. They have swallowed enough of that Old Spice stench to last a lifetime. They want the aroma of their own horse race floating past their nostrils. They want a winning scent they recognise as their own.

The 'yoof' want a place where they can drop anchor for the afternoon, swallow a mojito cocktail or a case of Penfolds Grange, sink the slipper into a few certainties and have a soft landing when they fall about legless at the end of the day.

On Everest day the soft spot on the track where a pissed punter can flop is the lawn out front of the Members' grandstand. They do not want to be bothered by the fossil set who pretend they know what Australian adolescents want. The old codger community are clueless – look where Australia is today, and it is all because of them.

Youngsters don't need fuds and OAPs telling them what they can and cannot do. Their outdated 'we know what is best' blather is a violation of young Australians' human rights. Remember, if you are under twenty in the twenty-twenties, if it did not happen in the last five years it simply did not happen.

They certainly do not need another long trip to Flemington. Randwick is the place to look good, roam about in extravagant footwear, see mates and drop a bundle. It is now. It has the light rail running past the front door. It's Woo Hoo! Who knows how lucky you might get after the sun sets!

The Everest is a disruptive race that has even changed the language of punting. The old language used by grey-beards and has-beens who cannot use a punting app is now associated with big losers, dud bets and never ever stabbing a winner. The new language from the TAB's 'World of Punt' is summed up with the phrase 'long may we play'. It makes everyone a winner, even if they drop the lot on a day of fourths and go home without a shirt and trouserless. It does not matter because they have been playing all day and not wasting their money punting.

The ATC brains trust keeps banging on about how disruptive it is. As racing supremo Peter V'landys said during a probing *The Project* interview:

> Waleed, my very good friend, if you don't get it, buddy, it is checkout time. You must be nearly cactus, hogging space in an aged care facility that others could use if you don't see what we are trying to do.

> Let me put it bluntly. Bugger off, granddad! Let a winner slip into those underpants stained with excitement . . . Waleed, it's the new language, it's the new idea. It is The Everest . . .

The race has disrupted the equine landscape completely. The races that precede The Everest and offer an insight into the form of horses entered to bag the fifteen million large are the VRC Sprint, which is now widely accepted by everyone under the age of twenty-five as a joke. Most serious punters, too young to have a driver's licence, laugh when anyone mentions the TJ Smith as a reliable form guide to anything except a one-way ticket to aged care. No one has thought seriously about the TJ since Steven Bradbury snared gold at the Salt Lake Olympics. The next two biggest sprint lead-up events are the Concorde Stakes and the Premiere Stakes. They are now the butt of YouTube gags by teenage race-going stand-up comics.

Even The Everest trophy talks to kids. The shiny bright bit of bling handed out to connections is a magnificent statuette of a stallion rearing on a frozen peak surrounded by a ring of precious metal. At last count, 8714 large diamonds were super-glued to the horse. These carefully placed rocks allow the image to sparkle from every angle in the spring sun.

This gem-encrusted gewgaw of success weighs fourteen kilograms. It was hand crafted by the necklace and earrings genius Nic Cerrone. Nic knows the horse and what young Australians want in an engagement ring. After all this bloke is an international superstar in the world of precious rocks. He has even made time in his busy schedule to visit the Vatican

*The Everest trophy is a great addition to the golden mile of Renaissance racing masterpieces.*

in Rome and natter on with the Pope about updating the papal trinkets and tiaras range. The Everest trophy is a great addition to the golden mile of Renaissance racing masterpieces.

Imagine the merchandise possibilities that this diamond rearing horse generates. There is already an avalanche of Everest-inspired Christmas gifts. Everest-themed bedside lamps, bunny rugs for the littlies with a matching set of flame-proof pyjamas, cake tins, steering wheel covers, eskys and earrings. The Everest store is a bottomless gold mine of licensing deals that is only limited by the racegoer's imagination.

Politics is never far from the track. No federal or state politician, minister or premier is without a tip in the lead-up to The Everest. Even if they admit they know nothing about the racing world, and most know bugger-all, they will stump in to do the breakfast television round offering their selections and some wry smiles about how Australia would not be Australia without The Everest. This race knocks down all barriers.

The promotion from the political class was important, but the race has to generate its own outrage. It has to generate copy and provide an endless supply of long-running issues for the tabloid press, digital channels and social media. There was an excellent early foray into the world of off-track marketing that unleashed public outrage and got all-important social media traction for free. It involved everyone.

In Sydney, from the low valley of Circular Quay and the foothills of the Museum of Contemporary Art, the nation looks east towards the Himalayas represented by the sails of the

Opera House. As the sun sets and the twilight glow glimmers, on that one night of the year a horse-mad nation sees the barrier draw of The Everest projected on those magnificent Opera House sails. It was an inspired move. It broke the promotional mould. It was a startling collision of sport and culture and cash. This was Peter V'landys's brain wave, the whizz kid from Wollongong, who pioneered The Everest as the race that pays for itself.

People were outraged when The Everest's first draw was plastered all over the Opera House sails. People understandably took to the streets in angry protest. Talkback radio and tabloids went berserk. It was considered a crime against humanity and art by opera lovers. *Carmen* and *Rigoletto* will never be the same. The critics demanded heads should roll. Bunnings was sharpening the blade.

At that moment in history, it would have been much easier if opera and racing had seen a way to walk together into a bright future. The Everest and *Rigoletto* wheeze should be a two-way street. Australia is big enough and is rich enough.

What was the last great horse-themed opera? Is this nation so devoid of talent that the story of Melbourne Cup winner Subzero or the life of the Cups King Bart Cummings could not be turned into a four-act opera? The Fine Cotton fairytale, a very funny saga of racing blokes who thought they could get away with painting a horse and running it in the first. Sadly, everyone heard about painted pony and went the plonk, so the collect was very skinny. This simple tale would make a top comic turn with tunes.

Australia is home to some of the best songwriters and musical stars on the planet. Horse stories write themselves. There is a start, heartbreak, a middle down in the dumps and a bright blast with a big ending. The operatic journey is populated with so many characters both good and evil. Everyone gets a chance to have a blast in B flat.

*These two great strands of Australian cultural life need to start singing from the same hymn sheet. What if the Australian Opera staged 'A Night of the Horse' on the eve of The Everest?*

These two great strands of Australian cultural life need to start singing from the same hymn sheet. What if the Australian Opera staged 'A Night of the Horse' on the eve of The Everest? There would be queues ten deep to see a crowd-funded programme of horsey tunes with musical theatre stars meeting the racing community halfway. Both promoting the big race. Imagine Chris Waller, Damien Oliver, Rachel King and Jamie Kah making up a musical foursome while top jockey Hugh Bowman conducts the Sydney Symphony Orchestra. The night could climax with the finalists in The Annual Everest horse song competition sung in a sumptuous setting before the announcement of the winner, the presentation of a cash prize and free tickets for The Everest race day.

But there are other options. The Theatre of the Horse at Randwick, home of The Everest, needs to be rebadged as a Centre of Equine and Operatic Excellence. It's a venue with great acoustic properties and plenty of space backstage. Purists will shout about opera invading Royal Randwick and devaluing a great sporting venue, and all that jazz. But bugger the fuds, let's dance!

Imagine racegoers on Everest eve being thrilled by a night of horse glamour and horse tunes. On a warm spring evening when the flowers along the running rail are in full bloom, romance and harmony are in the air. Everyone's a winner. The musical programme selects itself: George Jones' 'The Race is On', Spike Jones' 'Beetlebaum', 'I'm an Old Cow Hand from the Rio Grande', 'Up on Cripple Creek', from The Band's second album, The Pogues' 'Bottle of Smoke', then finishing up with an all-cast finale of tearjerkers, 'My Rifle, My Pony and Me' and 'Ghost Riders in the Sky'.

It is a lost opportunity to jab Melbourne in the eye yet again. They might have the Australian Open, the AFL Grand Final, the F1 and the MotoGP at Phillip Island, but tipping the horse into the Australian Opera will be Sydney's alone. A night out Melbourne cannot pinch.

This obvious synergy between opera and horse flesh would go a long way to normalise the 'long may we play' concept. University-conducted surveys have established that Australians will bet on any competition anywhere. From *MasterChef* finals to the Moonee Valley Cup, from Australian of the Year to cakes at the Royal Easter Show, from federal and state elections to Supercars, Australians love to have a crack. In all these top events the TAB drenches the punter with exotic options, from each-way bets and quinellas to trifectas, quaddies and trebles, the variety is mind-numbing.

With big-time opera and the musical theatre thrown at the race promotion, let us not overlook the Archibald Prize. This portraiture art prize has thrilled Australia for over a century. It is now time for the horse to take centre stage on this vast cultural canvas. For far too long, the great and the good Australians

*The prize committee should mandate that only horse-related subject matter will be accepted in the Archibald for the next decade.*

no one has ever heard of have been tapped as the subject matter in the Big A. The prize committee should mandate that only horse-related subject matter will be accepted in the Archibald for the next decade. Imagine the show featuring jockeys, owners, trainers, punters, colourful racing identities plus very nice pictures of horses. What a great challenge!

The TAB could be roped in to run the punting side of the equine Archibald, with bets available on the winner, plus odds and evens and pick fours. It is all there. All NSW racing boss and international art aficionado Peter V'landys has to do is put a rocket under it and light the wick.

Our betting agencies are world class at crow-barring money from a punter's wallet. Remember two decades ago, only the racing codes gave Australians a wide canvas of sporting investment options. Today no sport can exist without a return from the ever-expanding punting dollar. The nation has come a long way and culture is now part of the wallet-opening action.

All Australian punters want from the wagering industry is the opportunity to have another go. If gamblers lose in a photo finish, what they want is another race to chase winnings to fill the gaping hole in their wallet caused by the last.

Australian turf scheduling is such that if punters drop a load on a big one, they don't have to wait long for a chance to get square. Another race will be along in minutes with another winner. It would be madness to miss the jump in the next.

On every track there is the doyen of local tipsters, a Clarrie the Clocker type bellowing, 'Sport, in this next race at Strathalbyn there is an absolute certainty, it's fixed at twenty to one and has great blood numbers. It goes super first up after a spell. The horse has eaten everything in the bin for the past week. Its barrier trial last Monday was out of this world. Oh no, you would be mad if you did not go hard!'

In 2020, year one of COVID, The Everest ran at 4.15 pm Eastern Daylight Time. By the time you watched and calmed down after the excitement of winning, it was 4.18 pm. The next race in Australia jumped at 4.19 pm at Ascot. Like rust, racing never nods off. If punters dud out in the feature, they only wait two minutes for a chance to get square.

All racegoers accept that horses do not get that much from the racing industry. Not every horse can be a winner. It is often just another day. Ho hum! Wake up in the stable early, then a ride in the back of the horse float, followed by a bit of a jog out to the barriers; the crowd is back and being silly. Then into the barriers with a lot of other horses and 'Set and racing', the run, the crowd cheering the result, a hose off, then back in the float, another hose off, a bin of oats, salt lick and an early night back in the stable stall.

It's the punters who add a mad element to the caper. Hoping their win or each-way selection covers the outlay and a bucket of chips and a refreshing beer. But it is a simple mathematical truth that for every big win, there must be hundreds

*But it is a simple mathematical truth that for every big win, there must be hundreds of losing tickets, otherwise the whole shebang would fall over.*

of losing tickets, otherwise the whole shebang would fall over. Everyone is reminded of this fact whenever they look in the car park. It is the bookies and jockeys who have the flash set of wheels, the BMWs, the Mercedes, the Porsches and the Teslas; and lucky punters, well, they often travel to and fro on PT.

After every race, there is a brief moment to reflect on the lines tacked on to the end of every gambling ad. 'Remember to think of those who rely on you for support' and 'Bet with your head, not over it'. Fancy sticking that as a final line on punting ad copy.

There is the international interest in The Everest, from the wide world beyond. The 2020 million-dollar sprint was beamed into sixty-five countries. Punters in Hong Kong, Japan, Korea, Turkey and France saw the race live. In Russia, President Vladimir Putin suggested it would be 'anti-Russian' not to watch it.

Everyone overseas loves the race and its wild emphasis on youth. Dumping the Dad's Army contingent has breathed new life into the horse industry across Asia. The generation of ancient geriatrics has for years held back racing in Turkey and Korea where they associate the Colonel Blimp racing set with boat loads of losers. The idea that the winner in 2020, Classique Legend, was trained by eighty-two-year-old trackside legend Les Bridge freaks them right out. They don't know what to do with that snippet of biographical information.

For two minutes, millions of people across the planet downed the tools, tuned in to our national anthem, the introduction of the jockeys, all the action behind the barriers, and settled back for the 1200 metres of sprinting mayhem at Randwick before moving on with the rest of their lives.

The people of Vladivostok are captivated by The Everest and everything the race says about Australia. This eastern Russian city is in a wonderful time zone for live coverage. The mayor, Viktor Cherepkov, is a racing man. He has declared a public holiday across the region on Everest Day. The far east edition of *Pravda* publishes a form guide with a cut-out-and-keep sweep page. Many Russian business establishments run sweeps with a divvy-up of the pot for first, second and third, and a booby prize for the poor sod who drew the conveyance that plugs home last.

Last year across the thirteen time zones of Russia, regardless of the hour, people took the live feed from Channel Seven in English with Bruce McAvaney hosting the coverage, before going upstairs to Darren Flindell's call of The Everest with translation from SBS TV's Russian department.

In response to interest from around the world, the Department of Foreign Affairs and Trade has put together racing delegations and equine trade missions led by movers and shakers from all three Australian racing disciplines. It is a hands-across-the-water exercise. The ambition is to throw a petrol bomb on the glowing embers of horse racing in places like Russia. DFAT wants to fire up an out-of-control blaze on the steppes, producing flames that can be seen from the clocktower at Flemington.

*In response to interest from around the world, the Department of Foreign Affairs and Trade has put together racing delegations and equine trade missions led by movers and shakers from all three Australian racing disciplines.*

Rostov-on-Don, a great Russian horse-racing centre, is now twinned with Moonee Valley. This is a triumph of quiet diplomacy by the foreign affairs boffins. The proposed Northern Cox concept is a weight-for-age event for Russian and European horses. Russian racing is licking its lips. The Moonee Valley Racing Club is actively supporting the concept. Imagine a horse getting the Australian and Russian Cox Plates in the same year. The Everest and our racing diplomacy take Australian values to the world. The current prime minister is very bullish about the promotion of Australian values through racing in parts of the world that know nothing about our great mouse plagues and dud coral reefs.

The final challenge for Australian racing is normalising the punt for all sections of society. This will take time. Racing supremo in the pantaloons of plumage Peter V'landys, aka 'Saint Peter of the Punt', has an ambition to make the wagering caper the bedrock of a prosperous free market economy.

He knows there will be Victims of the Punt. The dud punter will always be part of Australian society. The refreshing V'landys view is that the problem gambler is a problem for others to worry about, not those involved in the punting, casino or poker machine industries. These so-called 'victims' will not need to be addressed for another thirty years, by which time he will have moved on to running the IOC.

But Pete is conscious of the caper's critics. He is very mindful that society's mores have changed. A modern sensitive approach is required for equine management during the horse's race career and this will continue once the hayburner is retired from the track. Belting a horse to make it go quickly is now considered cruel and inhumane. As V'landys maintained in a recent three-way turf talk with Ronnie 'The Duff' Dufficy and Troutie Hughes on *Racing Radio*:

> Troutie, you make a great point! Look, I understand where the woke generation is coming from. They see flogging a horse all the way down the straight, with great chunks of rump steak carved off from the entire flanks to get it home in a tight finish, as cruel. I get that! It is not a good look when our great jockeys are forced to reduce a horse to mince to score a win and earn a sling for the ride. It is unsightly. That is why we have invested millions in race-track technology so the stewards can get the whip issue under control.
>
> We have set out strict rules about whip use based on the modern understanding from the vets and horse shrinks that a horse does not mind being belted, say, three times every 100 metres, but every horse draws the line at being bashed twenty times in ten metres. That simply is a university-proven fact.
>
> Like you, Duff, I used to love seeing 'Fractious' Bruce Woodis and Mister Muscles, 'Brawny' Barry Lash, get to work on a bludging three-year-old, first up from a spell, at the top of the straight. But Troutie, vigour that was once admired, vigour that was remarked upon, is now a crime against horse humanity. The days when the whip ruled are long gone. This is a new age of racing. By the way, what do you like in this afternoon's Doomben 10,000?

As mentioned, the pinnacle of the new age of racing, The Everest, is the first fixture on the international racing calendar aimed directly at a new generation, the formally lukewarm, under thirty-five-year-old racegoer. It is their race. They have supported it as a meaningful entertainment option.

What can The Man of Feathers do for an encore? Disruption is a real bugger. Everything everywhere always needs another kick up the date. Change is constant. The next generation of racegoers do not want a bar of what satisfied their older brothers and sisters.

*The next generation of racegoers do not want a bar of what satisfied their older brothers and sisters.*

How long before the Australian racing industry's brains trust has to return to the drawing board? How long before it is forced to come up with a horse happening that will appeal to the nation's newly jaded appetites? How long before the bean counters demand an event that will capture the imagination of the under twenties? How long before the under thirty-fives move up into the under fifties age bracket and lose all interest in The Everest? Remember the hip groovers of today are the fuds of tomorrow.

What will Peter V'landys have to pull out of his feather-filled jodhpurs? Maybe an event called the Randwick Hustle aimed at the under twenties? A few years later will the trackside supremo have to dive back into his pantaloons for a race called, say, 'Spider-Man: The Tangled Web', a race that captures the imagination of under-fifteens?

Finally, will Saint Peter of the Punt do the impossible, and pluck a final quill out of the feathered flares and produce 'The Big Ted' – a race that fascinates the under sevens? To paraphrase the Jesuits, 'Give us the punter at the age of seven and we will have them for life.' That is Australia's racing nirvana. A race that hooks all seven-year-olds into the glories of the punt. Given the younger person's attention span, this may be a race over a distance of twelve metres. But that hard-to-reach younger set going the plonk is the Holy Grail of the TAB's 'long may we play' caper.

# CRICKET'S HOLY GRAIL

*The long-buried concrete strip made sense of it all. Like an oasis shining in the desert, there it was hiding in full view, the Don's lost pitch still chock-a-block full of runs.*

VERY HARD TO ADD anything original to the swirling vortex that is the knowledge pool of Australian cricket. No new ground broken here. This deep dive into the third leg swamp is just a lazy amble up to the crease off a very short run.

It's a blast at the tailenders with seven back in the pavilion. It is a roll of the arm over, giving the pill air, letting the ball do the work in flight. Hopefully there is a bit of grip and puff of dust off the pitch or a hint of reverse swing at the very least. If lucky, the delivery will be followed by a vigorous 'Howzat!' from behind the furniture and a simultaneous leap skywards from the slips cordon.

At the time this scorecard was inked, 460 fit Australian men had pulled on the pads or taken the new ball up the hill from the river end.

Since the first Test in 1877 against England at the MCG, Aussie blokes had donned the Gawler creams and baggy green in 834 tests. The team saluted in 394, flashed home for a fast-finishing second in 226, managed a be-on-me next time draw on 212 occasions and dead-heated twice.

Nine years earlier, between May and October 1868, there was a tour of England by an Australian First Nations team, made up of players largely from the Western Districts of Victoria. This first touring side played forty-seven matches throughout England, winning fourteen, loosing fourteen and drawing nineteen. The star with both bat and ball was Johnny Mullagh, who scored 1,698 runs and took 245 wickets. Everywhere they went, the tourists attracted big crowds who frequently put on displays of boomerang and spear throwing after stumps. After all that, on returning from the tour, restrictions on travel by the Victorian Government stopped First Nations involvement in the game at international level.

From very humble beginnings in the 1930s, 176 women have turned out in cricket Tests for Australia. Our women's Test team has played seventy-four big ones and snared the chocolates in twenty of them. They have lost ten and drawn forty-four.

They are impressive stats. But the number of players turning out for the nation is dwarfed by the collection of dedicated souls whipping up stump cam–inspired content for a wide variety of print, broadcast and digital outlets. This travelling circus of commentators slaves away, inhaling and exhaling every delivery across the planet in all forms of the game.

Many more than those actually out in the middle with the excellent hand–eye coordination, pulling on the pads looking for the quick single, are crouched behind the broadcast mike or slogging away in the press box trenches.

The scorebook devotees have the Bic biro poised over the notebook or are tapping loudly on the keyboard for every minute of play in every match. All are hoping for a hat trick or a ton in every over. Unlike the players, the vast cast and crew of the commentating community find something absorbing in every ball.

*On-air cricket chit-chatters are masters of the radio and television hook through.*

On-air cricket chit-chatters are masters of the radio and television hook through. This is the rare skill of encouraging listeners and viewers to stay tuned even when there is absolutely nothing happening and no chance of anything happening, on the off-chance that something might happen. An example being:

> Thanks very much for that excellent summary, Jim, of the morning session where only three overs were possible due to rain ... And join us right after the break for another session of spin from the Cathedral end and more of your fifth Test memories. As we go to lunch, Australia right on top, England 3 for 43.

The world of cricket commentating is always licking the lips in anticipation that something right out of left field will suddenly swirl centre stage and allow extended commentary and analysis of this shattering event. With hours of airtime to fill, there is space to unpack the implications of the latest discovery, rule modification or technological change on the future of the game and the wider world. It goes without saying that the best moments from the commentary box are often in those hours when no actual cricket was played due to rain or injury or drinks or at the end of overs. Commentators are at their best when they have a roaming commission to talk about anything, and not just the current game.

There is nothing the well-travelled press box huddle likes more than a day's play interrupted by an international betting scandal involving match fixing, or a subcontinental chucking imbroglio or a trio of players wandering on with a sheet of sand-paper wedged down the front of the Gawler creams. Suddenly, there's so much to talk about, so many incidents to recall and so little time.

The discovery of the Don Bradman concrete pitch in the scrub near the Bowral CBD in the Southern Highlands of NSW was right out of left field. News of this historic find landed with a loud clunk in the inbox of 4,980,027 ticketed cricket journalists. It has reignited and revitalised interest in the long history of cricket across Australia. The Don is always headline news wherever stumps are set up and the fielding team bursts out of the rooms and is told by the skipper to 'scatter' at the start of the day's play.

*News of this historic find landed with a loud clunk in the inbox of 4,980,027 ticketed cricket journalists.*

From evidence in TV news and eyewitness reports, this Bradman/Bowral number one strip looks in great nick. Cricket pundits have established that the site is a significant destination for any tragic wanting to understand the Don in his totality or for a traveller at a loose end on the prowl for something to do for the weekend in the Southern Highlands. Visiting this cricket ground zero site will fill in thirty minutes early Sunday morning before a hot breakfast. Many buffs and former players come and simply stare and wonder for hours.

Bradman freaks have placed this concrete pitch discovery alongside the quest for the Don's first cruet protector, the first ball the Don hit for six and the stump he used to bash the ball against the tank stand in the backyard.

The Bowral heritage strip was unearthed by Project Pucovski. This federal government probe uses revolutionary techniques adapted from archaeologists working on the Giza Plateau. It was funded by Kerry Stokes AO, BHP, Steggles Chicken and the Dannii Minogue Foundation Trust. Project P is tasked with unearthing lost cricket artifacts. So far, they have exhumed 374 significant finds, including 227 pitches that had been lost for over five decades.

The atmosphere that surrounds this stretch of Australian sporting history is incredible. Even today it is easy, with eyes half-closed, to imagine the young Don confidently striding through the gate in the picket fence at 11 am on a bright sunny day. His eyes take in the light before a couple of quick steps to make sure everything is moving. He notices the time on the St Jude's Church clock and sets his mind firmly on getting a quick 50 before lunch and pushing on to a fat ton before the tea break.

*Even today it is easy, with eyes half-closed, to imagine the young Don confidently striding through the gate in the picket fence at 11 am on a bright sunny day.*

One of the most amazing aspects of this discovery is that the concrete pour, all those years ago, is still vivid in the minds of those who witnessed the cement mixers arrive and drop a load.

At the time it caused genuine excitement across the cricket-mad tri-city hub of Moss Vale, Mittagong and Bowral. So many residents still remember with great enthusiasm, stunning clarity and incredible detail the day of the pour.

There was a very moving ABC *Australian Story* in October 2015 that allowed people who saw the cement arrive to recall their emotions on that day. And to discuss what it means to this cricket-obsessed area with its sky-rocketing real estate prospects.

Jarrad Reek Jr, who was captain at Bowral High School in 'the year of the pour', was overcome with emotion when recalling that hot day in late summer. Jarrad has never forgotten the seven green Pioneer trucks rolling into town looking for an oval or a vacant paddock where they could back up and dump a load of concrete. A load that had the future of Australian cricket written in every grain of sand embedded in the mix.

Reek, now well into his eighties, is a quiet man full of unexploded menace. He looks as if he still has an over or two left in him, at the highest level. It is not impossible to see him steaming in from the Punt Road end of the MCG in the first session on day one of the Boxing Day test against a lively Sri Lankan eleven. Reek would not let Australia down.

In a startling interview with Jarod 'JT' Tiffen, local ABC TV Wollongong-based news anchor, the former school skipper, Reek, was remarkably frank in an interview that took four days to record. Junior had a slow, measured and deliberate way of talking, often taking minutes to say a few words. The interview was controversial and had a shock at the start:

To be honest, Jarod, I didn't know what was going on. I was not that interested in cricket. Rugby league was my go. Like many I thought the Don was an overrated joke who hogged the strike!

I got him plumb first ball on three occasions and knocked over his leg stump more than once. After that I lost interest in the game. He just didn't move his feet. Like I say, I considered the bloke a joke. Fancy getting out for donut in your last dig for Australia ... How un-Australian is that?

And I simply don't believe that 99.94 rubbish.

What's more, Jarod, I had not given the pitch or the Don a moment's thought since the school bell clanged on that afternoon and we took off on our Speedwells to see what the concrete blokes were doing with that truck near St Jude's.

I did not realise the twenty yards of cement cricket magic was lost until your producer, Trevor Tartine, rang up. I had no idea the local council had a search party out for three decades and they finally found it using lolly from Project Pucovski. I knew where it was all the time. I could have saved them a lot of trouble.

The filming stopped for lunch. Eventually, a terrific spread of Lake Illawarra bream was served.

Jarrad barbecued the fish in a lime and ginger marinade. He served the fish with a fabulous pomegranate, sweet potato and mung bean salad. But tragedy struck when quite a sizeable bone got stuck in Jarrad's throat.

There was a substantial break in the recording at this point while Jarrad was rushed to Wollongong Hospital for three days.

When he came to in Ward 27, he picked up the Bradman story as though nothing had happened.

Filmed in his pyjamas in a hospital bed, Jarrad continued:

> Jarod, one thing that is firmly cemented in my mind from that wild afternoon. On the day of the big pour, I remember the cops bailing me up in Aitkin Road. Senior Sergeant Brucie Longbottom bellowed at me above the screech of the siren from the front seat of his Austin A30, 'Hey Reek, slow down! Where is the fire, sonny Jim? Where is everyone going?'
>
> I explained what was happening. He gave me a police escort down to the pour. That detail has always stuck in my mind. Remember, Jarod, any youngster never forgets his first grilling from the fuzz.
>
> The whole unearthing of the strip project left me pretty vacant until a few months ago when the blanks were finally filled in. The whole concrete circus escaped me.

There were tears in the eyes of the *Australian Story* crew when Jarrad finally stopped talking. The emotions were so raw and opinions unexpected.

The next eyewitness was Bruce 'Nubs' Nubbin, who takes up the story, setting the scene of life in Bowral at the time:

> Tiffy, you are too young to remember, but when the Don roamed these parts looking for a place to knock up a ton or two it was a different place. There was bugger-all going on and pouring a slab of concrete anywhere was big news. It always

pulled a crowd whether it was a four-bedroom house, a cheese factory or a servo.

As I recall it, I had tugged a sickie for the day from school. Got up late and had breakfast late. At lunchtime I was camped over a big bowl of Weet-Bix and SPC Two Fruits when bestie 'Stumpy' Bottomley let the cat out of the bag. He bellowed over the back fence, 'Hey Nubs, they are pouring a pitch in that rubbish tip alongside the Church of England.'

By the time I got there, the whole school had raced down for a sticky beak. I actually stumbled onto the cement stretch while it was still wet. Right on to it! There was a bit of push and shove, you know how mad a bunch of rowdy teenage boys can be, we all got involved and there is the footprint of one of my Clark's Ripple Sole Desert Boots in the town end just off the crease. You can still see it quite clearly.

Cyril 'Stumpy' Bottomley, who had a newspaper run at the time, clearly remembers pushing his Malvern Star with 359 copies of the *Telegraph* and the *Sydney Morning Herald* past the site in Church Paddock every morning. He had to distribute his load of 'fish wrappers' before 8.50 am and had a great vantage point from the back of the Malvern Star to witness history in the making.

Honestly, Tiffster, this site needs to be saved from the developers. Sure, the pitch could be broken up and sold off for souvenirs like the Berlin Wall. Real Australians would love to get a slab of it and make it the basis of a water feature in their front yard.

Is this humble stretch of cement and sand the missing link in the Don's development? At school, I can remember wandering over for a hit on the concrete every Wednesday. Scratch teams were selected but the Don's eleven always won. They had a big advantage: a skipper who could bat.

Tiffy, I'm a Don tragic. I love Bowral. The Bradman Museum has the lot. The suitcase he took on the road to stardom and actually, I was the one who unearthed his first set of Bonds Y-front underpants. It was my gift to the collection and the nation. I found them in a back room of a shop that used to be a Mittagong laundry. The CSIRO ran the eye over the stained artifact. The boffins said, 'Yes, Stumps, they're the Don's.'

The big one the Museum does not have is his first signature. Was it on a bat, a programme, a team list or an afternoon edition of a local newspaper? We just don't know! In later years, after retiring, everyone knows the Don spent several hours a day signing gear. He was a machine with a Bic biro in one hand and a fountain pen in the other. He learnt to do his signature with both hands such was the demand for his autograph. Club secretaries maintain he could scribble 1259 signatures between tea and stumps. That is some strike rate!

But now that the final piece in the Don puzzle has been found and the strip has been unearthed, I am completely drenched. I don't know why but it's a dream come true. I put it down to being Australian and having a vivid recollection of Shane Warne's first ball to Mike Gatting at Lord's and all the details of Dennis and Rod punting on the Headingley test.

> The brave crew who stumbled across these twenty-two yards of history deserve an Australia Day Award or one of those gongs Tony Abbott used to dish out to total strangers when he was PM.
>
> This discovery really does put everything into perspective. It is about the passing of time and those great knocks by the Don that schoolkids and cricket buffs will never see. No vision of them exists. Nothing! They have simply vanished, disappeared into the slimy sinkhole of stump cam history. People forget there was no YouTube, no Twitter, no Facebook back when the Don roamed the streets of Bowral.

It was at this point that *Australian Story* pivoted to the Don's impact away from the recent discovery of the pitch. The Cootamundra-born product was so good he had a song written about him.

'Our Don Bradman', the smash hit that still talks to kids, was written by songwriter Jack O'Hagan. The classic was recorded to promote the 1930 Ashes Test series in England. In the third Test, the Don knocked up a record 334 on a magnificent Leeds strip. He made it look easy, but that deck was a bugger to bat on.

The tune is a classic of its kind. Unsurprisingly, there are a lot of 'Don' references in the verse and chorus. Rhymes of 'Mickey Mouse' with 'house' and 'into bat' with 'record flat'. Honestly, the lyrics wrote themselves as the Don did the lyrical heavy lifting with the willow out in the middle.

Jack's cracker is right up there, pushing for inclusion in the great Australian sporting songbook alongside the selected works of Banjo Paterson, Mike Brady and Paul Kelly. The bloke could write and hold a tune.

O'Hagan burst out of inner-city Melbourne with a swag of radio commercials and campfire songs that featured on very popular radio shows like *Cabbage's Campfire* or Bob Dyer's *When a Girl Marries* and *The Long Paddock* featuring 'Backdoor' Bob Boot. This style of popular old-school radio show featured a stroll down memory lane, a joke, a scone recipe, a cup of billy tea and a tune about an Aussie hero.

O'Hagan's output was prodigious. He had a crack at 600 songs, of which 200 were published. Some critics argue Jack was the Don Bradman of song.

Jack sent a swag of his better tunes to Dean Martin, on the off-chance that the great crooner might have room in his act for a couple of hits from Down Under. There is no evidence that Dean got the packet of hits, and some music buffs wonder if Dean could read either lyrics or music. Others argue that the parcel simply went astray in the chaos of the overseas mail system.

But Dean may have been baffled by who the hell Don Bradman was and was scratching his head about why a dog would sit on a tucker box, and where the hell was Gundagai? That is, if Deano thought at all.

The *Australian Story* episode concluded with a provocative contribution from widely read cricket blogger 'Fragile' Frankie Grout, a distant relative of the great Australian wicketkeeper Wally Grout. Writing an editorial think-piece for 'In or out, it's worth a shout!', Fragile put forward a powerful argument that one last Test should be played on the concrete in Bowral:

Cricket Australia officials should look at giving the recently unearthed wedge of wonder a full Test when establishing future Test schedules.

Organisers at Cricket HQ must ask a simple question: Could this pitch take one more Test?

Sure, it looks buggered! The slab of cement is in an appalling state. It looks as though the Channel Nine key has been inserted into the cracks far too many times. But the strip and surrounds have character, history and the whole paddock complex exudes atmosphere.

Cricket needs novelty to keep it going. Look at the success of the new formats. The Big Bash has revolutionised interest, and the sandpaper incident in South Africa has brought hundreds of kids to the game.

Could this low-maintenance cement track host a celebratory five-day battle between England and Australia in 2028? What better way to commemorate the centenary since the Don's first waddle through the picket gate, to take guard in a Test match against the old foe in November 1928?

What an experience this test would be? What an event! One venue, one strip, one Test could encompass a century of cricket's rich history. To see this humble venue being used again at an international level would be a dream come true for all Australians!

Fragile finished his spray with the final button:

This Bowral pitch is the bridge that joins our heroic past to our sparkling present and our glittering future. A future that

> features so many players from a new generation who have not heard a thing about the Don and his final great innings of profound disappointment.
>
> Imagine the roar that would sweep the nation, on a Mexican wave of enthusiasm, if Cricket Australia said, 'YES!'

Obviously, a full array of punting options would be available on every ball.

# GOLF: IF IT'S NOT UP IT'S NOT IN

*It's an eighteen-hole stick-and-ball caper that explains the universe and why humans seek nirvana!*

THE 2020–21 COVID PANDEMIC has put golf front and centre in the national consciousness. With Greg Norman making his way back to Queensland and his trouser-off photo shoots grabbing recent social media attention, with ex-President Trump, D., still lurking around that great Florida links layout he owns, and with the man they call Tiger in trouble with cars again, is it any wonder that swingers around the world are shouting, 'Golf, count me in!'?

Joe Hockey tells a lovely story about playing the game with President Trump. Joe, one of our great Stateside ambassadors, loves his golf. He knew which end of the club to hold and which end of a cigar to light. He fitted right in. He could talk to anyone about anything. Small talk was his go, the smaller the better. He could tackle trade talks, defence treaties and joint exercises between the Australian and US navies, as well as keeping up a steady stream of Facebook posts and social news, and skate along the fake facts trail. The ambassador's work is never done. It meant our Joe had to have many rounds of slice and dice with President Trump. It was a real chore, an eighteen-hole grind.

Ambassador Joe knew Donald loved to cheat at golf. Whether teeing-off, puzzling over a difficult approach shot or putting for par, the President was a great head puller. He would tread on your ball, hide your putter, super-glue your clubs together. Donald T. was a whatever-it-takes golfer. He was the master of the foot wedge and hand wedge to improve a lie. Of course, he always played the executive course, which was several metres shorter than Joe's tee-off point.

Trump sledged, whenever Joe's back swing was in motion, with vicious put-downs. He dropped salacious dak-cacking gossip about stars and politicians when he saw Joe's confidence was shot. The Donald knew all the tricks. He wrote the book. He was very competitive, often putting a grand on a shot. If he wins, you pay; if you win, no one pays.

Whenever Joe played with Donald there were always twenty helicopters and forty golf buggies zooming about the course crammed to the brim with heavily armed, wired-up security personnel.

Once, halfway through a round with 'Comb-over' Don, Joe was a couple of strokes ahead when the President drove his buggy onto the green at the fifteenth. He always parked on the greens. His mobile pop-up food truck came to a halt dead centre on the green carpet, so the dual-cab V8 ute was between Joe's ball and the hole.

Joe shouts, 'Hey Don, can you move the bloody buggy? I have to play my shot!' This is from 150 yards away. Trump bellows, 'Come on, Joe, it's OK, play on! Hit me! Just hit me!' Joe responds, 'OK, you are the President. If you want me to hit you, I am happy to have a crack.'

As Joe lined up the shot, a quiet voice behind him mumbled in that White House drawl accompanied by the menacing click of a Glock being cocked, 'Hey Aussie Joe, hit it high! Hit it wide! If you hit the President, it will go very badly for you!' The secret service agent then handed Joe a five iron.

Joe's anecdote highlights the importance of golf to international diplomacy through the long decades of the ANZUS alliance. For years, golf has been the sport of international politics. Since World War Two, most American senior politicians have had a respectable game. Dwight D. Eisenhower played 859 rounds while President. That record was only broken when the forty-fifth President stepped up to the tee after putting his hand on the Bible and swearing. With Don, a new era of bag-dragging was underway and records were there to be broken.

Trumpy spent so much time on the dance floor with the putter that historians are waiting eagerly, for his golfing record to be released by the Ivanka Trump Library, to see if any presidential records have been broken. It will make fascinating reading for both golfers and op ed writers.

But with Don moving on, it will take time for international relations and the golfing landscape to settle down. It is reeling and punchy from the bunker-busting whacks that the Trump presidency unleashed from the driver's seat of the 'bigly' golf buggy. Don was a very disruptive influence.

*But with Don moving on, it will take time for international relations and the golfing landscape to settle down.*

The Trumpian golfing legacy will be a hot PhD topic in coming years, attracting the gaze of many sporting governance graduate students with an interest in golfing politics and Hot Dot ball technology, on-course water sustainability and greenkeeping.

Images of the President on the links during his time in office were not the best advertisement for the game. Course photographers were often on hand pointing the Nikon and the Apple iPhone at the sizeable presidential rear end camped under the bright red MAGA hat, bent over a difficult lie on the green, hoping to put away a nine-metre putt for par. These snaps often zeroed in on the presidential gusset, once seen never forgotten. Not sure if it was intentional or just art, but an unsettling amount of seepage and stainage featured on the wide expanse of rear end trouser pin snaps. The presidential trousers made headlines again in more recent times when it was suggested that Don had them on backwards at one of his post-presidential '2024 Here I Come' handshake tours.

After sinking the Hot Dot and inking the scorecard, Don clambered into a V8 buggy with four on the floor, room for the clubs, hot box groaning with barbecued chicken, French fries and an esky crammed to the brim with chocolate cream cake and Coke. That's the soft drink, not the nostril whizz, and never mind what Don Junior is having. That cake and Coke diet sustained Don in peak physical and mental fitness for four trying years in the top job. The bloke was super fit. He could put in a hard day's work spending ten hours out on the course before coming back to the clubhouse, watching all his shows and still able to tweet up a storm until 4 am on that balanced, uncomplicated diet. It's the sort of life-sustaining fuel intake that gave him the strength and stamina to consider the long march to the White House.

> *His doctor maintained the President had no need of the golf buggy because of his incredible levels of fitness.*

His doctor maintained the President had no need of the golf buggy because of his incredible levels of fitness. Trump's doctor was 'Unstoppable' Chuck Jackson, who was a very keen golfer and played off a handicap of four when he last played, back in 1967. Unstoppable snared an online degree in Medicine from Trump University in Macon, Georgia, and enrolled and graduated in a wellness PhD on the same day. He ran the stethoscope over Don on the seventh at the Turnberry, one spring afternoon in 2016, and declared that Don was the fittest President he had ever examined. It was a headline-grabbing diagnosis, even though no one is sure how many presidents Unstoppable had run the medical slide rule over.

For his White House years the Mar-a-Lago layout was Don's second home. He had mastered the layout and played many rounds yip free. His score card (often self-corrected in the rough behind the roses) showed he hammered every hole until he carded that elusive and difficult-to-grab one under par.

President Don, the Commander-in-Chief, played many courses but spent the bulk of his career pondering club selection at Mar-a-Lago. It is an exciting members-only layout in Palm Beach that caters for music and Hollywood celebrities, billionaires, the hardcore MAGA mob, the QAnon crew and four-star generals on the outer with the Washington military establishment.

'Mar-a-Lago', loosely translated, means 'sea to lake' as the property spans the gap between the Atlantic Ocean on one side and the Intercoastal waterway on the other. This fabulous Florida course was laid out between 1924 and 1927 by cereal company heiress and socialite Marjorie Post. In the heady twenties, that is, the nineteen twenties, the socialite concept and golf were a *Tender is the Night* tight fit. Back then, Mar-a-Lago was a byword for Florida pre-Depression glamour. It pulled the big names like F. Scott Fitzgerald, Clara Bow, Mary Pickford, Rudolph Valentino, Stan Laurel and Norma Shearer. It celebrated a past age when players had a drink in one hand, a club in the other, time on both hands and their eye on someone else.

*It celebrated a past age when players had a drink in one hand, a club in the other, time on both hands and their eye on someone else.*

Players always dressed for a round. On the first hole, canapés were dished up by handsome tuxedo-wearing, non-playing staff. A martini with olive was available on the third as nothing improves eighteen holes like regular alcoholic refreshment. The fourteenth was the party hole where Bing Crosby would often serenade golfers with the hits of yesteryear, like 'Don't Fence Me In', 'Buddy, Can You Spare a Dime?' and 'You Must Have Been a Beautiful Baby'. Bing often sang duets with contemporary stars like Grace Kelly and Joan Caulfield.

It is well known that Donald loves music. When he hoons back to the clubhouse after a round, he fires up the B and O sound system on the buggy to eleven and a half. He scares the bin chickens and homing pigeons with Twisted Sister's 'We're Not Going to Take It' blaring from the speakers, letting everyone and the birds know the big bloke is on his way.

Mar-a-Lago has always been associated with swingers and the romance of golf. Golf is a swinger's game and in Florida socialising is a big part of any round. Playing with friends, meeting new friends, hooking up with old friends and thinking about absent friends who may not be on Tinder yet is the best reason to take a bag of clubs out of the boot.

Australia was light years ahead of the States. The oldest Australian course is the Ratho Golf Links at Bothwell, seventy kilometres north of Hobart. This magnificent complex was established soon after the arrival of Europeans in 1821. It's the oldest course in the world outside Scotland.

This Tasmanian layout pre-dates the Mar-a-Lago set-up by a century. The Bothwell area of the Apple Isle boasted great Scottish connections. It was natural that the tartan kilt-wearers, once they tired of tossing the caber and eating haggis, began looking for a stretch of scrub where they could punch in eighteen holes and a few sand traps. The greens were square and surrounded by fences, to protect the grass from the sabre-toothed sheep that roamed the area. These peckish woollen jumpers on four legs with razor-sharp teeth had a go at anything featuring a tinge of green.

*Putting that achievement in historical perspective, a major NSW golfing organisation was up and running three years after the founding fleets turned up in Holdfast Bay and pegged out the streets of Adelaide.*

The first records of Australians swinging were left by Alexander 'Sparkie' Spark eighteen years later. The Spark diary records him playing a Grose Farm layout in 1839. These original eighteen holes are now buried under the suburbs of inner Sydney, but the course sowed seeds. Sparkie and fellow bag-draggers formed the New South Wales Golf Club in June 1839. Putting that achievement in historical perspective, a major NSW golfing organisation was up and running three years after the founding fleets turned up in Holdfast Bay and pegged out the streets of Adelaide.

Not sure what early controversial agenda items clogged the club's AGM. But the minutes of the first meeting indicate significant time was spent tackling the course dress code, as in appropriate footwear on the greens, sock length and decorations. There was the on-going scandal of horse dumps near the clubhouse front door. These were not a good look, and the tidy-up roster was not working effectively. Then there was that golfing evergreen, bad language, after a shocker on the fifteenth where children were often present. The issues then are much the same today on any golf club AGM agenda across Australia.

Back to Mar-a-Lago, and as the Trump presidency headed to the compost bin of history, an almighty stench emerged from the swamp near the par-four eleventh. The bubbles erupting from the open sewer were a concern, but even more alarming was the startling news that the ex-President could camp at Mar-a-Lago permanently, using the joint as his major residence. This would break the spirit of a letter of agreement signed by the Donald all those years ago. The three-page memo, on White House letterhead, signed by 136 concerned citizens, banned a permanent Trump settlement in the apartment above the pro shop with 24/7 access to the clubhouse buffet.

Understandably some of the 'You're fired!' man's Florida neighbours suggested the new arrangement broke the agreement. The feeling among the residents was that Donald camping out at the Winter White House would attract an unsavoury crowd of yahoos, spivs, late mail merchants and coat-tuggers. The locals saw Trump's decision as attracting many of the people he pardoned in the dying days of his stint as El Presidente.

But Donald knows golf and politics have always danced the rhumba cheek to cheek, buttock to buttock. He is the latest in a long line of White House club-swinging stars. JFK looked great out on the fifth in the check slacks with club in hand. His skill in the bunker with the sand wedge is the stuff of legends. Romance, atomic glamour, style and fashion all came together in the Kennedy game. His wife Jackie Kennedy could swing and once knocked in an ace, a hole in one, at Augusta, the home of the Masters.

Gerald Ford wandered into the White House when President Richard Nixon went for the long goodbye. Tricky Dicky vacated the Big House in a hurry, leaving the gas on. President Ford played a layout he designed himself in the White House grounds next to the rose garden.

Barrack Obama had a sensational game. He was always keen to get away from the thrust and tribulations of international politics and have a relaxing swing. Bill Clinton, cigar ablaze on the droop from the lower lip, eyes peeled for action, always looked as though he belonged. He often made up a foursome with Fuzzy Zoeller, Duffy Waldorf and the Australian champ Brett Ogle.

Trump lookalike 'Big Bill' Taft demonstrated that bulk is no hindrance to playing a top shot from the beach to save par. George W. Bush and his piano-playing Secretary of State, Condoleezza Rice, both had great games. The Veep, Dick Cheney, and 2003 Iraq war brains, Donald Rumsfeld, could hold up an end in a team event. Those two loved to have a bet and put something on every hole. Their boss, George W., looked magnificent in Bermuda shorts whenever he backed the Cadillac into his car park alongside the pro shop and pulled a bag of sticks out of the huge Caddy boot. He could destroy a course when he was in the right mood. George was on record as saying, 'You never remember how completely stuffed the world is while you are playing golf.'

Lyndon B. Johnson did the deals for the Civil Rights legislation on the back nine of the Whiskey Creek Golf Club. Vice President Dan Quayle played off a handicap of nine. Dan started dragging the bag aged seven. He played well into middle age. A late starter was Joe Biden, who only took up the game when he won the top job, but he now swings a very nice stick.

By comparison, there have been thirty-nine foreign ministers in Australia's history and thirty-seven of them have been great golfers. Our politicians always punched well above their weight on those hard-to-par international layouts. Bob Menzies was never lost in the rough, Paul Hasluck, William McMahon, Gough Whitlam, the soufflé Andrew Peacock loved playing from the beach, plodding Bill Hayden could get great length off the tee, and the fishnets and stockings swinger, Alexander Downer, had a great short game. He often played poorly but he always strolled into the nineteenth with tales of great shots he jagged by chance. He described these shots as 'haunting'. No one really knew what he meant. It was as though an unseen hand had played them for him.

There was that magnificent swing of Kevin Rudd's, as smooth as Carnation condensed milk being poured onto a Laminex table; 'Blinga' Bishop, who always looked the part and realised early in her time as Foreign Minister that 'you swing for show, but you putt for dough'. Finally, Marise Payne's club selection and uncanny understanding of distance was the envy of the foreign ministers' jet set community for some time.

*Our foreign ministers were all golf crazy and golf literate.*

Our foreign ministers were all golf crazy and golf literate. After a round they held up an end of the bar. Over a few beers or a tumbler of sweet sherry the international heavyweights discussed the big issues, like British champ Laura Davies, how good was she? Or who was a better player, the Language of Love man, Ernie 'The Big Easy' Els, or the Zimbabwean eagle machine, Nick Price? Did Spanish legend Seve Ballesteros have great golfer's hips?

The go-to person to organise a game or make up the numbers between the ambassadors and foreign ministers of either side of the Pacific was 'The Shark', Greg Norman, who had every ambassador's number in his phone and was willing to set the wheels in motion. With The Shark's help, our embassy staff are no strangers to the power of golfing diplomacy. But they have trouble selling the concept in Canberra in the current climate where China troubles swamp the Department of Foreign Affairs and Trade agenda.

News Limited and Institute of Public Affairs experts believe recent disagreements over trade and security with China could easily be settled over eighteen holes at any one of the great sand-based layouts around the country. Australia boasts a great variety of courses from the sand, rocks and bush layout at Lightning Ridge to the well-watered, demanding eighteen-hole monster at the Centre of National Golfing Excellence located on the south-west slopes in Young, NSW.

The failure of embassy staff in Canberra and Beijing to get a foursome of officials who matter out on the course and chatting is a national tragedy. For the sake of our trading future, we have to loosen this log jam. More importantly, no one in Canberra or the Chinese Communist Party wants to commit to breaking the ice or clearing the air by talking about the big issues during a round of golf. The pressing challenge in foreign affairs is to get the politicians together and thinking about a difficult lie and club selection instead of barley, wine, iron ore and heritage cheese futures.

*The failure of embassy staff in Canberra and Beijing to get a foursome of officials who matter out on the course and chatting is a national tragedy.*

There is always another approach. Should DFAT recruit our present and past golfing stars, like Karrie 'The Funnel' Webb, Adam Scott, Peter Senior and 'The Elk', Steve Elkington, to become our international diplomatic front line? Enrol them in a crash course in trade and international affairs, slip them into a bespoke suit, and ask them to pick up the phone and start inking in dates, teeing up times and courses.

## The Ivanka Response

*What can't we achieve with the knowledge, memorabilia and traditions of golf?*

With Donald Trump moving to the White House in 2016, a new era teed off with high hopes.

At the drop of a Twitter post he would down tools and make the numbers in a foursome for an afternoon on the swing. Often after three holes he was wishing he was back in the clubhouse watching his shows, by the ninth he was gnashing his teeth trying to think of places on the planet he could bomb, on the fifteenth he was ringing *Fox & Friends*, hoping to get put through to the on-air celebrities, and he was so catatonic on the eighteenth that he needed a couple of slices of chocolate cake before he could get the shoes off. But he always lobbed back in the White House later in the day saying he had a great round and felt better than ever.

There was always extensive media coverage of Donald out in the rough with a sand wedge in hand, and photos of him crouched over the Kool Mint hoping for a good connection that sent the nugget towards the pin were front-page news in the broadsheets.

The forty-fifth President arrived at the White House with a plan for international golfing domination. His concept involved world leaders, foreign ministers and ambassadors playing golf together and solving the world's problems. This international peace initiative was called the Ivanka Response (IvaRes). Don and Secretary of State Mike Pompeo imagined a circuit of Trump-owned and -operated golf courses around the world being used for summits and talkfests aimed at creating a greater understanding of the world: gabfests that focused on the interests of non-tax-paying American billionaires.

The IvaRes concept was tasked to take over all the duties of the United Nations, NATO, the WHO and the WTO. Funds raised from green fees, car parking, catering and club memberships were to be donated to international peace programmes that Jared Kushner was overseeing from the Trump 2024 re-election campaign headquarters. Obviously, administrative and day-to-day running expenses had been taken out by TRUMP International before Jared got his hands on a slimmed down slab of the charity lolly.

Greg Norman was a great supporter of linking the game to golf and world diplomacy. Greg thought the Ivanka Response was exactly what the world and the world of golf needed. The Shark proposed every nation should appoint a Minister for Golf who would be the official representative of the nation at all these major international meets.

Trump-controlled courses would be placed at strategic hot spots. All international diplomacy would be conducted on the course with a club in the hand. No decisions could be made without the golf shoes on. Foreign ministers and ambassadors were expected to turn up for a yak, dragging the bag and dressed for eighteen holes of red hot international diplomatic action.

The original Ivanka Response was linked to providing venues for all the majors from the Australian Open, the USPGA and the British Open at Trump-owned courses. It was hard to imagine the British Open, sponsored by Saudi Arabia, being played in Dubai, but according to the Don that was the new normal. He would bellow at moaners, 'Buddy, get used to it. Stop whinging, start swingin'.' Then give the whinger a forty-minute lecture on why the world was lucky to have inspirational international leaders with vision like Trump, D., Johnson, 'Banjo', B., Morrison, 'Sooty', S.

Jewels in the Ivanka Response crown included that magnificent Bedminster layout in New Jersey with its five star, all you can eat buffet available at every hole. The golf buggies at Bedminister are classic American cars from the fifties including a full range of Plymouth, Dodge and Desoto. Then there's the wonderful but challenging Great White Shark–designed eighteen holes in Charlotte, North Carolina. At this golfing experience, every hole is named after an American President or Vice President.

The thirteenth hole, The Tricky Dicky Nixon, lives up to its name. Many of the greats, including Tiger Woods and the forgotten man of Australian golf, Mark Hensby, have described the Dick Nixon hole as completely unplayable. Ivanka's SoCal jewel is located at Lunada Bay. This set-up has a very strong locals-only vibe. Whenever the surf rolls in, police patrol the beach breaking up fights between residents and blow-ins who have bobbed up looking for a surf. The Trump National Golf Club in Los Angeles, Rancho Palos Verde, is nearby. The RPV, with its eighteen holes of fun, needs its own police force to keep the riffraff from clod-hopping across the greens and bogging golf buggies in the expansive sand traps.

Then there are the European twin pillars, the Trump International Scotland and the Trump International Ireland. Not to mention the controversial six-and-a-half-star luxury golf resort, Trump Turnberry in Scotland. This links-style complex on the Firth of Clyde features two courses designed by cack-handed Martin Ebert.

A great lifestyle was attached to the Response. Ivanka created a special range of international on-course leisure wear for all sexes. The slacks and trousers had room to swing the hips and came in bright florals and moody pastels. Then there were the accessories: the shoes, the head gear, the sunglasses, the bags, the clubs, the buggy and membership were all part of the package.

Sadly, after the 2020 election, the international mood took a turn for the worse and the IvaRes Dream became a nightmare. Scotland has even gone cold on the whole 'swing and solve the world's snags' concept. The tartan set might even put up a wall and pull up the welcome mat, preventing Donald from playing at the game's spiritual home, the Royal and Ancient St Andrews layout.

IvaRes went down the tubes with the forty-fifth President. But Ivanka's dream is something that DFAT could get right up behind. This international dream would be an excellent addition to national Golf Month. Every year October promotes golf and asks all Australians to step outside and start swinging, for the good of the country.

Like our trade relations, golf today is at the centre of the swirling climate change debate, battles about sustainability and the extravagant use of shrinking resources like water. Even the very land the eighteen-hole layouts occupy is eyed off greedily by developers with high-rise plans in the hip pocket, and governments are looking to take over public courses for infrastructure needs. Bright sparks in the wealth creation business see golf courses as great locations for fifty-five-storey tower blocks with plenty of parking. Courses are being ploughed-in for housing and cut in half and reduced to nine holes to create park land.

It's an old story, and it is not yet time on in the first quarter.

Australia has 1500 golf courses. This is the third highest number of courses per capita in the world, taking the bronze after Scotland and New Zealand. There is a battle across the nation for the ground the Royal and Ancient stick-and-ball caper is played on. Unless they have the word 'Anzac' somewhere in the title, all courses are at serious risk of being buried alive under an avalanche of housing, high-rise,

*Unless they have the word 'Anzac' somewhere in the title, all courses are at serious risk of being buried alive under an avalanche of housing, high-rise, transport infrastructure and football stadiums.*

transport infrastructure and football stadiums. Battle-themed names like the Long Tan Golf Course, the Lone Pine Links or the Second Sixth Field Ambulance Memorial Course have a greater chance of survival. The AGM could ram through a name change at this late stage, but even that concession may not secure a future in these weird and changing times.

Then there is resistance to the game on the home front. Once upon a time, Australians of all ages would get out of the house any time of the day for a swing around the local eighteen before a few bevvies in the clubhouse after sinking a final putt.

If a space-consuming eighteen-hole course was a step too far away, there was a lively pitch and putt or an exciting par three within reach of public transport. The pitch-and-putt scene has disappeared into the dust of time like the dodo.

But the Australian game received a tremendous boost in 2020. The COVID plague year allowed locked-down citizens camping out in certain states to exercise playing golf while maintaining correct social distancing protocols. Golf is a game that is easily COVID compliant. Prior to COVID the game had been in the doldrums. Society was becoming time poor. In the modern age, who had time to spend waddling about swinging when there was a supermarket shopping to do at home and school sport occupied every Saturday and Sunday morning?

Commentators believe the game needs a makeover to make it relevant to a contemporary time-poor generation. They point to the example of cricket, which collapsed the madness of the five days of Test cricket into the One Day concept, then shrank the shebang even further to the twenty-over hit and run before experimenting with a 100-deliveries game. The jury is uncertain about what improvements can be made to the game of golf. How do you tinker with perfection? Sure, night golf is great, aqua golf is a blast, nude golf satisfies certain boutique sensibilities, but in essence the sport is a ball, a stick and a hole. What more does a sport need?

*The jury is uncertain about what improvements can be made to the game of golf. How do you tinker with perfection?*

Suddenly, the game was back in fashion. Club membership exploded across the nation. There was unprecedented growth. Forty-two thousand bag-draggers signed up to the code, allowing them to get 'fit' driving the buggy and relax out of the house in the healing COVID-free green. This was a five per cent rise in membership. What a boost to the sporting economy! It was the sort of boost the clay pigeon shotgun caper had given the GDP in September 2019. The figures were a real blast.

The inner-city course of Moore Park in Sydney hosted 60,000 rounds. It turned out to be one of the busiest courses on the planet. This one course made an extraordinary contribution to the mental health of the city. Number-crunching boffins calculated the game shaved $131 million off the national health budget. In the COVID months, everyone had time for eighteen holes.

Ten per cent of the adult population play the game because they love it. Many are playing into their Slow-go and No-go years, retaining membership well into their seventies and eighties. A stroll around the links is often the only exercise they get. In the COVID pandemic, the game got a tremendous boost with media stars like Sam Newman protesting the closure of courses during the long weeks of lockdown across Victoria. Sam waddled about town looking the part dolled up in crazy outfits that screamed, 'Yes you guessed it, swingers, I'm a golfer. And I love it!' He was a voice in the wilderness, but he kept at it and he triumphed.

Australians had not connected Newman with golf until May 2020. People of a certain age would remember Sam as the Geelong Cats super boot who played 300 games and booted 110 goals. Retiring from football in 1980, he pulled up a chair to the table on Channel Nine's long-running and notorious *The Footy Show*. The panel chat show began in 1994. It had no vision of the game, but it talked about what had happened last weekend and what was going to happen this weekend. It ground to a halt in 2019; by then, the game and society had moved on. At the death, the show had outlived its usefulness by about three decades.

Since being elbowed from the starting line-up at Nine, he has taken up the cause of golf at a political level. Many see the reinvented Slammin' Sam as the Che Guevara of golf. During lockdown he led a chorus of Victorian government critics who complained that Premier Dan Andrews combined the worst features of Pol Pot and Old Joe Stalin. Joe, who played every course in Russia, had a great long game, but he sadly never mastered what he called 'the thorny mystery of the greens'. He used to joke to firing squads, 'The world would be a better place if only Karl Marx had written a book about golf!'

During 2020, as well as leading the 'Open the Gates' movement, Sam began giving lectures via Zoom about the meaning of the game. His five-part lecture series entitled *Sit on My Broom Stick!* was the top-rating sports podcast for that year.

The first seventy-minute spray, 'Your swing reflects your soul', caught the imagination of both the world of golf and the wellness industry. Other topics in his *Sit on* series addressed stumpers like 'Why is the ball white?' 'Why are there eighteen holes?' 'Why do we keep score?'

In the final *Sit on* lecture, 'Wedged' Sam restated the great golfing truisms outlining the reasons the game exists in the modern world. Many who have heard the series liken Sam's handiwork to spiritual classics like *Zen and the Art of Pole Dancing* by former oriental weight loss tea expert Peter Foster, and *One in the Eye: The Mystery of Darts*, which was described by the renowned Buddhist scholar and international finance expert Alf Stewart from Summer Bay as 'a masterpiece on the mysticism of the bullseye'.

After a bit of pushing and shoving, with Sam up front bellowing into the loud hailer and outraged members from all courses bringing up the rear, the Victorian authorities caved in and threw open the gates, welcoming swingers of all ages back to their favourite pastime.

Speaking of winners, that imposing figure on the seventh tee with a toothy grin is the Great White Shark, Greg Norman, Australia's greatest golfer. Greg was struck down with COVID at the end of 2020. Through his social media posts, The Shark gave a chilling insight into how the illness had affected him and his son Greg Junior.

Today he does not have the time to swing the club in anger. He is a full-time fitness freak. He spends twenty-seven hours every day working out in the gym he built himself in the backyard. When he is not pumping up, he is flat out with business commitments in the condominium real estate and merlot wine space. There are great photo spreads showing The Shark's fitness. Some of these snaps are bizarrely revealing.

*There are great photo spreads showing The Shark's fitness. Some of these snaps are bizarrely revealing.*

Sensitive viewers are warned not to go poking around on the internet looking for the portfolio of 'Sharkie' pictures. Several snaps of the Shark sloop have created lively pushback from the digital comment community.

In the current era it is hard to imagine there was a time, in the not-too-distant past, when The Shark towered over all the majors caper and made golf compelling. He had the game that, once in the groove, could menace any golf course in the world. He could destroy eighteen holes and leave a smoking, screaming mess of rubble in his wake.

What a record it was! One hundred and thirty-one weeks at number one in the Official World Golf Rankings and 765 weeks in the unofficial rankings. He had the complete game and that touch of unhinged madness that accompanies golfing greatness.

On any course in a major, depending on par, a top pro needs around seventy great shots, every day, over four days of competition. Do the maths: 280 great shots have to be whacked around the fairways, roughs and greens to have a realistic shot of jagging the winner's claret carafe or lime green jacket that never fits and is never worn. The Shark always tried to get around in 272.

The Shark, on song, could complete the competition challenge with spectacular ease, but on occasions he was a spectacular choker. Maybe the best the world has seen. The golf course can be a lonely place. Only the player, with slim input from the caddie, can make the tough decisions. There is nowhere to hide when the ball slices into a dangerously placed hazard to the right,

150 metres from the pin. It is at those quiet moments of potential failure that the golf madness that stalks every swinger can set in. This Hot Dot lunacy makes the big names select a sand wedge instead of a putter and do the weirdest things.

The Shark could unleash a destructive genius equal to the creative brilliance he displayed at other times. There is an illustrated blog of The Shark's great chokes. It makes poignant reading as these are mistakes that any weekend hacker would make. A world number one should have cut this rubbish out of his game before he left golf school.

Greg could stroll up the fairway on the last, having teed off to perfection. In this major, the world number one was coming home secure at the top of the leaders' board with one hand gripping the winner's jug and the other on a brightly coloured jacket ensemble. The Shark's final approach shot was from 139 metres away – what could go wrong? The Shark swung and the crowd groaned as one; all they saw was total carnage of the shot. The Shark had over-egged the shot. There was far too much grunt and poke. The ball flew past the pin. It was a total shank. No one saw where the dimpled Jaffa finished up. It was not on the green. A search party was organised. Greg knew where it was. The Shark's shot ended up with a challenging lie in the green-keeper's garage under the blades of the ride-on Victa mower.

Another major was slipping down the gurgler on the final hole. But if anyone could rescue the round, Greg could. Who knows why the number one gave the final whack too much chilli? This was bad. But then came the brain explosion. Instead of taking the common-sense, conservative approach and taking a drop, Greg wanted to give the crowd a wild and crazy pure golf finish to a memorable day.

In the double garage behind the clubhouse, The Shark calculated that if he played the shot out of the blades onto the petrol tank of the Victa, the ball would jag a deflection from the tank, clear the shed door, dribble down the clubhouse path and back onto the green, and with a bit of luck it would end pin high with a three-metre putt to make one over par and a certain green jacket win. At least this was the view from the Channel Seven commentary team, who said they knew what The Shark was thinking. With hindsight it was always hard to know what The Shark was actually thinking.

*With hindsight it was always hard to know what The Shark was actually thinking.*

It was a brilliant conception in the mind, not so good off the stick. Suddenly, after twenty minutes swinging and swearing in the greenkeeper's shed, Greg was eight over par for the hole and powdering into fifth place. But that was The Shark, genius and loon, all in the one package.

If after The Shark's return to Queensland, his real estate and wine set-ups go pear shaped, our greatest golfer may have time to return to an earlier career using his name to market cars or anything that needs a leg-up in the sales caper. With the pandemic loosening its grip, Australia may be about to experience another golden era of Great White Shark promotional magic. Wind the clock back to 1997, the big unit of the year was the Holden Statesman International Greg Norman Signature Series.

The days are long gone since Australians made cars. But in the decades when Australia was a player in the car manufacturing caper, the public eagerly waited out front of the local dealer's showroom for the curtains to be drawn back, revealing the latest Holden sedan in all its glory. It is hard to imagine that people in the Barossa Valley queued for days and gasped in amazement when the vertical blinds were lifted to reveal the 1975 Monaro in the Steinborner Barossa Holden showrooms in Craker Drive, Nuriootpa. It was a different Australia, less to do.

Not all cars are big hits, moving swiftly out of the showroom and on to roads across the nation at speed. Never mind the appealing promotion. The car-buying public are sometimes reluctant to take the risk with a new model or a new idea. No matter what inducements car dealers offer.

The limited edition can rescue slow-selling models. The personality touch up can turn a lemon into a bestseller. The Australian car history is littered with duds that required a star power push. The Carla Zampatti Ford Laser is a classic in the celebrity makeover story. Carla, no stranger to the fashion world, was involved in adding value to the Laser KB and KC range.

The KB range featured Carla's touch with two-tone duco and colour-coded grill. Then Carla went crazy, adding yellow and red pinstripes to the KC. Plus there was a bonus key holder and, surprising many interior designers, the upholstery was dyed in a hard-to-miss fetching shade of S-bend brown. Some of these features may not have shifted this citrus from the showroom floor, but dealers were desperate.

Other examples of rebadged, touched-up cars are the Reebok Pulsar and the Sportsgirl Holden Barina. So when Holden dealers struck trouble moving 250 units of the 1997b Holden, golf-mad Theo Simpson, in head office, had a brainwave and roped in Greg Norman, the world number one and golf course design guru. Greg was asked to, as they say in the automotive industry, 'put the polish on a turd'. A once-over with the chammy and hey presto, the Statesman International

*Greg was asked to, as they say in the automotive industry, 'put the polish on a turd'.*

Greg Norman Signature model was ready to drive away from a dealer in your suburb.

The Series 3 touch-up was jam-packed with extras, including sixteen-inch alloy wheels, leather and suede upholstery, fog lights, a sun roof and that special Shark styling in the detailed badging. Early adopters of the range also scored a set of King Cobra golf clubs and Norman's signature on the boot lid. Running the practised eye over that lot, Australian car buyers could see it was a total package and represented incredible value.

Today, these Shark Statesmans change hands for about $11,352. Not sure if the King Cobra clubs are part of the deal. But if the Cobras were in the boot untouched and unswung, it would make this a great purchase for any genuine car collector or golf memorabilia enthusiast. Even just knowing that The Shark had fiddled about with the donk of this Statesman would make this a priceless package.

The COVID years were a boom time for the car industry as people were wary about public transport and wanted to keep to themselves. Both new and used cars were sold in record numbers. But tough times may return and then car sales managers will be hollering for The Shark to come back to the showroom and weave his winning magic on another case of lemons.

# SPORTS RORTS: EVERYONE KNOWS EVERYONE DOES IT!

*Our shotgun queen takes her A-game to Canberra and hits the federal pork target dead centre.*

WHEN SPORT BOBS UP on the national agenda, money and duffle bags crammed with folding tossed casually into the club secretary's car boot are never far from the first order of business.

Australia has a proud and long-standing tradition of dumping truckloads of cash into sporting organisations based in marginal seats across the nation. It is a simple way of thanking the citizens for doing the right thing last time and reminding them it is not long before they need to do the right thing again.

It's a time-honoured and widely applauded part of the electoral cycle, along with the democracy sausage on election day out front of the local school. The taxpaying public grumble at every 'sports cash splash scandal' but if the scattering of cash was not a proven election strategy major parties would stop doing it. The key trick, as with all political intrigues that involve large slabs of taxpayers' moolah, is not to get caught. But in 2020 even getting caught was no crime. In today's electoral landscape everyone knows everyone does it.

The pattern of federal sports pork (or should that be smashed avocado in these vegan-tinged times?) allows federal loot to trickle its way out of Canberra through grants and end up in the pockets of club officials and committees. And, if the trickle-down effect worked, some of these sports dollars would end up in the pockets of coaches, players and suburban ground staff. In charge of the grand grant largesse is the federal Minister for Sport. This nation has been blessed with wonderfully talented Australians who offered to plug away in the federal Sport portfolio.

The Minister for Sport wheeze was unleashed in 1972 when Labor leader Gough Whitlam shoehorned Frank Stewart into the job. Gough had no real interest in sport, but he knew Frank was well credentialled for the portfolio, having played first-grade rugby league for the Canterbury-Bankstown Bulldogs in that golden run for the top NSWRL side between 1948 and 1952.

The Bulldogs over the years have turned out as the Berries, Dogs, Doggies, Dogs of War, the Family Club and the Entertainers. Their home ground was the Kennel at Belmore Oval. They always produced a hard-core rugby league–style entertainment on and off the paddock. They have bagged eight premierships and been runners-up ten times. The club have been at the forefront of Mad Monday, end-of-season trip and pre-season trial match outrages for decades.

The Dogs have kept the wick turned up on league scandals, creating headlines that have the great code front of mind during the long hot summers of cricket and tennis when everyone thinks only of the beach.

Frank Stewart, our original Minister for Sport, had a great set of rugby league and political genes, which he inherited from his dad, the founding president of Canterbury-Bankstown Club. Frank was very active in the sport policy space for the Whitlam government. He laid the foundations for the Australian Institute of Sport. Incidentally, for a lifetime of effort at the coalface Frank had a stand named after him at the Kennel.

Since 1972 and Frank's early efforts at running the ball up, there have been twenty-six federal Ministers for Sport. The portfolio has been a revolving door in the big house with a new minister sworn in approximately every 1.84 years.

*The portfolio has been a revolving door in the big house with a new minister sworn in approximately every 1.84 years.*

In later Labor times, when our greatest sporting all-rounder, Bob Hawke, was at the helm of the Canberra runabout struggling with a sputtering outboard, sport was a central issue. Bob knew what the electorate liked. He knew it liked winners.

Labor front-bench talents like John Brown, Graham Richardson and Ros Kelly were all tapped to hand out the cheques in the winnable seats. Minister Kelly was connected with one of the best sports rorts cash handouts the nation has seen. The term 'sports rort' was coined to acknowledge her great handiwork. Her Texta pen and whiteboard, on which the original carve-up was sketched, is now in the entrance way of the National Sport Museum in Canberra. Remember, Minister Kelly's handiwork would have been encouraged by those at the very top.

It was a similar tale when another sport mad PM, John Howard, took over steering the Lake Burley Griffin moored runabout.

Skipper John squeezed the best out of Sport Minister Jackie Kelly (October 1998 to November 2001). When it came to money and handouts, Jackie always asked, 'What would John Eales do?'

When J.K.'s reign ended, she was followed by the greatest to serve in this plum post. The 'Eh, Er, Eh!' man Rod Kemp was our longest-serving Sport Minister. Rod kept a tight hold of the scorecard and felt-tipped pen from November 2001 to January 2007. It was a long, sustained dig. His spell included the Winter Olympics in Salt Lake City and that magnificent Stephen Bradbury come-from-behind speed skating gold, a Rugby Union World Cup in Sydney and the Athens Olympics, to name three of the big ones.

But other great Australians served with distinction in this political post that allowed free entry to the big events, car parking near the main gate, passes to the head of the catering queue any time day or night and a chance to have a selfie snapped with the sporting champions of the day who were paid to put in for our nation.

*Politicians were always camped near the finish line or podium looking good for a happy snap with a winning Aussie.*

Politicians were always camped near the finish line or podium looking good for a happy snap with a winning Aussie. Or maybe a late tap to present the medals at a gold medal ceremony if the appointed IOC official did not front, thinking the event was beneath them.

The list of ministers is long and features many who appeared to be completely unsuited to the task – like the man who was always filmed in front of empty bookshelves and was a great lover of interpretative dance, George Brandis (January 2007 to December 2007). Or Peter 'Spud' Dutton (September 2013 to December 2014). To give Spud his due he still looks as though he has a quick 50 in him if needed to stabilise an innings in a Pollies v Press ODI stinkarama at Manuka Oval. Or the marathon man, Greg Hunt (January 2017 to December 2017), who is no stranger to running the hard yards; or the Gold Coast real estate expert, Sussan 'Time to Shine' Ley (December 2014 to September 2015), who has done wonders for spearfishing on the Great Barrier Reef.

Cynics might moan that this plum is available to anyone who puts their hand up. Nothing could be further from the truth.

The post is so highly rated that in 2020, the whip-cracking, aged care numbers man, Richard 'Big Dick' Colbeck, was tapped for the job. In his heyday Dick was always one out and one back until he spotted a rails run in the shadows of the post, and burst through a gap to salute.

That is a quick roundup of the heroes and heroines who have served in the portfolio. The gaze now zeroes in on more recent adventures in the 2019 sports budget carve-up.

The idea all ministers share is the understanding that federal sporting loot for votes is central to Australian politics. The sport pork racket barely rates a mention in the media unless it goes horribly wrong.

The attitude to this distribution of largesse was summed up in late 2020 by NSW Premier Gladys Berejiklian. Aunty Glad mumbled to a startled press pack, after the exposure of her government's latest barrel of avocado and single origin cream hurled from the back of the moving ute towards vulnerable seats, 'Everyone knows it is wrong, but it is not illegal, so it must be OK!' Or words to that effect. Gasps all round followed by everyone quickly moving on.

In the lead-up to the 2019 federal election, Prime Minister 'Gold Standards' Morrison could see a few marginal electorates on the wobble, so he opened the play book that Glad referred to in the presser, the one that has served all politicians so well since Federation.

The 2019 dishing out of big lolly for sport was guided through the rough rapids of parliamentary scrutiny by Senator Bridget 'Bang Bang' McKenzie. Bridget was perfect for the job. Elected as a senator in July 2011, she rose quickly to the top, becoming deputy leader of the National Party.

The then PM, Malcolm Turnbull, a great swimmer, bus enthusiast, walker and amateur fitness guru, tipped Bridget into three portfolios. Her responsibilities were Sport, Rural Health and Regional Communications.

Sport was her passion. The shotgun was her sport. She shot with the Wangaratta Trigger Pullers, who were thrilled when the wombat trail tapped her for the top job in Canberra.

Bridget was in great company. Australia has had so many great shooters and wonderful success at the highest levels of international competition. Our stars have climbed the heady heights to the top step of the Olympic podium. Remember, it's the only sport to feature in both the Summer and Winter Olympic Games.

No one can forget the golden joy unleashed across the nation by Australian shooters in Atlanta in 1996. Michael Diamond, gold in the trap, and Russell Mark, gold in the double trap. Michael backed up and blew the competition away in the trap for a second time, getting gold in Sydney. This early nugget of precious metal unleashed a golden shower of success in Sydney, making it our best Games ever.

Australians can shoot. Our politicians can shoot. The sport looks easy but requires total stillness, a dead eye, trigger coordination, concentration and the ability to shout 'Pull' and then pull the trigger.

Our master blasters were not forgotten in the election of 2019. Bridget, dubbed Minister for Hunting, produced a compelling report that suggested a gun- and shooting-led economic recovery was the most likely pathway to the nation's continued economic success. The income generated by the shooting industries from gun sales to bullets, from travel to hospital admissions, from clothes to merchandise, was eye-watering.

This timely report was accompanied by an equally startling online survey in which participants, mainly shooters, were asked how they were travelling health-wise in their work–life balance battle.

Once the survey votes were in, researchers discovered that shooters and, especially, shotgun shooters, were among the most well-adjusted members of the Australian community. Between them they contributed $17.47 billion annually to the nation's economy simply by pulling the trigger and blazing away at clay targets and bush junk across the nation.

Remember this was a survey of shooters. There was nothing technical about the sample but look at those results! Other sports were green with envy.

Sadly, climate activist PM, Malcolm T., was dumped by his colleagues in the night of the long gladiolus before he could finish the sport cash dish-out job. In a three-way run-off for the crown on 24 August 2018, 'Our Miners Are the World's

Best' Scottie Morrison saw off the challenges of Spud Dutton and Blinga Bishop. There was a cabinet reshuffle once the new PM, with an all-trade, have-a-go agenda, located the keys to The Lodge.

'Shotgun' McK clung tenaciously to the Sport portfolio in the subsequent ministerial reshuffle. She was put in charge of the 2019 election sport pork strategy. Her department was allocated $98.5 million large to tip into the nation's sporting clubs. Seasoned observers maintain this was a sensible and well-targeted cash splash. All federal seats were on the table, apart from safe Labor seats, obviously.

*She took a steady bead on those pesky marginal seats. She drew up a map, aimed truly and pulled the cashflow trigger.*

Bridget was quite capable of dishing out the money. She took a steady bead on those pesky marginal seats. She drew up a map, aimed truly and pulled the cashflow trigger.

As the election day approached, the boss, 'On Water Matters' Morrison, wasn't happy. He could see the handiwork was not good enough and picked up the phone.

But when the PM involved himself in the details the troubles began. Here the nation is indebted to the work of Australia's number-one sports-rorts researcher, Theo 'Red Ted' Damp. Theo anchors a podcast, *Sink Your Teeth into This, Australia!*

Damp's extensive research, using FOI requests, revealed that the marginal seat sporting loot plans went backwards and forwards many times between the PM's office and the Minister for Sport's parliamentary cubby hole. They were amended and amended again. The gravy train of sports rorts dough only ground to a halt on election day when the polls closed.

'It's not a race' Morrison went above and beyond. He tasked Bang Bang McKenzie to roam the country pleading with sporting organisations to go for a grant whether they needed it or not! Many grant applications came in late. It did not matter. If there was time to swing a vote, there was money in the kick.

Once the vote was counted, the ABC's Anthony Green declared at 7.04 pm that the government was returned. It was a stunning night of nights for federal politics. How good? But as so often happens in the corridors of power post hooter, tongues started wagging.

After a vigorous probe putting chilli on the in/out stick, Red Ted Damp unearthed emails which suggested that everyone in a marginal seat had been offered something. Here is a sample of how it worked:

To 'Mouse' Brown
Hon. Sec. Budgewoi Smugglers and Shooters Club
Budgewoi NSW
21 April 2019

Dear 'Mouse' Brown,

Thanks for the dozen frozen mullet, the kids and the neighbours loved them. And regards to Breffnie, Shelby and the glamorous Nadine.

Now to business. I know that the date for lodging any application for the current round of sports grants has passed. Don't worry! It is never too late to get a snout deep into the federal pork trough. And every snout deserves something.

My office can tidy up loose ends and do any backdating required.

Never mind that you don't have a women's team in any competition, apply for a grant because you never know what might happen in the future. We just need an indication that your committee could be considering gender diversity sometime in the next fifty years.

To make it easy, there is a tick box form attached. If you need any help working out whether 'yes' or 'no' is the right answer, please ring Vera in my office.

Bang away, Mouse, and win big!

Yours at the trigger end of a shottie!

Bridget McKenzie

Min. for Sport

The Big House

Canberra ACT

This email struck gold. A response came from the Budgewoi (Budgie) Smugglers and Shooters Club. This progressive club is located in downtown Budgewoi, that NSW Central Coast jewel which draws holidaymakers from across the world ... well, it will when COVID travel restrictions are lifted.

This area has a wonderful sporting history, home of rugby league's Ray Price (the Parramatta great, dubbed 'Mister Perpetual Motion'), and tough nut, front row forward and Kangaroo, Mark O'Meley, the Bear who became an Eagle, then a Dog and ended up a Rooster (he played ten games for NSW and fifteen for Australia).

After several days the minister's office received an application for federal funds by email from the Budgie Smugglers. It was a heartfelt plea for a grant to build a toilet block in Slade Park just off the Central Coast Highway.

The club president and 2011 Lake Munmorah Shooter of the Year, Albert 'Knocker' Toole, wrote a covering note, which ran:

To Minister for Sport
The Big House
Canberra ACT
31 July 2019

Dear Shotgun,

How are you?

How are they coming out? Are you getting a few?

Mouse Brown passed your letter dated 21/04/2019.

Sorry for a case of the slows in replying.

This is a covering letter for our application for a grant of seventeen hundred and ninety-five dollars. I hope we have completed the tick box form to your satisfaction.

We are not a big club like the some of the shooting outfits on the Central Coast of NSW. The Wyong Mad Bastards or Port Macquarie 303s come to mind. They are very go-ahead with millions of dollars in poker machine and clubhouse bar action turnover. We are a very modest outfit. But we are doing our bit to keep the feral pest load in our area under control.

Our night shoot records show that last month we put away fifteen stray cats (at least I hope they were strays), nine foxes, four goats, 245 Indian mynas and a wild camel.

Sadly, we managed to drop quite a few koalas when a member unfamiliar with night shoot protocols, young Harry 'Houseboat' Hunt, went silly. He let a few go in all directions and collected nearly two dozen of our gumleaf-chewing furry friends.

The kid was spooked by an extremely rare night parrot flying towards him. In the gloom, as dusk turned to night, he swore, in the post-shoot debrief, that he thought it was an ambush of aliens coming to get him. He let a few go and winged a brush-turkey on the prowl nearby.

With Houseboat letting loose, everyone opened up without thinking or pausing to look. Suddenly we were walking on a carpet of fur and feathers. From body armour video evidence, the alien attack turned out to be nothing more threatening than a pair of parrots flying in formation close to young Hunt's melon.

The birds were featherless when the shooting stopped. We rushed towards the kill zone to tend to the wounded and found we had brought down twenty-three koalas, a couple of dozen black cockatoos and the endangered parrots that started the firefight. They lay dead among the feathers on the forest floor

They were listed in the shoot record as collateral damage. Thank God none of the Smuggler membership caught a stray bullet.

The kill numbers are estimates taken from post-shoot conversations with recording secretary 'Bagpipes' Bruce Blinkhorn. Bruce was tasked to conduct a full-on probe into the incident. It was a devastating and sobering report that the Blinkhorn Committee handed down after three weeks of quiet deliberation. The Club had no option but to suspend young Houseboat for nine months and twenty-one days.

It's the biggest penalty imposed by our club in a decade and recalled the time we had to expel 'Stubbie' Prendergast after he went silly in the main street and took out thirty-five car windscreens in a single night of MDMA-fuelled madness.

I mention these actions taken by the Smuggler's management team to give you an idea that we are a serious club with an eye always on the correct safety protocols.

As to the grant for toilet facilities, you can understand, with environmental issues front and centre, the days when club members could take a leak in a creek or squat with the pants around the ankles and drop the load on an endangered toad are long gone.

Shotgun shooting in Australia has left all that hoo-ha behind in the sewage treatment works of history.

Bridge, we are a humble club. We are not looking for much. We want enough to bolt on a Portaloo to a box trailer. We want to tow the trailer behind the Club's Ford F-100 out on site when we go a full-on night shoot. Plus, we would like an outdoor shower with solar-heated hot water back at base to wash off the dirt and muck from ten hours of crawling through the swamps taking out vermin.

We don't own any land in Slade Park. But if it was OK your end, could we have a grant to allow us to buy three Portaloos and the outdoor shower as a stop gap? I am sure the local council will eventually green light the plans for a five-storey amenities structure to be erected on a block of land owned by club patron, retired Major General Sir William 'Wobbly' Monk.

Remember the Budgie Smugglers motto . . .

'If it's feral, it's in peril!'

Love to see you up this way for a bang any time.

Thanks very

Yours sincerely

Albert 'Knocker' Toole

Bang Bang!

Minutes later an email reply winged its way to Knocker's inbox from the federal Department of Sport.

> Dear Knocker,
>
> Thanks for the letter and the Budgie Smugglers' very thorough application. If only all our requests for grants were this accomplished.
>
> Please find enclosed a cheque for $227,000.00.
>
> Use it however you see fit.
>
> Good luck with the dunny build.
>
> And Knocker, keep banging! If you run out of bullets, you know who to call.
>
> Yours with Both Barrels
>
> Bridget McKenzie
>
> Minister for Sport (Rorts) Ha Ha

Red Ted says it is literally that simple. And Ted thought the subtext of the message was quite clear. If you want us to deliver in the future, there is only one way you and your members can vote on the big day. As in, vote for us!

And according to Ted, in that federal election of 2019, Knocker and the Smugglers shooting crew got the ham bag message loud and clear.

# SONGS OF PRAISE AND SONGS OF REDEMPTION

*'When the rugby league flock welcomes back those who have strayed, the sideline assembly will sing out 'Halleluiah! Brothers and Sisters, the sinful will be blessed and returned to the flock once the Steeden is kicked off in anger.'*

AS REVEALED ELSEWHERE, RUGBY league's great hidden strength is its redemptive power. The chaplain of the Central Coast church Our Lady of the Heaving Sea, Monsignor the Very Reverend Brodie Grundie, had this to say in a recent issue of the *Catholic Weekly* when interviewed by South-East Asian Vatican correspondent Bishop Dom Bloodknock:

> Dom, I wish the church had the same ability as rugby league to save souls. Imagine welcoming those who have strayed from the true path into the weeds of temptation and found themselves doing the devil's work on TikTok and the like. Imagine getting them back to the flock in front of 20,000 cheering fans filling the stands at the new Parramatta Stadium or the Adelaide Oval. That is what the good book is all about!

The redemptive act before the kick-off in a top-of-the-table clash is the powerful message of a life reborn in Christianity writ large in club jumper and shorts. Rugby league is the gospel made flesh with a kick to come after the try has been scored. Remember all the action is filmed live for Channel Nine with Ray 'Rabbits' Warren going upstairs to the bunker should there be any controversial decisions. Upstairs to the bunker that keeps the eternal score, says it all.

For the less religiously inclined, rugby league is a mechanical bull of a sport. Spectators throw a leg over the bouncing, corkscrewing, machine-powered beast and hang on for the ride, never knowing how long the trip will last or where it will dump them. When the congregation throw a leg over the Texas Cannonball, they know they will be tossed off onto the beer-sodden bar room carpet sooner or later.

*For the less religiously inclined, rugby league is a mechanical bull of a sport.*

One of the go-to sounds of rugby league is the soothing, smooth strains of the cabaret classics canon smeared with a dollop of burlesque. The game is so tough it seeks out, for post-hooter relaxation, the easy listening, the familiar tunes. Those songs that swerve around the reality of the game. The reality of the big hits, the aches, the injuries, the weeks on the sidelines, the pain and the concussion – all need the soothing balm of chart-topping tunes.

League fans are familiar with the sweet noise of scraping the bottom of the barrel. On occasions, the bottom of the top barrel is scrapped away completely and the sound that emerges is the sound from the barrel beneath. This tune is a deep dive into aural liquid manure. It is in this gooey goop nourishment of the barrel beneath that the game has found sonic guano gold. It is the sound of success.

The game's musical culture straddles a tricky balance. One boot in the greatest hits and the other boot sunk into slabs of the totally duff.

These choices are woven into the fabric of the game. Both cabaret styles and hard rock blasts are baked into its DNA. This is what is known around the grounds as the code's culture. Popular culture has served the G.G.A. extremely well as the code wobbled along the tightrope strung between the sound of success and the cacophony of noise.

Beginning nowhere in particular, Frank Hyde, the game's great radio caller, found time mid-week to record three albums in the 1970s, once again proving rugby league players can do anything. In his playing days Frank packed down for ninety matches, scoring twenty-seven tries with the Newtown Bluebags before moving to the Balmain Tigers (premiers in 1939), and finishing up pulling on the shorts thirty-seven times for the North Sydney Bears (RIP).

Frank then took up the clipboard and coached the Bears for forty-six matches before he moved to the seat behind the sideline card table and began a long stint of calling all the game-day action. His great contribution to the language of league was his catchphrase used whenever the kick for a try conversion was on its way from the kicking tee towards the black dot: 'It's long enough, it's high enough and it's straight between the posts.' This was a regular dollop of the Hyde magic the public loved. A career can be built on a line like that! Frank's multi-pronged career featured a substantial stint behind the card table. He camped on the sideline stool for thirty-three Grand Finals.

Hyde was a great contributor on many levels. His astounding and outstanding musical gift to the game began with *Frank Hyde Sings* (1973). This heartfelt collection featured songs like 'Who Threw the Overalls in Mrs Murphy's Chowder?', 'Right! Said Fred', 'Surfin Bird' and standards like 'Somewhere My Love', and the track that he made his own, the Irish tearjerker 'Danny Boy'. This song, Frank's party piece, reached number seven on the top forty charts in 1973.

He was back in the studio later that year, when he put down the cabaret classic *The Frank Hyde Party Sing-a-long* (1973). This selection of toe-tappers featured tunes tinged by the green of the Emerald Isle, like 'Galway Bay', 'Ramblin' Rose', 'Get Me to the Church on Time', 'Baby, Let's Play House', 'When Irish Eyes Are Smiling' and that great 'Irish' seasonal heart-tugger 'White Christmas'. The song selection alone indicates it must have been a 'helluva party' when the genial host laid this solid gold twelve inches of Frank onto the Stromberg-Carlson turntable and lifted the needle. The fans wanted more from the game's number-one caller. He was lured back to the recording studio for a final hit out with *Frank Hyde Sings for the Good Times* in 1976.

As Frank said in a long interview with *Rolling Stone* magazine's Wendy Williams:

> Wen, cabaret is my thing. I loved the greats, Ian 'Turps' Turpie, the singing jockey Donny Sutherland, Barry Crocker, the 'I Go to Rio' man Peter Allen, the country classics from 'The Sheik from Scrubby Creek' Chad Morgan, the lanky yank Don Lane and Ernie Sigley. All great Australians who could hold a tune.

> It was the razzle-dazzle that talked to me. It's the whole package – the big wigs, the ill-fitting suits, the shoes with pointy toes, the shoulder pads, the champagne glass in hand, the Craven A ablaze on the lip, the hot band and that loveable rugby league audience. They were wonderful cabaret years when the NSWRL premiership trophy came home in the back of the FB Holden station wagon.

Wholesome rugby league cabaret, packaged in living stereo, spoke to a gentler concept of the code devoid of all the concussion-inducing grunt and poke required to play the greatest game of all for eighty action-packed minutes in the modern era.

Frank – a player, a coach, a commentator and a cabaret star – was the sound of the sport. The game was supported by the leagues clubs of NSW, and after dark in the big showrooms these clubs supported the nation's great cabaret artists. But music was everywhere in the code. All rugby league clubs had a song known by every true supporter. These simple songs, of heartfelt 'our team is the greatest' sentiment, were familiar to all fans.

Club songs were belted out tunelessly with impressive gusto by the team in the rooms after every win. The winners bellow the lyrics across the space filled with happy club members, families, friends and officials. The enthusiastic rendition is accompanied by the bashing of esky lids and hammering on the doors of the change cubicles. The lyrics are drivel. The aim of the post-hooter bellow is to reduce the song to a barrage of annoying noise.

*The enthusiastic rendition is accompanied by the bashing of esky lids and hammering on the doors of the change cubicles.*

There are some breathtaking club songs. For the St George Illawarra Dragons, well, it is an obvious selection:

Oh when the Saints!
Oh when the Saints go marching in!

No melody, no need. The team shouting accompanied by the rowdy percussion ensemble is perfect.

North Queensland Cowboys have a country-tinged offering to gather the supporters around the campfire. No surprise it's a big sound for a big-hat town:

The Cowboys are my team
And it's my dream to see them at the top

Repeat these chorus lines. They say it all.

AS MENTIONED, POST-HOOTER CLUB singsongs are fraught with danger. Players forget, in their enthusiasm to get involved with the celebrations, that there is a vast TV audience tuned in down the local pub or on the couch at home. They forget for a few minutes that they are rugby league players and role models. They imagine they are part of the world of show business where seemingly anything goes. Images of semi-nude players during these

*They forget for a few minutes that they are rugby league players and role models. They imagine they are part of the world of show business where seemingly anything goes.*

rowdy post-hooter renditions often flaunt aspects of the league anatomy that once seen can never be forgotten.

The league's modern era of musical promotions dates from the late eighties. The G.G.A. was very active in linking existing hit songs to the marketing of the game during the season. But endless repetition in television advertising reduces any song to incomprehensible gibberish.

'Boys Are Back in Town', Thin Lizzy's 1976 rough-and-tumble anthem, got the rugby league promotional ball rolling. Thin Lizzy were a rowdy, hard-drinking, hard-rocking Irish band fronted by a Black Irishman on the bass. They had a run on the top forty charts, but this was their signature tune. It could have been written about the greatest game of all. The lyric is wildly offside in today's more inclusive times. Not sure what 'the Thins' knew about Australian rugby league, but ten years after the gang recorded this number one, the tune was pressed into service to let everyone know the weekend thump, dump, bump action was back. That is the right timeline for a rugby league promotional gambit. The game's culture is approximately ten years behind mainstream recognition.

The Lizzy posse saddled up and rode the high suburban range, rounding up the herd for rugby league from 1985 through to 1988. The NSWRL were on a winner. In the future, head office promotional efforts focused on songs that summed up the emotion of the game in its totality. They got lucky when someone in the office knew someone who knew the boss of Tina Turner's management company. Tina had a long history of emotive, pedal-to-the-metal rhythm and blues classic chart-toppers like 'River Deep Mountain High', 'Nutbush City Limits' and 'What's Love Got to Do with It', to name three smouldering top ten bangers.

The first cab off the Tina rugby league rank was 'What You Get Is What You See'. This tune promoted the game in 1989. In its essence it was pure rugby league: a simple song for a simple game. The lyrics celebrated fit blokes looking great with their shirts off. On the original recording there is a blistering guitar contribution from god-like Eric Clapton. Then the 1989 song 'Simply the Best' lurched into view. The league pounced. Thin Lizzy were great but 'Simply' was even greater. With 'Simply the Best', Tina proved to the world that rugby league was the greatest game of all.

It was the smash the musical maestros at League HQ were after. This song of praise, penned by Mike Chapman and Holly Knight, started life as a tune for Bonnie Tyler called 'The Best'. The musical idea and promotional film clips captured the rawness of league. Players from all clubs packed down in the bash-and-barge videos and looked 'simply' stunning.

Tina brought the exotic to the table. She was way more exotic than rugby league, but this song and her appearance demonstrated that rugby league could rock and attract the biggest names of international show business. Therefore, it must be simply the best.

As Tina said in a recent long-form TV documentary on Foxtel when asked by Molly Meldrum about the rugby league involvement:

> Honestly, Molly, it was the highlight of a long career to be tapped to be the voice of rugby league. The boys were wonderful. From the Door, the Puller, Stomper, Tiptoes and Barbs I learnt the importance of ball security, knowing when to

> spread it wide and the importance of putting the ball down under the black dot.
>
> On the first morning of the shoot when they opened *Fatty and Chook: Laughing at League* as we settled down for a mid-morning cup of tea, I was rubble. I have never laughed so hard. I had heard that league was a funny old game. I had no idea it was an absolute riot.

Tina looked very fit, running with the players along the sand, passing the football like a professional. Tina was there with our stars doing the hard yards in the sand hills. What a great image for the game. Not burlesque, as theatrical types would understand it, but not far from it. The television campaign was a highlight of the season, for once everything came together. It worked. The big moment, the strawberry on top of the whipped cream, on top of the three-layer chocolate cake, came when Tina blew into town for the season-ending big dance at the Sydney Football Stadium in 1993. She mimed 'Simply' before kick-off.

*What a great image for the game. Not burlesque, as theatrical types would understand it, but not far from it.*

'Hullo Sydney!' That's all the capacity crowd wanted! Acknowledgement that one of the world's entertainment greats knew about rugby league and the 1993 league journey. Everyone could have left the SFS after her performance and wandered away completely happy, in the certain knowledge that they had had the best day of their lives.

No band, no need – just Tina, a backing tape, a wig, footsteps and Sydney! It all came together, when a sax player burst onto the stage with the horn to the lips and a leather codpiece strapped on below to mime the mincemeat out of the sax solo. Everyone was rubble!

It was pure league. This bump-and-grind floorshow up the Randwick end of the SFS would not have been out of place in any one of Sydney's great after-hours clubs of the era along Oxford Street or in Kings Cross.

The league lost its mojo for a couple of years after Tina was benched in 1995. It was so hard to find someone who could plug the yawning gap Tina left. In 1997 the G.G.A. promotion machine gave the game's supporters 'Two Tribes' by Frankie Goes to Hollywood. No one was sure of Frankie's league credentials. But the song summed up the struggle for the very soul of the game in that troubling time of the News Limited Super League breakaway era. That is a story for another book which has already been written, several times.

Eventually a peace deal was plonked on the table. With a peace treaty ready for signatures, 'Tubthumping' by Chumbawamba was the song of the hour, as peace pens were poised. The Chumbas, a one-hit wonder cabaret collective, was tasked to do the heavy promotional lifting, applying the soothing balm to the code's blackening bruises. The repeated lyrics of getting knocked down and getting up again were rugby league in a nutshell.

In 1999, to usher in the new millennium, the promotions crew in League HQ went right out to the left field fence and then right over it for a promotional campaign. The committee commissioned a poem by league lover and prize-winning novelist Tom Keneally. Tom came down from the hills with a poignant scribble, 'Blow that Whistle Ref'. It was completely weird. There was no beat, no melody, no chorus. What were the dancers to do with their feet? It made no sense. What was Tom going to do at the Grand Final? Poetry did not talk to footy freaks. It was a oncer!

*Poetry did not talk to footy freaks. It was a oncer!*

2000 was the year of the Sydney Olympics and so sports fans' gazes were elsewhere, but the 'What's New Pussycat' man, Tom Jones, knocked up a jingle with the catchy tagline 'What a Game!' It had the right elements: a simple lyric with few words that said it all, images of fit players, big hits, incredible tries, fabulous footsteps from the dance troupe and Tom blasting away flat out. The package had a beautiful simplicity, and there was the tantalising carrot that Tom might be available for the Big Frolic on that Sunday in October.

A couple of years flew by now and the league promotion crew were relocated to new digs in the garden shed out back of League HQ, just beyond the toilets. Between 2003 and 2007 'That's My Team', a rewrite of The Hoodoo Gurus hit 'What's My Scene', did the promotional chore. The Hoodoos were league lovers. They were in town and very keen to strap on the Fenders and run amok at the end-of-year Steeden big day out. The code was cooking with gas.

Moving on, in 2011–12 'This Is Our House' by Bon Jovi was tapped to let Australians know the big show was on the lurk again. Bon Jovi's connection with rugby league was vague, but it must have made sense when the idea was floated at the marketing meeting in the garden shed lean-to. The 'Our House' concept spoke to fans who easily made the jump from 'this is where we live' to 'rugby league is our game'.

It was big hair, big guitars, big blokes and a right-on message. But as in all things slaved to league or the charts, the rise and fall is a continuous wheel of ups and downs. Popular culture is a restless sea, and what was great last season rapidly becomes last year's model. Suddenly, that tune, that style, that noise is old hat and set to sink without trace. The lid is always flapping on pop culture's FOGO bin of history.

Over the years, many were called to put their shoulder to the rugby league wheel. They had a crack and moved on. Whenever the league was really stuck for an idea they slid back to the glory days of the 1990s for one more squeeze of the juiciest lemon. As luck would have it, Jimmy Barnes and Tina Turner had recorded a duet version of 'Simply the Best'. In 2020 the league touched up the duet with a veneer of modernity, tasking Jimmy Barnes to reheat the league's great anthem.

And in 2019, in one of NSW's many golden ages of infrastructure expenditure, the jewel in the rugby league real estate crown, the Sydney Football Stadium, was tapped for demolition. When the stadium was built, rugby league was for blokes. Blokes meant there were never enough alcohol outlets, and blokes, unlike women, always need a leak at the footy. When these arguments were considered ridiculous, late suggestions maintained that the stadium was a firetrap and the stairways had never been completed in the original build.

The closing night of the SFS action, before the bulldozers went in, was a night of fabulous league cabaret. There was only one name who could do the event, the game and the venue justice. To bring down the curtain and the stands it was over to Michael Bublé.

Michael loves Australia. He loves cricket. He had heard all about the Sydney Football Stadium. He had a look at the joint and loved it even more when he was told the stories. He was reduced to tears when he stood on the stage and looked out across the field where so many league dreams had come true. He understood immediately why they had to knock it down.

There were no surprises on the night. Toe-tapping, finger-clicking, easy-listening standards. There are never any surprises with Bublé: 'Cry Me a River', 'I Have the World on a String', 'Howzat', 'Up There Cazaly', 'Haven't Met You Yet'. But where were the celebrated rugby league classics in this farewell set? There was no medley of 'The Boys Are Back in Town', 'This is Our House', 'Simply the Best' and 'That's My Team'. A Bublé medley like that would have brought down the house – and wasn't that the aim of the night?

# ACKNOWLEDGEMENTS

THE PANDEMIC WAS A golden age for the book. The present and the immediate future seemed so uncertain and yet people who were struggling with health, work, relationships and life in general found time to read books in great numbers. Thanks to all Australians who took an interest in the written word during this troubled time.

A big thanks to the team from Pan Macmillan: Cate Blake, who suggested I have a go at something as the virus took hold, knocked the flight plan into shape after take-off. Belinda Huang was a great editor; she got the idea straightway and made sense of it all, especially the humour in the simple idea of making up history. Of course, I was not the first person to turn that wheeze into a book.

Many ideas and themes for *The Fairytale* first surfaced in the programmes I made over the last forty years with my companion at the coalface of commentary, Rampaging Roy Slaven aka John Doyle. I thank him for letting me nick the good ones.

As a sounding board on the cultural curve, I picked the brains of two well respected practitioners of *The Fairytale*, Dare Jennings and James Valentine. They provided the prongs of stability for the flimsy table of knowledge that supports this version of the truth.

A special thanks to Lucille Gosford for the title and IT support, and thanks to the Queen of the Nile, who puts up with the endless practise, Kate Gosford.

Lastly, thanks to all the players who made *The Fairytale* possible and all the fans who have followed these adventures from near and far.